LIBRARY OF HISTORICAL JESUS STUDIES

Volume 8

Published under
LIBRARY OF NEW TESTAMENT STUDIES

413

Formerly Journal for the Study of the New Testament Supplement Series

Editor
Mark Goodacre

JESUS' LITERACY

Scribal Culture and the Teacher from Galilee

Chris Keith

t&t clark

Published by T & T Clark International
A Continuum imprint
80 Maiden Lane, New York, NY 10038
The Tower Building, 11 York Road, London SE1 7NX

www.continuumbooks.com

Visit the T & T Clark blog at www.tandtclarkblog.com

© 2011 by Chris Keith

Library of Congress Cataloging-in-Publication Data
A catalog record for this book is available from the Library of Congress.

ISBN: HB: 978-0-567-11972-8

Typeset and copy-edited by Forthcoming Publications Ltd. (www.forthpub.com)
Printed and bound in Great Britain

CONTENTS

FOREWORD

The traditions about Jesus often remember him as having quoted, alluded to, and rewritten the law and the prophets. But if he did such things, how did he learn to do so? Was he educated into Jewish scribal culture? Or did later Christians make him out to be more scripturally sophisticated than he actually was? Did Jesus learn to read in a synagogue school? Or did his father teach him at home to read and perhaps write? Or did he, as a Jewish peasant, never learn to read or write at all, so that his knowledge of the Scriptures was necessarily limited to what he heard others recite during religious services? Everybody agrees that Jesus was a teacher, but what sort was he—an uneducated text-broker or a scribally educated text-broker?

Luke 4:16–30, where Jesus unrolls a scroll of Isaiah and then recites from ch. 61, traditionally settled the main issue. For many modern scholars, however, the testimony of Luke is not enough to establish what Jesus could or could not have done, especially given how uncommon the ability to read appears to have been in his time and place. Some have accordingly doubted that Jesus could read.

This is the immediate context for Professor Keith's work, which is the first book-length treatment of the topic. Happily, it is first-rate. Indeed, all subsequent discussions will inevitably take their bearings from *Jesus' Literacy*. The work is comprehensive, well-informed, and well-argued, and time and time again it reveals that almost everybody who has addressed the pertinent issues has come to premature conclusions. As Keith himself puts it, historians of early Christianity "have underestimated the complexity of literacy in the ancient world, the complexity of the claims concerning Jesus' scribal-literate status in the earliest sources, the complexity of scholarly evaluation of those claims, and the complexity of Jesus' relationship to various audiences" (p. 5).

One of Keith's major contributions is the revelation that previous treatments have all-too-often failed to make necessary distinctions. To ask, for example, whether Jesus was literate or not is to ignore that there were differing degrees of literacy in his Jewish world. The query also misdirects the discussion, which should not be whether Jesus could read anything at all in any language but whether he was scribally literate, that is, whether he had been trained to interpret the Tanak. Scholars have, in addition, often failed to see that one could be textually adept without being textually literate: it is possible to dictate texts without the ability to read, just as it is possible to recite and interpret, even with some facility, texts one has only heard because one cannot read them.

Keith's volume further commends itself by virtue of the self-conscious care with which it goes about reconstructing the past. For over fifty years now, most critical historians conducting the so-called quest for the historical Jesus have tried to answer their questions by employing the so-called criteria of authenticity. Their method has involved subjecting individual units to a gauntlet of authenticating tests. Keith is keenly aware of the problems that surround those criteria, and he sensibly abandons them for an alternative strategy. His approach is, in essence, to construct a plausible narrative that explains the various conflicting traditions—at least some of which must be inaccurate—regarding Jesus' literacy. The prudent strategy pays off.

Perhaps the most important thing to say about *Jesus' Literacy* is this. It does not just summarize previous work and add a nuance here or a new argument there. Rather, by discussing at length important topics heretofore contemplated much too briefly or even not at all, it reboots the discussion. Indeed, it is no exaggeration to say that this book renders everything else written on this subject well-nigh irrelevant.

Dale C. Allison, Jr.

PREFACE

I had the idea for this book on a Lufthansa flight between Frankfurt, Germany and Edinburgh, Scotland. At the time, I was working on John 8:6, 8 for my doctoral thesis at the University of Edinburgh. That thesis argues that the account of Jesus writing in the ground in John 8:6, 8 in the *Pericope Adulterae* (John 7:53–8:11) is a claim that Jesus was able to write (grapho-literate).[1] Its focus is entirely upon the social significance of the claim of grapho-literacy for Jesus and its relation to how and why a scribe inserted the story between John 7 and 8. Since my hands were full with the exegetical and text-critical matters, I left historical matters unaddressed. Judging by many conversations during that time, however, this was not a popular decision. In addition to *what* Jesus wrote in the ground, whether Jesus *really could* write was almost all that anyone else wanted to discuss. The issue came up in my review boards in my first year of doctoral work. It came up at my viva at the end of my course of study. It came up at all points in between, with specialists and non-specialists alike. If I said, "Well, that is not really the focus of my study" once, I said it a thousand times. So, as I hovered somewhere between Frankfurt and Edinburgh and considered where my thesis work could lead next, I decided to address whether Jesus could read and write.

This work builds further upon research originally undertaken at New College, University of Edinburgh, so it is only proper to thank my *Doktoreltern*, Helen K. Bond and Larry W. Hurtado. Their examples, guidance, and encouragement have meant the world to me. I also thank the following individuals for reading various sections of this study and offering helpful feedback: Dale C. Allison, Jr., Samuel Byrskog, Bart Ehrman, Alan Kirk, Patrick D. Miller, Jack Poirier, Benjamin Reynolds, Rainer Riesner, Rafael Rodríguez, Barry Schwartz, Tyler Stewart, Neal Windham, and Walt Zorn. Worth singling out for thanks is my colleague at Lincoln Christian University, Anthony Le Donne. To his continuing disapproval, I insist that our interoffice debates really happened, and

---

1. Now published as Chris Keith, *The* Pericope Adulterae, *the Gospel of John, and the Literacy of Jesus* (NTTSD 38; Leiden: Brill, 2009).

were not simply perceptions on my part, and I will point to several improvements in the manuscript of this book as evidence. I also thank my colleague Chris Simpson for a conversation that drastically improved the shape of Chapter 4. Leslie Starasta and Michelle Rodgers of the Jessie C. Eury library at Lincoln Christian University were immensely helpful in obtaining articles and books, as was Nick Alexander. In Clay Alan Ham, I am fortunate to have a Provost who not only understands the importance of academic scholarship for institutions of theological education, but is a New Testament scholar in his own right and is willing to add to his administrative duties the task of offering feedback on my work. I am also grateful to Carol Bakhos and Ruben Zimmermann, each of whom provided pre-publication copies of essays.

I presented versions of Chapter 2 at Eastern Kentucky University, Yale Divinity School, Illinois Wesleyan University, the University of Edinburgh, Western Kentucky University, and the Winners Colloquium for the 2010 John Templeton Award for Theological Promise at the Forschungszentrum Internationale und Interdisziplinäre Theologie, University of Heidelberg. I presented a version of Chapter 3 at Cincinnati Christian University and the University of Chicago Divinity School. I thank those institutions and the participants in those discussions for their feedback. The lectures were made available through the John Templeton Award for Theological Promise. I thank Prof. Dr. Michael Welker and his staff at FIIT, including Jennifer Adams-Massmann and Alexander Massmann, for their generous help and kindness, and the John Templeton Foundation for their endowment of the award.

It has been a pleasure to work with Bob Webb, editor of the Library of Historical Jesus Studies series, and Dominic Mattos, Biblical Studies editor for T&T Clark. I thank them for accepting this volume for publication.

Chapter 2 modifies and expands "Memory and Authenticity: Jesus Tradition and What Really Happened," *ZNW* 102 (forthcoming 2011) (Walter de Gruyter; used with permission). Several sections of the Introduction and Chapter 4 appeared first in "The Claim of John 7.15 and the Memory of Jesus' Literacy," *NTS* 56, no. 1 (2010): 44–63 (Cambridge University Press, 2010; used with permission). All Scripture citations are from the New Revised Standard Version unless noted otherwise.

More than anyone else, I must thank my wife, Erin, son, Jayce Andrew, and daughter, Hannah Louise. There is nothing better in the world than coming home to you guys at the end of the day.

ABBREVIATIONS

AAW	Approaching the Ancient World
AB	Anchor Bible
ABD	David Noel Freedman, ed. *The Anchor Bible Dictionary*. 6 vols. New York, 1992
ABRL	Anchor Bible Reference Library
ACAF	Ancient Context Ancient Faith
AO	Anecdota Oxoniensia
ASP	American Studies in Papyrology
BASOR	*Bulletin of the American Schools of Oriental Research*
BASP	*Bulletin of the American Society of Papyrologists*
BBR	*Bulletin for Biblical Research*
BDAG	Walter Bauer, Frederick William Danker, William F. Arndt, and F. Wilbur Gingrich. *A Greek–English Lexicon of the New Testament and Other Early Christian Literature*. 3d ed. Chicago, 2000
BECNT	Baker Exegetical Commentary on the New Testament
BETL	Bibliotheca ephemeridum theologicarum lovaniensium
Bib	*Biblica*
BRS	Biblical Resource Series
BS	Biblical Seminar
BTB	*Biblical Theology Bulletin*
BTZ	*Berliner Theologische Zeitschrift*
BZNW	Beihefte zur Zeitschrift für die neutestamentliche Wissenschaft
CBQ	*Catholic Biblical Quarterly*
CCS	Cambridge Classical Studies
CCSA	Corpus Christianorum: Series Apocryphorum
CGTC	Cambridge Greek Testament Commentary
CM	Christianity in the Making
CMP	Cultural Memory in the Present
ConBNT	Coniectanea neotestamentica or Coniectanea biblica: New Testament Series
COQG	Christian Origins and the Question of God
CPP	Critical Perspectives on the Past
CRINT	Compendia rerum iudaicarum ad Novum Testamentum
CSHJ	Chicago Studies in the History of Judaism
DNTB	Craig A. Evans and Stanley E. Porter, eds. *The Dictionary of New Testament Background*. Downers Grove, 2000
DSD	*Dead Sea Discoveries*

ECLS	Early Christian Literature Series
EKKNT	Evangelisch-katholischer Kommentar zum Neuen Testament
ES	European Sociology
ESCJ	Études sur le christianisme et le judaisme/Studies in Christianity and Judaism
ESCO	European Studies on Christian Origins
ExT	*Expository Times*
GBIU	Göttinger Beiträge zur Internationalen Übersetzungsforschung
GBS	Guides to Biblical Scholarship
GRBS	*Greek, Roman, and Byzantine Studies*
HNT	Handbuch zum Neuen Testament
HS	The Heritage of Sociology
HTKNT	Herders theologischer Kommentar zum Neuen Testament
ICC	International Critical Commentary
JBL	*Journal of Biblical Literature*
JCM	Jews, Christians, and Muslims from the Ancient to the Modern World
JECS	*Journal of Early Christian Studies*
JGRChJ	*Journal of Greco-Roman Christianity and Judaism*
JRASup	Journal of Roman Archaeology: Supplement Series
JSHJ	*Journal for the Study of the Historical Jesus*
JSJ	*Journal for the Study of Judaism in the Persian, Hellenistic, and Roman Periods*
JSJSup	Journal for the Study of Judaism: Supplement Series
JSNT	*Journal for the Study of the New Testament*
JSNTSup	Journal for the Study of the New Testament: Supplement Series
JSOTSup	Journal for the Study of the Old Testament: Supplement Series
JTS	*Journal of Theological Studies*
LAI	Library of Ancient Israel
LCL	Loeb Classical Library
LJ	Lives of Jesus
LNTS	Library of New Testament Studies
LSE	La scuola di epicuro
LXXG	Septuaginta: Vetus Testamentum Graecum Auctoritate Societatis Litterarum Gottingensis editum
MBMC	Matrix: The Bible in Mediterranean Context
MNTS	McMaster New Testament Studies
Neot	*Neotestamentica*
NIBCNT	New International Biblical Commentary, New Testament
NICNT	New International Commentary on the New Testament
NIDNTT	*New International Dictionary of New Testament Theology*. Edited by C. Brown. 4 vols. Grand Rapids, 1975–85
NIGTC	New International Greek Testament Commentary
NovT	*Novum Testamentum*
NovTSup	Novum Testamentum Supplements
NPP	New Perspectives on the Past

NTOA	Novum Testamentum et Orbis Antiquus
NTS	*New Testament Studies*
NTTh	New Testament Theology
NTTSD	New Testament Tools, Studies, and Documents
OBO	Orbis biblicus et orientalis
OCPM	Oxford Classical and Philosophical Monographs
ÖTBK	Ökumenischer Taschenbuchkommentar zum Neuen Testament
OTM	Oxford Theological Monographs
PSN	Paul's Social Network
PTS	Patristische Texte und Studien
PVTG	Pseudepigrapha Veteris Testamenti Graece
RFCC	Religion in the First Christian Centuries
RLS	Rockwell Lecture Series
SBEC	Studies in the Bible and Early Christianity
SBLABS	Society of Biblical Literature Archaeology and Biblical Studies
SBLEJL	Society of Biblical Literature Early Judaism and Its Literature
SBLSP	Society of Biblical Literature Seminar Papers
SBLTCS	Society of Biblical Literature Text-Critical Studies
SBLTT	Society of Biblical Literature Texts and Translations
SBT	Studies in Biblical Theology
SCJ	*Stone-Campbell Journal*
SemEd	Seminar Editions
SemeiaSt	Semeia Studies
SGJC	Shared Ground among Jews and Christians
SJ	Studia judaica
SL	Scribner Library
SLFCS	Studies in Literacy, Family, Culture, and the State
SNTSMS	Society of New Testament Studies Monograph Series
SNVA	Skrifter utgitt av Det Norske Videnskaps-Akademi i Oslo
SP	Sacra pagina
SPNT	Studies on the Personalities of the New Testament
STDJ	Studies on the Texts of the Desert of Judah
STI	Studies in Theological Interpretation
SUNT	Studien zur Umwelt des Neuen Testaments
TAPA	*Transactions of the American Philological Association*
TENTS	Texts and Editions for New Testament Study
TDNT	G. Kittel and G. Friedrich, eds. *Theological Dictionary of the New Testament*. Translated by G. W. Bromiley. 10 vols. Grand Rapids, 1964–76
ThS	Theorizing Society
TLNT	C. Spicq. *Theological Lexicon of the New Testament*. Translated and edited by James D. Ernest. 3 vols. Peabody, Mass., 1994
TS	*Theological Studies*
TSAJ	Texte und Studien zum antiken Judentum
TTKi	*Tidsskrift for Teologi og Kirke*
VPT	Voices in Performance and Text

VSI	A Very Short Introduction
VT	*Vetus Testamentum*
WBC	Word Biblical Commentary
WMANT	Wissenschaftliche Monographien zum Alten und Neuen Testament
WUNT	Wissenschaftliche Untersuchungen zum Neuen Testament
ZNW	*Zeitschrift für die neutestamentliche Wissenschaft und die Kunde der älteren Kirche*

INTRODUCTION:
JESUS, READING, AND WRITING

For, as regards any writing professing to come immediately
from Christ Himself...[1]

But we must first discuss a matter which is apt to present a
difficulty to the minds of some. I refer to the question why
the Lord has written nothing Himself.[2]

And so the Savior left his teaching in no book of his own.[3]

This study is the first book-length treatment of Jesus' literacy. It is also the first study to argue that there is substantial disagreement and confusion over the issue in our earliest sources, and likely was in Jesus' own life. The topic of Jesus' relationship to reading and writing, however, has a long history. This history has concerned itself mainly with the fact that Jesus did not author texts. As the quotations above indicate, Augustine and Jerome were invoking Jesus' lack of authorship in the early fifth century C.E. as responses to pagan critics[4] or heretical Christians who claimed to possess writings of Jesus.[5] Among modern scholars, Fredriksen begins her *From Jesus to Christ* by also observing that Jesus was not an author: "Jesus of Nazareth announced the coming Kingdom of God; but he did not write it."[6]

1. Augustine, *Faust.* 28.4 (*NPNF*[1]).
2. Augustine, *Cons.* 1.7.11 (*NPNF*[1]).
3. Jerome, *Comm. Ezech.* 44.29 (PL 25.443); author's translation.
4. Augustine, *Cons.* 1.7.11–12.
5. Augustine, *Faust.* 28.4; Jerome, *Comm. Ezech.* 44.29.
6. Paula Fredriksen, *From Jesus to Christ: The Origins of the New Testament Images of Jesus* (New Haven: Yale University Press, 1988), ix.

1. *Why Did Jesus Never Write a Book?*

As Augustine, Jerome, and Fredriksen (to name but a few who discuss Jesus and literary activity[7]) indicate, some scholars stress only that Jesus did not compose writings. Others, however, are concerned with providing an explanation for this fact. For example, in 1932 Sangster published *Why Jesus Never Wrote a Book*.[8] Ultimately, his answer to why Jesus never wrote a book is one of a devotional nature: "Because it would have become a fetish: because it would have lent itself to bibliolatry: because men would have given a reverence to it as a book that belongs only to God himself."[9]

Much more recently, Crossan offers an entirely different answer to why Jesus never wrote a book by raising an issue that Sangster does not appear even to consider; namely, whether Jesus *could* have written a book. Crossan pronounces negatively on the prospect: "Jesus did not—and, in my opinion, could not—write."[10]

As Chapter 1 will demonstrate, Crossan is not alone in explaining Jesus' lack of literary activity in terms of his lack of literate ability. His claim is important to note here at the outset of this study, however, because it reveals a tremendous difference between the state of biblical scholarship in the times of Sangster and Crossan. In the period between these two scholars, our understanding of ancient Jewish scribal culture has experienced nothing short of a sea change. Questions concerning who could read and write, how many could read and write, how one learned to read and write, and the role of literacy in the distribution of power have received intense scholarly interest in light of their important implications for the socio-political structure of Second Temple Judaism and early Christianity. The burden of this book is to bring the insights of this burgeoning field of enquiry to bear upon the figure of Jesus of Nazareth.

2. *Why Does Jesus' Literacy Matter?*

An initial step in this regard is to establish why Jesus' literacy matters, or should matter, to New Testament and historical Jesus scholars in the first place. The question of Jesus' literacy matters because not all Second

---

7. See further Chapter 1.
8. W. E. Sangster, *Why Jesus Never Wrote a Book and Other Addresses* (London: Epworth, 1932).
9. Ibid., 12.
10. John Dominic Crossan, *The Birth of Christianity: Discovering What Happened in the Years Immediately after the Execution of Jesus* (New York: HarperCollins, 1998), 235.

Temple Jewish teachers were created equal. More specifically, the dividing line between recognized Torah authorities and unofficial teachers was one of education, which led to mastery (whether presumed or actual) of the holy text rather than mere familiarity. In this context, literacy equaled power.[11] This is not to suggest that uneducated Torah teachers had no authority or were unable to resist the literate elite. As purveyors of local traditions and interpretations, they too could have served as Torah teachers.[12] It is, however, to observe that the locus of Torah authority resided with those teachers or groups of teachers who(m everyone knew) were most capable of accessing the text; that is, the pedagogically qualified text-brokers.[13] In the words of Schwartz, "*Mastery* of the Torah was a source of power and prestige."[14]

Yet, the vast majority of the Jewish population in the Second Temple period was illiterate, and thus incapable of attaining such power and prestige. Harris's assertion of a general 10 percent literacy rate for the Roman Empire is now well-known.[15] Chapter 3 will give further attention

---

11. On this topic, see especially M. D. Goodman, "Texts, Scribes and Power in Roman Judaea," in *Literacy and Power in the Ancient World* (ed. Alan K. Bowman and Greg Woolf; Cambridge: Cambridge University Press, 1994), 99–108, as well as Robin Lane Fox, "Literacy and Power in Early Christianity," in Bowman and Woolf, eds., *Literacy and Power*, 126–48.

12. John P. Meier, *A Marginal Jew: Rethinking the Historical Jesus* (4 vols.; New York: Doubleday, 1991–2009), 1:268: "But in an oral culture, one could theoretically be an effective teacher, especially of ordinary peasants, without engaging in reading or writing." Also, Craig S. Keener, *The Gospel of John: A Commentary* (2 vols.; Peabody: Hendrickson, 2003), 1:712 n. 86: "An uneducated peasant might be a more credible prophet on the popular level."

13. See, for example, Jer 8:8, where Jeremiah's prophecy against scribes and their control of the law simultaneously witnesses to their authority in matters of the law. In this sense, it is important that Jeremiah accomplishes his lasting counter to scribal authority through a written text. He ultimately challenges them as a co-literate, displaying the very connection between authority and scribes and their pens ("false pens" for Jeremiah) that he rails against. On the apt description of Jewish and Christian "text-brokers" who mediated the holy text, see H. Gregory Snyder, *Teachers and Texts in the Ancient World: Philosophers, Jews and Christians* (RFCC; New York: Routledge, 2000), 122–217. More broadly on the power of literates in illiterate cultures with a holy text, see the well-known study of Brian Stock, *The Implications of Literacy: Written Language and Models of Interpretation in the Eleventh and Twelfth Centuries* (Princeton: Princeton University Press, 1983).

14. Seth Schwartz, *Imperialism and Jewish Society, 200 B.C.E. to 640 C.E.* (JCM; Princeton: Princeton University Press, 2001), 74 (emphasis added).

15. William V. Harris, *Ancient Literacy* (Cambridge, Mass.: Harvard University Press, 1989), 22, states that in the Roman Empire illiteracy was "above 90%". Also,

to Harris and the literate landscape of Jesus generally. Worth noting briefly, however, is that Hezser's detailed assessment of the Jewish literate scene has furthered Harris's research by suggesting that, if anything, illiteracy was even more common in Roman Palestine.[16] Similarly, and while there are detractors,[17] the most recent thorough studies of Jewish scribes, orality, textuality, and education have also affirmed Harris.[18] In other words, the common anthropological description of Judaism in the time of Jesus as a world of "haves and have-nots" applies as equally to education and its benefits as it does to wealth and food.

Thus, while there is nearly universal agreement that the historical Jesus was, in one form or another, a Jewish teacher,[19] and Keck can even claim, "To a considerable degree the history of the quest is the quest of Jesus the teacher,"[20] the question remains for critical scholarship: On which side of the literacy line did Jesus fall? Stated otherwise, *what type* of Jewish teacher was Jesus?

3. *This Study*

In what follows, I will argue that Jesus most likely did not hold the form of literacy known as scribal literacy. Unlike Crossan and many others,

"[It is] unlikely that the overall literacy of the western provinces even rose into the range of 5–10%" (272).

16.   Catherine Hezser, *Jewish Literacy in Roman Palestine* (TSAJ 81; Tübingen: Mohr Siebeck, 2001), 496.

17.   See Paul Rhodes Eddy and Gregory A. Boyd, *The Jesus Legend: A Case for the Historical Reliability of the Synoptic Tradition* (Grand Rapids: Baker Academic, 2007), 242–45, whom I find unpersuasive and discuss further in Chapter 3.

18.   David M. Carr, *Writing on the Tablet of the Heart: Origins of Scripture and Literature* (New York: Oxford University Press, 2005), 116 (cf. 270 n. 51); generally, 111–73; Richard A. Horsley, *Scribes, Visionaries, and the Politics of Second Temple Judea* (Louisville: Westminster John Knox, 2007), 8–9, 91, 211 n. 27, 225 n. 6; Christopher A. Rollston, *Writing and Literacy in the World of Ancient Israel: Epigraphic Evidence from the Iron Age* (SBLABS 11; Atlanta: Society of Biblical Literature, 2010), 127–35 (esp. 128 n. 1); Karel van der Toorn, *Scribal Culture and the Making of the Hebrew Bible* (Cambridge, Mass.: Harvard University Press, 2007), 10–11. Cf. also Albert I. Baumgarten, *The Flourishing of Jewish Sects in the Maccabean Era* (JSJSup 55; Atlanta: Society of Biblical Literature, 1997), 49 n. 36. See Chapter 3 for further affirmations of Harris among biblical scholars.

19.   Dale C. Allison, Jr., *Constructing Jesus: Memory, Imagination, and History* (Grand Rapids: Baker Academic, 2010), 24: "It is more than a safe bet that Jesus was a teacher…"

20.   Leander E. Keck, *Who is Jesus? History in Perfect Tense* (SPNT; Columbia: University of South Carolina Press, 2000), 65.

however, and based upon the background of scribal culture just mentioned, I will argue further that the issue is not quite as simple as a statement affirming or denying literacy for Jesus. Any attempt to answer the question of Jesus' literacy must sort through confusion in the sources and the likelihood of confusion over the issue in Jesus' own lifetime. My general criticism of the majority of prior attempts to answer the question of Jesus' literacy, then, which will find more detail in the pages that follow, is that they have underestimated the complexity of literacy in the ancient world, the complexity of the claims concerning Jesus' scribal-literate status in the earliest sources, the complexity of scholarly evaluation of those claims, and the complexity of Jesus' relationship to various audiences.

In giving greater attention to these matters, the present study will unfold in the following manner. Chapter 1 will provide a history of research that will also highlight the manner in which Jesus' literacy, and scholarly disagreement concerning it, is an overlooked yet central aspect of larger reconstructions of Jesus. Two of the most prominent differences between these prior studies and this book are my approach to the historical Jesus, which is undergirded by social memory theory rather than criteria of authenticity, and my attention to the varieties of literacy in Second Temple Judaism and their social manifestations. Chapters 2 and 3, respectively, will address these topics. Chapter 4 will discuss the primary evidence concerning Jesus' literacy, focusing prominently upon first-century sources but also including evidence from the second to sixth centuries C.E. This chapter will feature two original contributions. The first contribution will be my argument that, in narrating Jesus' return to his hometown synagogue, Mark and Luke disagree over whether Jesus was a scribal-literate teacher. The second contribution will be my interpretation of John 7:15. Chapter 5's hypothesis concerning the scribal-literate status of Jesus will also be an original contribution. I will argue that Jesus most likely was not a scribal-literate teacher, but that many of his audiences likely thought he was. Brief concluding remarks at the end of the book will summarize its contributions and offer comments on the implications of my argument for the interpretation of the controversy narratives.

With regard to nomenclature, I have attempted to avoid unnecessary and pedantic distinctions between "Jesus," "the historical Jesus," "the real Jesus," and so on. This is not because I am blind to the potential usefulness of such terms. With the majority of scholars, I affirm that one cannot equate the Jesus who walked the earth with the Gospels' portrayals of him. Part of the present study's argument, however, is that scholars have been overly confident in their ability to separate cleanly one from the other.[21] Thus, I will refer to Jesus as a person who existed in the past as "the historical Jesus" only when unnecessary confusion would result otherwise or in reference to historical Jesus research (mostly in Chapter 2). Other than these instances, I will refer simply to "Jesus" and Jesus as he appears in a given text or source (e.g. "Mark's Jesus").

4. *Interest in Jesus' Literacy*

As final introductory comments, I want to address what I perceive as occasional motivating factors in both scholarly and popular interest in the topic of Jesus' literacy. Although some find Jesus' literacy to be of the utmost insignificance,[22] I have found that others care strongly, even adamantly, about it. They sense that something important is at stake when one discusses Jesus' literacy.

After many conversations about this topic over the past six or so years in SBL meetings, invited lectures, classrooms, and ecclesial contexts, I am utterly convinced that one of the reasons that some (certainly not all) are willing to fight vehemently about Jesus' literacy is that the topic is something of a battleground for Christology. Asking whether Jesus *could* read or write causes assumptions about Jesus' identity and limitations to surface, whether one finds him- or herself inside or outside the faith community. As a result, it is nearly impossible to discuss Jesus' literate abilities without bumping into the Christological commitments of one's interlocutor; again, regardless of what those commitments are. I do not pretend to avoid entirely my own commitments in this regard (although I would add that my argument has not typically found a welcome home among those who fall on my side of the aisle). Nevertheless, I find it necessary to state that the following argument does not reside upon, address, or have a stake in matters Christological. Others may disagree, but I have had no success in finding a mention of Jesus' literate abilities in any of the creeds.

Along similar lines, and often in conjunction with Christological assumptions, some (again, not all) specialists and non-specialists seem heavily invested in affirming or denying Jesus' literacy based on a misunderstanding of the relationship between literacy and intelligence. To speak of literate abilities in the ancient world was not to speak directly of intelligence. A charge of illiteracy could function as a slur under certain circumstances, and I will present several examples. But these instances

---

21. This study thus joins a recent, but nonetheless vocal, minority in rejecting the criteria of authenticity. See further Chapter 2.
22. Meier, *Marginal Jew*, 1:268: "Some would say that the question is ridiculous."

are not truly comparable to modern derogatory references to someone as illiterate, since literacy is the norm in the industrialized world and it was not in the ancient world. Stated more bluntly, asking "Was Jesus literate?" is not the same as asking "Was Jesus stupid?" This point may seem painfully clear, but since many of my conversation partners have seemed to respond to the second question when I raised the first, I believe it bears mentioning explicitly here at the beginning of this book.

Of course, I carry no illusion that asserting these caveats will deflect all criticism of my proposal. In this sense, my modest goal for this volume would be that even those whom my argument does not persuade will recognize it as an advancement of the discussion that demonstrates that the matter of Jesus' literacy is significant and deserves greater attention.

Chapter 1

JESUSES LITERATE AND ILLITERATE

That he was able to write
may be assumed.[1]

It must be presumed that Jesus
...was illiterate.[2]

This chapter will present previous proposals of Jesus as both literate and illiterate, highlighting the roles that Jesus' socio-historical context and particular biblical texts have played in those proposals. The discussion will also demonstrate the intrinsic connection between scholars' views on Jesus' literacy and their larger reconstructions of the historical Jesus as a Jewish teacher. This presentation of previous research inevitably is not exhaustive, but will suffice for demonstrating that Evans is entirely correct when he claims, "Scholars are divided on this question."[3] At the end of the chapter, I will note the manners in which my proposal in the rest of the book will reflect the *status quaestionis* in some ways, but also depart significantly from it in other ways.

 Related to the relationship between this study and previous considerations of Jesus' literacy, a comment on terminology is necessary. Although useful as general descriptors and perhaps unavoidable in that capacity, the terms "literate" and "illiterate" are ultimately unhelpful due to their lack of precision. Such classifications do not accurately reflect the literacy landscape of Roman Judea where individuals could hold different

---

 1. J. H. Bernard, *A Critical and Exegetical Commentary on the Gospel of John* (ed. A. H. McNeile; 2 vols.; ICC; Edinburgh: T. & T. Clark, 1928), 2:719.
 2. John Dominic Crossan, *Jesus: A Revolutionary Biography* (New York: Harper-Collins, 1994), 25.
 3. Craig A. Evans, *Fabricating Jesus: How Modern Scholars Distort the Gospels* (Downers Grove: InterVarsity, 2006), 35.

levels of literacy with different literate skills implied, and in different languages.[4] I will return to this issue, too, at the conclusion of this chapter (and more thoroughly in Chapter 3). It is important to recognize it at present, however, because I will adopt the traditional approach for heuristic purposes since the *status quaestionis* resides upon the dichotomy of literate/illiterate. Also, since the primary purpose of this chapter is to present previous opinions, I will refrain from offering thorough criticisms or prolonged discussion of the primary evidence and reserve these tasks for subsequent chapters.

1. *The Literate Jesus*

Historically, the most popular scholarly position on Jesus' educational status has been that he was literate to some degree. As Foster observes in his brief survey, the members of the First Quest were at times rather confident in their abilities to know Jesus' educational background.[5] Renan, for example, dedicates an entire chapter of his *Life of Jesus* to the matter of his education.[6] He claims Jesus could "doubtless" read and write in Aramaic, but likely did not know Hebrew or Greek.[7] Their assertions could be tempered also, however, as is the case with D. Strauss. D. Strauss claims that John 7:15, where Jesus' opponents "explicitly assert" that he is illiterate and "he does not contradict them," indicates that Jesus "did not pass formally through a rabbinical school."[8] Nevertheless, this emphasis may reflect an early Christian desire to portray Jesus as completely independent from human learning and, in turn, also may witness latently to the fact that "Jesus may not have been so entirely a stranger to the learned culture of his nation."[9] In other words, John 7:15 may be an early Christian cover-up that Jesus received his wisdom from

4. Cf. Harry Y. Gamble, *Books and Readers in the Early Church: A History of Early Christian Texts* (New Haven: Yale University Press, 1995), 3: "A Christian in first-century Palestine might have been thoroughly literate in Aramaic, largely literate in Hebrew, semiliterate in Greek, and illiterate in Latin, while a Christian in Rome in the late second century might have been literate in Latin and semiliterate in Greek but ignorant of Aramaic and Hebrew."

5. Paul Foster, "Educating Jesus: The Search for a Plausible Context," *JSHJ* 4, no. 1 (2006): 7–12.

6. Ernest Renan, *The Life of Jesus* (trans. unknown; London: Watts & Co., 1935; repr., San Diego: Book Tree, 2007), 41–46.

7. Ibid., 41–42 (quotation p. 41).

8. David Friedrich Strauss, *The Life of Jesus Critically Examined* (ed. Peter C. Hodgson; trans. George Eliot; LJ; London: SCM, 1973), 201, 202.

9. Ibid., 202.

human schools rather than divine bestowal. (D. Strauss's theory is interesting since, as we will see below, Bauer argues that the early Christian
cover-up in John 7:15 ran in the opposite direction.)

1.1. *Appeals to Jesus' Socio-Historical Context*

Some scholars assert Jesus' literacy by locating him in a Jewish context
where it is presumed that "most Jewish boys" went to school,[10] a
presumption that Chapter 3 will demonstrate is unlikely. For example, in
his short *Life of Christ*, Cadoux claims that Jesus' "educative influence…
would from an early age be supplemented at the local synagogue—where
with his younger brothers and other small boys Jesus would be taught in
class to read and say by heart portions of the Mosaic Law, and perhaps
also to write."[11] In his important study, *Reading and Writing in the Time
of Jesus*, Millard likewise says, "As a well-taught, observant Jewish boy,
Jesus would also have learnt to read the Scriptures in Hebrew."[12] Lee goes
so far as to say that an uneducated Jesus is implausible: "It seems safe to
presume that he attended a *bet sefer* and *bet talmud* as a child and young
man, because most Jewish males would have. His style of interaction with
the Pharisees is not intelligible without presuming education."[13] In a
similar vein, Flusser claims, "When Jesus' sayings are examined against
the background of contemporaneous Jewish learning…it is easy to
observe that Jesus was far from uneducated. He was perfectly at home
both in holy scripture and in oral tradition, and he knew how to apply
this scholarly heritage."[14] He claims further that, despite the fact that "the
historically less reliable John" records a charge in John 7:15 that Jesus

---

10.   John C. Poirier, "The Linguistic Situation in Jewish Palestine," *JGRChJ* 4
(2007): 87, refers to the idea that "virtually all male Jewish youths were schooled in
reading Torah" as "once a universal belief among scholars, and…still dominant in
many circles."

11.   C. J. Cadoux, *The Life of Jesus* (Gateshead on Tyne: Pelican, 1948), 37. See
also, Markus Bockmuehl, *This Jesus: Martyr, Lord, Messiah* (Downers Grove: IVP,
1994), 38. Cf. A. Morris Stewart, *The Infancy and Youth of Jesus* (London: Andrew
Melrose, 1905), 126–29, whose account is quite imaginative.

12.   Alan Millard, *Reading and Writing in the Time of Jesus* (BS 69; Sheffield:
Sheffield Academic, 2001), 146.

13.   Bernard J. Lee, *The Galilean Jewishness of Jesus: Retrieving the Jewish Origins
of Christianity* (CRNT 1; New York: Paulist, 1988), 126–27.

14.   David Flusser with R. Steven Notley, *The Sage from Galilee: Rediscovering
Jesus' Genius* (4th English ed.; Grand Rapids: Eerdmans, 2007), 12; repeated in David
Flusser, "Jesus, His Ancestry, and the Commandment of Love," in *Jesus' Jewishness:
Exploring the Place of Jesus in Early Judaism* (ed. James H. Charlesworth; SGJC 2;
New York: Crossroad, 1991), 161.

was uneducated, in reality, "Jesus' Jewish education was incomparably superior to that of St. Paul."[15] In a 1995 study of Jesus, Flusser's student, Young, repeats this claim: "Jesus' training and experience as a learned teacher of Torah far surpassed that of Paul the Jewish apostle to the Gentiles."[16]

Although he agrees with Dodd that Jesus could meet "scholars learned in the Scriptures upon their own ground,"[17] Riesner rightly considers Flusser's claim regarding Jesus' pedagogical superiority to Paul "gewiß falsch."[18] Nevertheless, in perhaps the most thorough consideration of Jesus' education to date, he too argues that Jesus was literate and empha- sizes Jesus' socio-historical context. Riesner is willing to grant that pas- sages such as Luke 4:16 and texts where Jesus asks his opponents "Have you not read?" imply that Jesus himself could read, and John 8:6 may even claim he could write.[19] But, for Riesner, these abilities certainly did not come from formal scribal education and need not even have come from elementary education, since he could have attained some degree of reading and writing ability in the home,[20] or via his attendance at syna- gogue.[21] He claims, "Die beiden stärksten Argumente für eine Elementar- schulbildung sind aber die Existenz einer Synagoge in Nazareth und seine Herkunft aus einem frommen Elternhaus."[22] Riesner thus concludes his section on Jesus' education by appealing not to any particular New Testament text, but rather to Jesus' supposed pious home and participa- tion in synagogue, as well as pilgrimages to Jerusalem, as an explanation for his "biblical knowledge":

15. Flusser, *Sage*, 12; Flusser, "Jesus," 161.

16. Brad H. Young, *Jesus the Jewish Theologian* (Peabody: Hendrickson, 1995), xxxiv.

17. C. H. Dodd, *The Founder of Christianity* (New York: Macmillan, 1970), 120.

18. Rainer Riesner, *Jesus als Lehrer* (WUNT 2/7; Tübingen: Mohr Siebeck, 1981), 242.

19. Ibid., 231.

20. Ibid.; cf. 112–15.

21. In his earlier essay, Rainer Riesner, "Jüdische Elementarbildung und Evan- gelienüberlieferung," in *Gospel Perspectives*. Volume 1, *Studies of History and Tradition in the Four Gospels* (ed. R. T. France and David Wenham; Sheffield: JSOT, 1980), 218, he claims, based on rabbinic evidence, that the synagogue attendant could have functioned as an elementary teacher: "Nazareth besass eine eigene Synagoge (Mt 13,54/Mk 6,2/Lk 4,16), in der alttestamentliche Schriften zugänglich waren (Lk 4,17). Der Synagogendiener (Lk 4,20) konnte, wie wir das aus rab- binischen Quellen wissen, als Elementarlehrer fungieren. Interessierte Nazarethaner vermochten sich eine gründliche Schriftkenntnis erwerben."

22. Riesner, *Jesus*, 232.

> Jesus hat keine 'höhere' schriftgelehrte Ausbildung absolviert. Aber sein frommes, in davidische und priesterliche Traditionen eingebettetes Elternhaus, der Besuch der Synagogen in Nazareth und Umgebung sowie die regelmäßigen Wallfahrten nach Jerusalem konnten ihm ein großes Maß vor allem an biblischem Wissen verschaffen.[23]

Elsewhere, he again underscores the importance of the synagogue: "The synagogues provided even in small Galilaean villages such as Nazareth a kind of popular education system. Many men could read and write…[and] Jesus could presuppose a knowledge of the Old Testament."[24] Herzog too claims, "It is very likely that [Jesus] learned to read and argue Torah in the local synagogue gathering."[25]

More recently, in an introduction to Jesus and the Gospels, M. Strauss continues this line of thinking by presenting a trilingual synagogue-educated Jesus:

> Like most Jewish boys, Jesus would have been educated in the local synagogue, where he learned the Scriptures and the Hebrew language. We know from his Nazareth sermon that he could read (Luke 4:16–20). This means Jesus was probably trilingual, speaking Aramaic in the home and with friends, using Hebrew in religious contexts, and conversing in Greek in business and governmental contexts.[26]

Ehrman is less convinced of Jesus' ability to speak Greek, but he also affirms the likelihood that Jesus spoke Aramaic and could read the Hebrew Scriptures.[27] (Nevertheless, for Ehrman, despite the possibility that Jesus "had some modicum of education…he was not considered an intellectual superstar by the people who knew him as he was growing up."[28]) In another recent textbook, one again finds the combination of Jesus being like other Jewish boys with the role of the synagogue in securing literacy for him: "Like other boys in his village, from the age

23. Ibid., 244. Similarly, Ben Witherington III, *The Jesus Quest: The Third Search for the Jew of Nazareth* (2d ed.; Downers Grove: IVP Academic, 1997), 38.

24. Rainer Riesner, "Jesus as Preacher and Teacher," in *Jesus and the Oral Gospel Tradition* (ed. Henry Wansbrough; London: T&T Clark, 2004), 191. See also Riesner, "Jüdische Elementarbildung," 218.

25. William R. Herzog II, *Prophet and Teacher: An Introduction to the Historical Jesus* (Louisville: Westminster John Knox, 2005), 68.

26. Mark L. Strauss, *Four Portraits, One Jesus: An Introduction to Jesus and the Gospels* (Grand Rapids: Zondervan, 2007), 421. Similarly, Mark Strauss, "Introducing the Bible," in *The IVP Introduction to the Bible* (ed. Philip S. Johnston; Downers Grove: InterVarsity, 2006), 14.

27. Bart D. Ehrman, *Jesus: Apocalyptic Prophet of the New Millennium* (New York: Oxford University Press, 1999), 100.

28. Ibid.

of six to ten Jesus became literate in Hebrew through study of the Torah in the Nazareth synagogue, and he memorized vast quantities of Scripture."[29]

1.2. *Appeals to Biblical Texts*

As the quotation from M. Strauss above indicates, some scholars foreground a particular portrayal of Jesus in the New Testament in order to affirm his literacy. M. Strauss cites Luke's presentation of Jesus reading the scroll of the Hebrew Scriptures in the Nazareth synagogue in Luke 4:16–20.[30] Others too appeal to this passage in affirming that Jesus was, or may have been, literate. Barclay points confidently to Luke 4:16 as evidence that "he learned to read" and John 8:8 as evidence that "he learned to write."[31] Dunn claims that, although "it is unclear how much weight can be put on Luke 4:16–21," "the picture painted in Luke 4:16–17 is in essence quite credible."[32] Foster concludes his cautious article on Jesus' education by claiming, "The balance of probabilities appears to favour the contention that Jesus at least possessed a basic reading ability."[33] During his discussion of the primary evidence, he claims Luke 4 is "the strongest piece of evidence in the New Testament for seeing Jesus as possessing some level of functional literacy" and (similarly to Dunn) states, "Luke's portrayal of Jesus' ability to read is not implausible…[and] can be assessed as feasibly fitting into the context of wider Galilean culture in the first century C.E."[34]

In a sustained treatment of Jesus' literacy, Meier considers Luke 4:16–30 along with John 8:6 and John 7:15.[35] In contrast to Foster's statement, however, Meier concludes that the last of these texts offers the most

29. Gary M. Burge, Lynn H. Cohick, and Gene L. Green, *The New Testament in Antiquity: A Survey of the New Testament within Its Cultural Contexts* (Grand Rapids: Zondervan, 2009), 128–29.

30. Presumably, Mark Allan Powell, *Introducing the New Testament: A Historical, Literary, and Theological Survey* (Grand Rapids: Baker Academic, 2009), 66, has this passage in mind as well: "Some process of education is implied by the fact that, as an adult, he is able to read and is knowledgeable of the scriptures."

31. William Barclay, *The Mind of Jesus* (New York: Harper & Row, 1961), 8–9. Barclay also appeals to Jesus' socio-historical context: "There was a village school in Nazareth; to that village school Jesus must have gone" (9). Leslie T. Hardin, *The Spirituality of Jesus* (Grand Rapids: Kregel, 2009), 56, also cites Luke 4:16–20 and John 8:6, 8 in affirming that Jesus could read and write.

32. James D. G. Dunn, *Jesus Remembered* (CM 1; Grand Rapids: Eerdmans, 2003), 314 n. 280, 315, respectively.

33. Foster, "Educating Jesus," 33.

34. Ibid., 12, 13–14, respectively.

35. Meier, *Marginal Jew*, 1:268–71; more broadly on the issue, 1:268–78.

evidence that Jesus had some level of literacy: "Of the three New Testament texts proposed, [John 7:15] at least provides some indirect basis for supposing that Jesus could read and comment on the Hebrew Scriptures."[36] For Meier, although John 7:15 rules out any formal education for Jesus,[37] it does indicate that he "could...read the Hebrew Scriptures... [and] enjoyed a fair degree of literacy in Hebrew and—a fortiori— Aramaic, the language he usually spoke."[38] Like Riesner, Meier posits that Jesus could have received what training he had in a Nazareth synagogue, but ultimately for Meier one "has to allow for a high degree of natural talent—perhaps even genius—that more than compensated for the low level of Jesus' formal education."[39] In a predominantly illiterate culture, though, Jesus' limited literacy would have been sufficient to distinguish him from the majority. Meier concludes:

> In at least one aspect Jesus was atypical of most men and women of the Greco-Roman world in the 1st century A.D.: he was literate, and his literacy probably extended beyond the mere ability to sign one's name or to conduct basic business transactions ("tradesman's literacy") to the ability to read sophisticated theological and literary works and comment on them ("scribal literacy"). Jesus comes out of a peasant background, but he is no ordinary peasant.[40]

Meier's assessment of Jesus' literacy exhibits both a sophisticated reflection on the literacy landscape of Jesus, but also a certain lack of precision when placing him within it. He correctly observes the general low-literacy environment and notes that literacy in Jesus' socio-historical context existed in gradations ("tradesman" and "scribal" literacy). However, despite concluding that Jesus did not receive a formal education— which would have undergirded "scribal literacy"—he nevertheless claims

36.   Ibid., 1:269; also 271, 278. Following Meier is Thomas E. Boomershine, "Jesus of Nazareth and the Watershed of Ancient Orality and Literacy," in *Orality and Textuality in Early Christian Literature* (ed. Joanna Dewey; SemSt 65; Atlanta: Society of Biblical Literature, 1995), 22–23. On pp. 23–24, Boomershine compares Jesus to Socrates since both left no writings of their own. Augustine, *Cons.* 1.7.12, had already made this comparison. See also Werner H. Kelber, *The Oral and the Written Gospel: The Hermeneutics of Speaking and Writing in the Synoptic Tradition, Mark, Paul, and Q* (VPT; Bloomington: Indiana University Press, 1983), 18.

37.   Meier, *Marginal Jew*, 1:269, 278.

38.   Ibid., 1:278.

39.   Ibid.

40.   Ibid. See also Craig A. Evans, "Jewish Scripture and the Literacy of Jesus," in *From Biblical Criticism to Biblical Faith: Essays in Honor of Lee Martin McDonald* (ed. William H. Brackney and Craig A. Evans; Macon: Mercer University Press, 2007), 54: "Jesus was no typical Galilean Jew."

that Jesus' literate abilities extended to scribal literacy. In the least, Meier's comments demonstrate the complexity of the issue.[41]

Another scholar who argues that Jesus was not formally educated but nonetheless could at least read the Hebrew Scriptures, and points to John 7:15 as evidence, is Evans. In several contexts, he argues against the idea that Jesus was illiterate.[42] Like Meier, he views John 7:15 as a statement of Jesus' lack of scribal education, but also as an indication that he held some degree of literate ability.[43] Specifically, he claims:

> The comments in John 7:15 and Acts 4:13 should not be taken to imply that Jesus and his disciples were illiterate. In fact, the opposite is probably the intended sense, as most commentators rightly interpret. That is, despite not having had formal training, Jesus and his disciples evince remarkable skill in the knowledge of Scripture and ability to interpret it and defend their views. These texts, more than Luke 4:16–30 and John 8:6, lend some support to the probability that Jesus was literate.[44]

Evans, however, also appeals to "considerable contextual and circumstantial evidence" in support of his overall argument, such as Jesus having followers who called him "Rabbi" or his references to Scripture in his teachings.[45] He is aware that "it is not easy to determine to what degree Jesus was literate" and that "there is no unambiguous evidence for the literacy of Jesus."[46] Nevertheless, for Evans, the cumulative force of the evidence is in favor of a Jesus who could at least read Hebrew Scriptures and interpret them in Aramaic.[47]

---

41. Eddy and Boyd, *Jesus Legend*, 247–49, follow Meier. They begin by noting that there is "no absolute proof" that Jesus was literate but claim it is "quite conceivable" (247) in light of their reconstruction of his context, and then cite John 7:15 and Luke 4:16–30 as supporting texts.

42. Craig A. Evans, "Context, Family, and Formation," in *The Cambridge Companion to Jesus* (ed. Markus Bockmuehl; Cambridge: Cambridge University Press, 2001), 15–21; Evans, *Fabricating*, 35–40; Evans, "Jewish Scripture," 41–54. The last essay is something of a compilation of the first two and a direct response to Pieter F. Craffert and Pieter J. J. Botha, "Why Jesus Could Walk on the Sea but He Could Not Read or Write: Reflections on Historicity and Interpretation in Historical Jesus Research," *Neot* 39, no. 1 (2005): 5–35.

43. Evans, "Context," 16; Evans, *Fabricating*, 36; Evans, "Jewish Scripture," 42–43. Similarly on John 7:15, Craig S. Keener, *IVP Bible Background Commentary* (Downers Grove: InterVarsity, 1993), 282: "This issue here is not that Jesus is illiterate (he is not), but that he has never formally studied with an advanced teacher."

44. Evans, "Context," 16; Evans, "Jewish Scripture," 43.

45. Evans, "Context," 19–20 (quotation from p. 17); Evans, "Jewish Scripture," 48–50.

46. Evans, "Context," 15, 17, respectively; also Evans, "Jewish Scripture," 44.

47. Evans, "Context," 21; Evans, *Fabricating*, 39; Evans, "Jewish Scripture," 51.

Scholars therefore find different reasons for asserting that Jesus was literate. While some state simply that his literacy may be assumed, others emphasize Jesus' socio-historical context in a Jewish culture where, it is presumed, boys normally received an education, sometimes attributing this to a synagogue. Still other scholars see particular images of Jesus in the Gospels, such as Luke 4:16 or John 7:15, as requiring a Jesus with some degree of literate skills. The most popular position on a literate Jesus is that, while he was not the recipient of a scribal education, he nevertheless could at least read the Hebrew Scriptures.

2. The Illiterate Jesus

Compared to assertions that Jesus could read and/or write, viewing him as illiterate has been a more recent phenomenon within historical Jesus research. This is not to suggest that the matters of Jesus' academic credentials or literary activity were never discussed previously. Indeed, already in the third century C.E., Origen is wrestling with Celsus' accusations and insinuations regarding Jesus being an uneducated τέκτων ("carpenter/craftsman") and the disciples being "fisherfolk and tax collectors who had not even a primary education."[48] As noted in the Introduction, in the early fifth century C.E., Augustine twice addresses the fact that Jesus never wrote anything,[49] as does Jerome in his *Commentary on Ezekiel*,[50] although neither mention his literacy or lack thereof as the reason. In the early twentieth century, Deissmann too cites Jesus' lack of literary activity: "Jesus of Nazareth is altogether unliterary. He never wrote or dictated a line."[51] Quite independent of these ancient and modern authors, Chapter 4 will demonstrate that Jesus' literate status was already a discussion topic for Christians in the *first* century C.E.

2.1. *Foundations for Recent Conceptions of Jesus as Illiterate*
Nevertheless, it remains that modern scholars have pursued the question of Jesus' illiteracy with a renewed vigor in light of recent social-scientific developments and subsequent applications to the field of New Testament studies. Among those developments, one can cite at least two landmark studies that have laid new foundations for viewing Jesus as

---

48.   Origen, *Cels.* 1.28–29; 6.34–36 (Chadwick), respectively.
49.   Augustine, *Faust.* 28.4; *Cons.* 1.7.11.
50.   Jerome, *Comm. Ezech.* 44.29 (PL 25.443).
51.   Adolf Deissmann, *Light from the Ancient East* (trans. Lionel R. M. Strachan; rev. ed.; London: Hodder & Stoughton, 1927 [original German, 1908]), 245; see also 246.

illiterate: Werner H. Kelber's *The Oral and the Written Gospel* and William V. Harris's *Ancient Literacy*.

Inspired especially by Walter Ong's work on oral hermeneutics and by folklorists Albert Lord and Milman Parry, Kelber's groundbreaking *The Oral and the Written Gospel* (1983) made New Testament scholars acutely aware of the impact of the oral environment of Jesus and the early Christians.[52] Since its initial publication, this book has generated significant critical response,[53] but also received widespread praise for its overall argument regarding the importance of Jesus' culture being an oral culture.[54] Kelber's primary contribution in *The Oral and the Written Gospel* regards the impact of orality on the transmission of the Jesus tradition, as his primary target was the hegemony of form-critical conceptions of that process based on literary models. Significant for present purposes, he situates Jesus within his oral culture at the beginning of the study. Kelber traces the "phenomenon of early synoptic orality" to Jesus himself, whom he claims the canonical Gospels present "as speaker of authoritative and often disturbing words, and *not as reader, writer, or head of a school tradition.*"[55]

52. Kelber, *Oral.*

53. See, for example, John Halverson, "Oral and Written Gospel: A Critique of Werner Kelber," *NTS* 40 (1994): 180–95; Larry W. Hurtado, "Greco-Roman Textuality and the Gospel of Mark: A Critical Assessment of Werner Kelber's *The Oral and the Written Gospel,*" *BBR* 7 (1997): 91–106. Kelber responds to his critics in Werner H. Kelber, "Introduction," in his *The Oral and the Written Gospel: The Hermeneutics of Speaking and Writing in the Synoptic Tradition, Mark, Paul, and Q* (VPT; Bloomington: Indiana University Press, 1997), xix–xxxi.

54. Although few have accepted Kelber's thesis *in toto*, the recent publications of a tribute to Kelber (Richard A. Horsley, Jonathan A. Draper, and John Miles Foley, eds., *Performing the Gospel: Orality, Memory, and Mark* [Minneapolis: Fortress, 2006]) and a tribute to *The Oral and the Written Gospel* itself (Tom Thatcher, ed., *Jesus, the Voice, and the Text: Beyond* The Oral and the Written Gospel [Waco: Baylor University Press, 2008]) demonstrate scholars' acknowledgment of Kelber's seminal insights. Consider Tom Thatcher, "Beyond Texts and Traditions: Werner Kelber's Media History of Christian Origins," in Thatcher, ed., *Jesus, the Voice, and the Text*, 2: "But while many of the specific points of [*The Oral and the Written Gospel*] have been disputed, time has shown that the book was a milestone in biblical studies, significant less for the answers it gave than for the questions it raised."

55. Kelber, *Oral*, 18. Sixteen years later, Kelber reiterated, "Jesus was a speaker, not a scribe, and not even a rhetorical composer by way of dictation" (Werner H. Kelber, "The Quest for the Historical Jesus from the Perspectives of Medieval, Modern, and Post-Enlightenment Readings, and in View of Ancient, Oral Aesthetics," in John Dominic Crossan, Luke Timothy Johnson, and Werner H. Kelber, *The Jesus Controversy: Perspectives in Conflict* [RLS; Harrisburg: Trinity, 1999], 75).

A second landmark study that created interest in Jesus as an illiterate is classicist William Harris's *Ancient Literacy* (1989). As mentioned in the Introduction, Harris argues against the idea of widespread literacy in the ancient world and claims that literacy rates in the Roman Empire likely never rose above 10 percent.[56] Subsequent research has qualified Harris' study for specific geographical and chronological locales, but in general his thesis is broadly accepted.[57] Also aforementioned, subsequent research on Jewish literacy and scribal culture has affirmed Harris's findings for the Jewish context.[58] Gamble's *Books and Readers in the Early Church* has similarly affirmed Harris's conclusions for the early Church.[59] Already on the third page of this book, Gamble places the issue before his readers as such: "So the question remains unanswered: To what extent could early Christians read and write?"[60] Gamble's question is indicative of the renewed interest in such matters in the wake of Harris, including interest in asking the question specifically of Jesus. Harris himself acknowledges that several passages imply literacy for Jesus, but regards him as "a poorly educated provincial."[61]

Although I mention their opinions on Jesus here, Kelber's and Harris's respective impacts on seeing Jesus as illiterate are not primarily due to their individual statements on him, but rather to their description of his socio-historical context. Furthermore, Kelber's and Harris's studies are clearly not the only ones effecting a scholarly shift towards an illiterate Jesus. One could also cite the work of Horsley, for example, who emphasizes the importance of class distinctions within the imperial context and argues that Jesus was a member of the oppressed peasant class who resisted the power of the scribal-literate elite.[62] It would seem that Kelber

---

56.   Harris, *Ancient*, 22, 272.

57.   Mary Beard et al., *Literacy in the Roman World* (JRASup 3; Ann Arbor: Journal of Roman Archaeology, 1992); Eldon Jay Epp, "The Codex and Literacy in Early Christianity and at Oxyrhynchus: Issues Raised by Harry Y. Gamble's *Books and Readers in the Early Church*," in *Perspectives on New Testament Textual Criticism: Collected Essays, 1962–2004* (NovTSup 116; Leiden: Brill, 2005), 541–42; repr. from *CRBR* 11 (1998): 15–37.

58.   See the Introduction and, more extensively, Chapter 3.

59.   Gamble, *Books*, 5. Accepting Harris and Gamble is Philip Esler, "Collective Memory and Hebrews 11: Outlining a New Investigative Framework," in *Memory, Tradition, and Text: Uses of the Past in Early Christianity* (ed. Alan Kirk and Thom Thatcher; SemSt 52; Atlanta: Society of Biblical Literature, 2005), 154.

60.   Gamble, *Books*, 3. Note the methodological appropriateness of Gamble's question; he asks not if they were literate, but to what extent they were.

61.   Harris, *Ancient*, 281 n. 527, 213, respectively.

62.   In addition to Horsley's earlier studies, see his recent succinct presentation of this view of Jesus in Richard A. Horsley, "A Prophet Like Moses and Elijah: Popular

and Harris are the primary catalysts, however, as Kelber argued thoroughly for the impact of the oral environment and Harris argued that Judea and Galilee, like the rest of the ancient world, were indeed predominantly non-literate.

Not all of the following scholars who argue for or assume an illiterate Jesus are explicitly dependent upon Kelber or Harris, although many are. The current suggestion, however, is not that they all are explicitly dependent upon them, but rather that Kelber, Harris, and others such as Horsley have generated a shift in the state of the discussion. Whereas some scholars of a previous generation would have, and did, find the idea of an illiterate/uneducated Jesus inconceivable, some present scholars argue the exact opposite. For example, two recent scholars, Bond and Thatcher, assume Jesus' illiteracy or lack of education but do not argue it in detail. Bond claims, "Jesus was uneducated; he was not a priest, he claimed no learning in the law."[63] Thatcher argues throughout his *Jesus the Riddler* that Jesus was a Jewish teacher who consistently outwitted his opponents and "uses his riddles both as a teaching tool and as a means of establishing his academic credentials."[64] He claims, however, that Jesus "probably couldn't write at all, or at least very little" and "possessed no official academic credentials."[65] For Bond and Thatcher, it is simply unnecessary to argue at length that Jesus was not formally educated.

Memory and Cultural Patterns in Mark," in Horsley, Draper, and Foley, eds., *Performing the Gospel*, 166–90. More generally on the peasantry, see Horsley, *Scribes*, 24–26. Note Crossan's acknowledged dependence on Horsley for his identification of Jesus as a peasant in John Dominic Crossan, *The Historical Jesus: The Life of a Mediterranean Jewish Peasant* (New York: HarperCollins, 1991), 124–25. (He references Horsley's *Jesus and the Spiral of Violence: Popular Jewish Resistance in Roman Palestine* [San Francisco: Harper & Row, 1987].) On Crossan's view of an illiterate Jesus, see below, p. 20.

63. Helen K. Bond, *Caiaphas: Friend of Rome and Judge of Jesus?* (Louisville: Westminster John Knox, 2004), 69. Cf. Allison, *Constructing*, 32 n. 4: "Jesus was not a scribe."

64. Tom Thatcher, *Jesus the Riddler: The Power of Ambiguity in the Gospels* (Louisville: Westminster John Knox, 2006), 112.

65. Ibid., 136, 102, respectively. Thatcher claims that whether Jesus had "official rabbinic credentials" is beyond the scope of his study (168 n. 11). His consistent reference to Jesus' lack of formal/official academic credentials, however, demonstrates the importance of the issue of Jesus' (lack of) education to his overall argument (102, 107, 117; cf. 110, 112, 168 n. 11). My argument in this book strengthens Thatcher's suggestions.

2.2. *Appeals to Jesus' Socio-Historical Context*

Just as some scholars cite Jesus' socio-historical context as primary evidence for his literacy, others cite the same context as primary evidence for his illiteracy. Foremost among the latter group is Crossan. In several contexts, he argues that, since Jesus was a Jewish peasant, he must be considered illiterate. For example, after citing Harris' study on ancient literacy, Crossan says, "Jesus was a peasant from a peasant village. Therefore, for me, Jesus was illiterate until the opposite is proven."[66] On the same page, he states more emphatically, "Jesus did not—and, in my opinion, could not—write."[67] In another context, he likewise claims, "Since between 95 and 97 percent of the Jewish state was illiterate at the time of Jesus, it must be presumed that Jesus also was illiterate."[68] Crossan acknowledges that Luke's account of Jesus' synagogue activities claims literacy for Jesus, but, like Kelber before him,[69] he sees the image of a scribal Jesus as due to theological elaboration rather than accurate reflection of the historical Jesus.[70] For Crossan, the identification of Jesus as a "carpenter" (τέκτων) in Mark 6:3 more accurately reflects his non-scribal peasant origins.[71]

The identification of Jesus as a peasant and the concomitant implications for his literate status have proven persuasive to several scholars. In his biography of Jesus, for example, Chilton refers to Jesus' illiteracy in this manner when he says of Galilean Jewish peasants, "For the most part, like Jesus, they were illiterate."[72] The Jesus Seminar, of which Crossan was a member, reiterates his position in their *The Acts of Jesus*. They print the entirety of Luke 4:16–30 in black ink, indicating their judgment that such an episode did not happen, and offer the following commentary:

> The Fellows of the Jesus Seminar are dubious that Jesus could read and write. That he was an oral sage is attested by ample evidence. But that does not mean that he had learned the scribal skills, in his day a rare achievement among peasants. It is by no means certain that Jesus could read Hebrew.[73]

66. Crossan, *Birth of Christianity*, 235. Cf. also his quotation of Carney on peasant illiteracy in Crossan, *Historical Jesus*, 3; cf. 421.

67. Crossan, *Birth of Christianity*, 235.

68. Crossan, *Jesus*, 25. See also his *The Essential Jesus: What Jesus Really Taught* (New York: HarperCollins, 1989), 21.

69. See above, n. 55.

70. Crossan, *Birth of Christianity*, 235; Crossan, *Jesus*, 26.

71. Crossan, *Jesus*, 23–26.

72. Bruce Chilton, *Rabbi Jesus: An Intimate Biography* (New York: Doubleday, 2000), xx; see also p. 99.

73. Robert W. Funk and the Jesus Seminar, *The Acts of Jesus: The Search for the Authentic Deeds of Jesus* (New York: HarperCollins, 1998), 274.

As in the work of Crossan, one can see here that placement of Jesus in the peasant class trumps the claim of the Lukan narrative. (The Seminar prints Mark 6:3's identification of Jesus as a "carpenter" in grey ink, indicating its possible reflection of the historical Jesus, and claims it "may be accurate, although it is difficult to verify."[74]) Elsewhere, the founder of the Jesus Seminar, Funk, claims, "Economically and socially Jesus was a peasant. He was probably technically illiterate—he may not have been able to read and write."[75] Initially, Oakman entertains the possibility that Jesus held some level of literacy: "Jesus was either illiterate (unable to read or write at all), or possessed at best craft literacy."[76] Thereafter, however, he refers to him as "the illiterate Jesus" and "an illiterate peasant."[77]

Rather than emphasizing Jesus as a peasant, Burge portrays him as a Middle Eastern storyteller and implies his illiteracy when appealing to his socio-historical context. He says, "Jesus lived in a world where literacy was rare and books (or scrolls) were rarer still…. The Gospels were penned by Jesus' followers, but we have no evidence that he wrote down any of his own sayings—much less that he wrote a book."[78]

2.3. *Appeals to Biblical Texts*
Although Crossan primarily points to Jesus' identity as a peasant and the realities of peasant life in order to assert his illiteracy, he demonstrates that advocates of an illiterate Jesus also can appeal to scriptural support. In Crossan's case in particular, he sees Mark 6:3 as corroborative evidence for an illiterate peasant Jesus and the scribal Jesus of Luke 4:16 as an inaccurate reflection of the historical Jesus.

Although initially considering Mark 6:3 as a possible indication of a *learned* Jesus (!),[79] Vermes cites the combination of the silence of gospel tradition on Jesus' education and John 7:15's "explicitly stated denial of formal training" for Jesus as indications of his lack of education.[80] He

---

74. Ibid., 84.

75. Robert W. Funk, *Honest to Jesus: Jesus for a New Millennium* (New York: HarperCollins, 1996), 158.

76. Douglas E. Oakman, *Jesus and the Peasants* (MBMC 4; Eugene: Cascade, 2008), 303.

77. Ibid., 305, 308, respectively.

78. Gary M. Burge, *Jesus, the Middle Eastern Storyteller* (ACAF; Grand Rapids: Zondervan, 2009), 18.

79. Geza Vermes, *Jesus the Jew: A Historian's Reading of the Gospels* (Philadelphia: Fortress, 1973), 21–22.

80. Geza Vermes, *The Changing Faces of Jesus* (New York: Penguin, 2000), 165.

thus considers Jesus "apparently untaught and unqualified."[81] Bauer also sees John 7:15 as evidence for an illiterate Jesus. Whereas D. Strauss posits John 7:15 as an early Christian attempt to cover up the fact that Jesus was educated, Bauer believes John 7:15 is the opposite—a Christian assertion for Jesus' literacy and thus a cover-up for the fact that "Jesus wäre ein Analphabet gewesen."[82]

In one of the more recent arguments for Jesus' illiteracy, Botha briefly mentions the role of John 7:15 and 8:6 in previous discussions of Jesus' literacy, but then focuses exclusively upon Luke 4:16.[83] (He never returns to the other passages.) Botha argues that scholars must view Jesus' activities in the Nazareth synagogue as a "cultural event" and interpret them in terms of Galilean peasants, for the majority of whom "literacy was of little concern"—"To be Jewish *and* literate are demands of a different time and not of the first century."[84] As with Crossan, for example, Botha emphasizes Jesus' historical context as a Galilean Jewish peasant in order to assert, "The historical Jesus could not read or write."[85] Botha, however, does not discount Luke 4:16 entirely and insists, "There is an association with reading which can plausibly be ascribed to him."[86] According to Botha, Jesus' "reading" in the synagogue (he appropriately notes that the text technically never claims Jesus read) was actually a performance—"a highly rhetorical verbal presentation of stories and oral interpretations"—rather than a literal reading from the text.[87] Luke is, for Botha, showing an expert interpreter of the Hebrew Scriptures at work. Therefore, although Jesus was illiterate from our perspective, "Seen as a report of a cultural event, Luke 4:16 should be related to Jesus' authoritative and demon-conquering activities. He is the son of God who can employ various techniques, including 'reading'."[88] In this heavily qualified sense, for Botha, Luke 4:16 presents an illiterate Jesus.

Scholars who argue for an illiterate Jesus, therefore, like those who argue for a literate Jesus, support their arguments with a variety of evidence. Appealing to Jesus' socio-historical milieu as a context that would

---

81.   Ibid., 165.

82.   D. Walter Bauer, *Das Johannesevangelium* (2d ed.; HNT 6; Tübingen: Mohr Siebeck, 1925), 105.

83.   Craffert and Botha, "Why Jesus," 21–31. In this co-authored article, Botha writes the section concerned with Jesus' illiteracy.

84.   Botha, "Why Jesus," 22, 26 (emphasis original), respectively.

85.   Ibid., 29; also, 32.

86.   Ibid., 29.

87.   Ibid., 30.

88.   Ibid., 31.

have precluded literate education is popular, although some scholars also cite biblical passages, or both. Especially popular is connecting Jesus' illiteracy to his identity as a peasant.

3. *Summary and Conclusions*

In light of the previous discussion, one must consider Craffert and Botha wrong when they claim, "Current scholarship is fairly unanimous that Jesus could read and write."[89] If anything, there has been a slight shift towards seeing Jesus as illiterate, although there are still advocates of a literate Jesus. Furthermore, confusion exists not only over whether Jesus was literate or illiterate, but also over the nature of the evidence upon which one makes a decision. Both John 7:15 and Luke 4:16–30 appear in the discussions as evidence for a literate Jesus (John 7:15—Evans, Meier; Luke 4:16–30—M. Strauss) *and* as evidence for an illiterate Jesus (John 7:15—Bauer; Luke 4:16–30—Botha). Similarly, scholars appeal to Jesus' socio-historical context as a Galilean Jew as evidence for a literate Jesus (e.g. Riesner, M. Strauss) *and* as evidence for an illiterate Jesus (e.g. Crossan, Chilton). Equally perplexing, scholars assert propagandistic influence on the gospel tradition in opposing directions. D. Strauss sees John 7:15 as early Christian cover-up for a literate/educated Jesus while Bauer sees it as early Christian cover-up for an illiterate Jesus. I shall return to many of the preceding suggestions in subsequent chapters, but offer now several remarks regarding the current book in light of this confused *status quaestionis*.

3.1. *The Question Matters*
First, to reiterate the point of the Introduction with emphasis, the *question* of Jesus' literacy matters because how one answers that question impacts how one will answer other questions about Jesus. As a particularly salient case in point, and one to which I will return in Chapter 5, how one answers the question of Jesus' literacy will impact how one views Jesus as a teacher, and thus how one interprets the controversy narratives. Do the Gospels portray an intra-Pharisaical dispute? Or do they portray an attempt by Jesus, a renegade scribal authority, to challenge his former comrades? Or do they portray an attempt by known scribal authorities to shame Jesus as an unqualified imposter? One's assumptions about Jesus' educational background will affect these broader exegetical matters. Thus, it is completely unsurprising that

---

89. Craffert and Botha, "Why Jesus," 5.

Young's Jewish theologian Jesus exhibits pedagogical superiority in Scripture, that Thatcher's riddling Jesus, who uses wit to compensate for official authority on interpretive matters, is himself devoid of formal academic training, and that Crossan's Jesus, preaching a brokerless kingdom as a form of resistance against the scribal elite, is himself outside that culture as an illiterate peasant.[90]

Crossan, however, deserves praise for at least answering the question of Jesus' literacy explicitly and acknowledging the role it plays in his larger portrait of Jesus. Others do not address the issue, or address it insufficiently, when it is clearly pertinent to their topic. Clear examples are scholars who suggest that Jesus was in fact a member of the Pharisees (or at least that the Gospels portray him as a Pharisee).[91] Maccoby, for instance, argues that Jesus was a member of the Chasidim, a non-mainstream group of Pharisees, stating that the "central proposition" of his book is "that Jesus was a Pharisee."[92] *En route* to this argument, he suggests that Pharisees and scribes in the Gospels are "members of the same movement" and that the two identities are interchangeable.[93] In light of Maccoby's image of a Pharisaic Jesus, it is likely not coincidence that his index of scriptural references does not list Mark 6:3 or John 7:15, passages that have the capacity to challenge the notion of a scribal Jesus.[94] Rather, he addresses the issue indirectly and briefly: "The idea, commonly held, that Jesus' upbringing as a carpenter somehow disqualified him from entering the ranks of the Pharisees (regarded as rich aristocrats, or, more recently, as pen-wielding bureaucrats) is entirely wrong."[95] He offers the matter no further reflection other than noting that Hillel and other Pharisees were laborers as well. Surely, however, (in addition

---

90. I am not the first to make this point. Luke Timothy Johnson, "The Humanity of Jesus: What's at Stake in the Quest for the Historical Jesus," in Crossan, Johnson, and Kelber, *Jesus Controversy*, 66, comments on the usage of categories such as literacy in order to establish "boundaries to what Jesus could and could not have done": "A charismatic Jew would not be interested in observance of the law, an apocalyptic Jew must have been committed to the restoration of the temple, a peasant Jew could not read and write."

91. This is the approach taken by Harvey Falk, *Jesus the Pharisee: A New Look at the Jewishness of Jesus* (New York: Paulist, 1985); Hyam Maccoby, *Jesus the Pharisee* (London: SCM, 2003); Paul Winter, *On the Trial of Jesus* (SJ 1; Berlin: de Gruyter, 1961), 133.

92. Maccoby, *Jesus the Pharisee*, 180.

93. Ibid., 2.

94. Ibid., 220.

95. Ibid., 181.

to his identity as a carpenter,) Jesus' education/literacy is relevant for whether he was part of a movement that Maccoby categorizes as scribal.

The present point is not simply to criticize Maccoby and others for failing to discuss an issue they did not set out to discuss.[96] Rather, it is to observe that there is indeed an intrinsic connection between what one thinks about Jesus' literate abilities and what one thinks of Jesus' fuller identity. *Jesus' literacy is a foundational issue in historical Jesus research and is thus long overdue for a critical treatment.*

3.2. *Abandoning the* Status Quaestionis

The present book will therefore fill this lacuna in Jesus research. It will share some similarities with previous investigations of Jesus' literacy insofar as it will enlist Jesus' socio-historical context (Chapter 3) and particular texts and traditions about Jesus (Chapter 4) in order to offer a statement on the literacy of Jesus (Chapter 5).

More important, however, this study will abandon the *status quaestionis* in other manners and forward a thesis that is, to my knowledge, original. First, I will abandon the literacy/illiteracy dichotomy upon which almost all prior studies have been based.[97] This dichotomy is too simplistic for proper understandings of literacy and its social manifestations in Second Temple Judaism. Chapter 3 will thus concentrate on various gradations of literacy, the social factors that affected the acquisition of literate skills, and the perception of literate abilities, among other issues. I will argue that the early Jesus traditions allow us to address not whether Jesus was literate or illiterate at all, but specifically whether he held scribal literacy. Second, I will not assess the historical trustworthiness of each Jesus tradition that is relevant to his scribal-literate status and proceed only with those traditions that "pass."[98] Rather, my argument will begin with the various images of Jesus' scribal-literate status in early Christianity's corporate memory of him and posit a Jesus who, in

---

96.   See the remarks regarding Thatcher's riddling Jesus in n. 65, above. See also the discussions of Jesus' literacy in relation to his possible consultation of the Jewish Scriptures for his identity and mission in Sean Freyne, *Jesus, A Galilean Jew: A New Reading of the Jesus-story* (London: T&T Clark, 2004), 150–51; Scot McKnight, *Jesus and His Death: Historiography, the Historical Jesus, and Atonement Theory* (Waco: Baylor University Press, 2005), 189 n. 1; cf. 177–87.

97.   Exceptions who note the existence of gradations of literacy are Botha, "Why Jesus," 26–27; Meier, *Marginal Jew*, 1:278 (see the quotation above on p. 14).

98.   This method is especially clear in Foster, "Educating Jesus," 12–21; Meier, *Marginal Jew*, 1:268–71.

one form or another, was capable of setting into motion this particular "history of his effects."[99] Chapter 2 lays the methodological groundwork for this approach and Chapters 4 and 5 put it into practice.

In light of these differences, the remainder of this study will argue that the most plausible explanation for why the early Church remembered Jesus as both a scribal-literate teacher and a scribal-illiterate teacher is that Jesus did not hold scribal literacy, but managed to convince many in his audiences that he did.[100]

99. Gerd Theissen and Dagmar Winter, *The Quest for the Plausible Jesus: The Question of Criteria* (trans. M. Eugene Boring; Louisville: Westminster John Knox, 2002), 212.
100.   As Chapter 5 will emphasize, my argument does not require that Jesus *intended* to convince his audiences that he was a scribal-literate teacher, only that he did convince them.

Chapter 2

JESUS TRADITION, MEMORY,
AND WHAT REALLY HAPPENED[*]

*Historical portrayals of Jesus, therefore, are also
hypotheses about how things could have been.*[1]

*Everywhere memorial sensibilities run up against
the limits of historical criticism's
analytical categories.*[2]

The question "What really happened?" is the Rock of Gibraltar of historical studies generally and historical Jesus studies specifically. Waves upon waves of scholars using various methodologies have insisted, persuasively even, that answering that question is ultimately impossible.[3] Nevertheless, as the waves of Jesus scholarship crash against the Rock and retreat, the question of historicity stands today, as it has in every generation since the Enlightenment, as the primary generating force

[*]   This chapter expands and modifies Chris Keith, "Memory and Authenticity: Jesus Tradition and What Really Happened," *ZNW* 102 (forthcoming 2011) (Walter de Gruyter; used with permission).

1.   Jens Schröter, "Jesus of Galilee: The Role of Location in Understanding Jesus," in *Jesus Research: An International Perspective* (ed. James H. Charlesworth and Petr Pokorný; Grand Rapids: Eerdmans, 2009), 38 (emphasis removed). See also Jens Schröter, "New Horizons in Historical Jesus Research? Hermeneutical Considerations Concerning the So-Called 'Third Quest' of the Historical Jesus," in *The New Testament Interpreted: Essays in Honour of Bernard C. Lategan* (ed. Cilliers Breytenbach, Johan C. Thom, and Jeremy Punt; NovTSup 124; Leiden: Brill, 2006), 77.

2.   Werner H. Kelber, "The Work of Birger Gerhardsson in Perspective," in *Jesus in Memory: Traditions in Oral and Scribal Perspectives* (ed. Werner H. Kelber and Samuel Byrskog; Waco: Baylor University Press, 2009), 203.

3.   Consider Ernst Fuchs, *Studies of the Historical Jesus* (trans. Andrew Scobie; SBT 42; London: SCM, 1964), 179: "It can *never* be certainly decided whether any indisputably genuine saying of Jesus has been handed on to us" (emphasis added).

behind any and every quest for the historical Jesus.[4] It may indeed be naïve to think we can answer the question of historicity in a final sense and without subjectivity; it is equally naïve to think that either of these matters will stop us from trying to answer it at all.

As Chapter 1 demonstrated, "what really happened" with regards to Jesus' education and literacy is an overlooked, yet important, matter. Scholars portray Jesus, however, as both literate and illiterate, with both sides appealing to biblical texts and Jesus' socio-historical background in support. The *status quaestionis* thus reveals an overall lack of progress since 1835 when D. Strauss claimed regarding Jesus' education: "But from the absence of authentic information we can arrive at no decision on this point."[5] As a case in point, note the similarity in Evans's statement in 2006: "Scholars are divided on this question because the evidence is somewhat ambiguous."[6] This chapter will argue that this protracted stalemate is a result of a commonality between Strauss in the nineteenth century and the dominant approach to the historical Jesus today—the search for "authentic" tradition. In contrast to the majority of scholars using the "criteria approach" to the historical Jesus, which employs criteria of authenticity to sanitize Gospel traditions as authentic before connecting them to the historical Jesus,[7] this study joins other recent

---

4. This is the case even for the so-called No Quest associated primarily with Bultmann, whose negative conclusions on the ability to quest after Jesus nevertheless demonstrate the primary role of the question in the research agenda. As a related note, the inaccuracy of the moniker "No Quest" for Jesus research in the first half of the twentieth century has been well demonstrated (see Dale C. Allison, Jr., *Resurrecting Jesus: The Earliest Christian Tradition and Its Interpreters* [New York: T&T Clark, 2005], 1–26; Stanley E. Porter, *The Criteria for Authenticity in Historical-Jesus Research: Previous Discussions and New Proposals* [JSNTSup 191; Sheffield: Sheffield Academic, 2000], 28–59 [esp. pp. 40–45], 238–39; Fernando Bermejo Rubio, "The Fiction of the 'Three Quests': An Argument for Dismantling a Dubious Historiographical Paradigm," *JSHJ* 7 [2009]: 211–53; Walter P. Weaver, *The Historical Jesus in the Twentieth Century: 1900–1950* [Harrisburg: Trinity, 1999]). It remains an accurate description of Bultmann's approach to the historical Jesus, however.

5. Strauss, *Life*, 202. On the date of the publication of the first edition, see Peter C. Hodgson, "Introduction," in Strauss, *Life*, xxiv.

6. Evans, *Fabricating*, 35.

7. Alternatively, David S. du Toit, "Der unähnliche Jesus: Eine kritische Evaluierung der Entstehung des Differenzkriteriums und seiner geschichts- und erkenntnistheoretischen Voraussetzungen," in *Der historische Jesus: Tendenzen und Perspektiven der gegenwärtigen Forschung* (ed. Jens Schröter and Ralph Brucker; BZNW 114; Berlin: de Gruyter, 2002), 118–19, refers to the "das Authentizitäts-modell," and McKnight, *Jesus*, 43, refers to "the criteriological approach to the Gospels."

voices in employing (what I term) the "Jesus-memory approach" to the historical Jesus.

Foundationally, arguments about the Gospels and historicity are actually about the nature and development of the Jesus tradition, and thus its possible connections to the actual past. In this regard, this chapter will break into three sections. First, I will argue that the criteria approach inherited a form-critical conception of the development of the Jesus tradition, which then determines how scholars employ the Gospels in search of the historical Jesus. Second, I will observe previous dissatisfactions with the criteria approach to the historical Jesus. Third, the remainder of the chapter will propose the Jesus-memory approach, which differs from the criteria approach both in its conception of the Jesus tradition and its determination of the historian's task in search of the historical Jesus. This chapter will thus lay the groundwork for the rest of this study, establishing why one must factor Jesus' socio-historical context (Chapter 3), as well as all the traditions about Jesus' literate status in the early Church (Chapter 4), into an opinion on Jesus' literate status (Chapter 5).

1. *The Criteria Approach to the Historical Jesus*

The dominant approach to the historical Jesus since at least the advent of the so-called Third Quest has been criteria of authenticity. Although most of the criteria considerably pre-date this period of Jesus research, they are a particular fixture of this most recent period and still the majority approach to the historical Jesus. As recent as 2007, after claiming, "Exegesis is now united in the view that the quest of the historical Jesus is historically possible and theologically necessary," Schnelle presents the criteria as the answer to the question "But how is this to be done?"[8] Even more recent, Keener's 2009 *The Historical Jesus of the Gospels*, which at least one reviewer claims "sets the standard for current historical Jesus work,"[9] continues to affirm some criteria of authenticity.[10] Although there are many criteria, up to twenty-five according to one

8.   Udo Schnelle, *Theology of the New Testament* (trans. M. Eugene Boring; Grand Rapids: Baker Academic, 2009), 68; trans. of *Theologie des Neuen Testaments* (Göttingen: Vandenhoeck & Ruprecht, 2007).

9.   Craig L. Blomberg, review of Craig S. Keener, *The Historical Jesus of the Gospels*, *RBL* (2010), n.p. (cited 10 September 2010). Online: http://www. bookreviews.org/pdf/7385_8048.pdf.

10.   Craig S. Keener, *The Historical Jesus of the Gospels* (Grand Rapids: Eerdmans, 2009), 155–62. He notes criticisms of the criteria, however, particularly with regard to the criterion of dissimilarity (pp. 156–57).

scholar,[11] it is not necessary to treat them in detail here; others have provided useful introductions and descriptions.[12] The most significant points for the present discussion are the criteria approach's conception of the composition of the Jesus tradition, the form-critical influence upon this conception, and the manner in which this conception defines the historian's task for scholars who use the criteria. These are the most significant points because I will propose that the Jesus-memory approach affirms what is correct in the form-critical conception of the Jesus tradition while addressing constructively what is incorrect.

1.1. *Form Criticism and the Pre-Literary Jesus Tradition*
Several scholars note that the formative development of certain criteria of authenticity occurred concomitantly with the rise and practice of form criticism, and thus the criteria reflect form-critical influence.[13] My argument, however, is that the *entire enterprise* of criteria of authenticity is dependent upon a form-critical framework. For, the criteria approach adopts wholesale the form-critical conception of the development of the Jesus tradition and thus its method for getting "behind" the text. Dibelius and Bultmann, the two most prominent practitioners of form criticism, will serve as representative examples of the method.[14]

---

11. Dennis Polkow, "Method and Criteria for Historical Jesus Research," in *Society of Biblical Literature 1987 Seminar Papers* (ed. Kent Harold Richards; SBLSP 26; Atlanta: Scholars Press, 1987), 338. Craig A. Evans, *Jesus and His Contemporaries: Comparative Studies* (Leiden: Brill, 2001), 13 n. 34, refers to Polkow's numeration of the criteria as "finely nuanced...at times 'hair-splitting.'"

12. Inter alia, M. E. Boring, *The Continuing Voice of Jesus: Christian Prophecy and the Gospel Tradition* (Louisville: Westminster John Knox, 1991), 192–206; D. G. A. Calvert, "An Examination of the Criteria for Distinguishing the Authentic Words of Jesus," *NTS* 18 (1972): 211–18; Evans, *Jesus*, 13–26; Polkow, "Method," 336–56; Porter, *Criteria*, 63–123; Riesner, *Jesus*, 87–95; Robert H. Stein, "The 'Criteria' for Authenticity," in France and Wenham, eds., *Gospel Perspectives*, 225–63; Gerd Theissen and Annette Merz, *The Historical Jesus: A Comprehensive Guide* (trans. John Bowden; Minneapolis: Fortress, 1998), 115. For convenient collections of applications of various criteria, see Bruce Chilton and Craig A. Evans, eds., *Authenticating the Words of Jesus and Authenticating the Activities of Jesus* (2 vols.; NTTS 28; Leiden: Brill, 1999).

13. Keener, *Historical*, 155; McKnight, *Jesus*, 45; Porter, *Criteria*, 63–102; Gerd Theissen and Dagmar Winter, *The Quest for the Plausible Jesus: The Question of Criteria* (trans. M. Eugene Boring; Louisville: Westminster John Knox, 2002), 8–9; cf. Klaus Haacker, "Die moderne historische Jesus-Forschung als hermeneutisches Problem," *TBei* 31 (2000): 64–67.

14. Edgar V. McKnight, *What is Form Criticism?* (GBS; Philadelphia: Fortress, 1969), devotes an entire chapter to Dibelius's and Bultmann's articulations of the

1.1.1. *Primary Task of Form Criticism.* Form criticism's primary task was to conceptualize and explain the pre-literary history (*die Geschichte*) of the Synoptic Jesus tradition.[15] Accepting the now disproved sharp distinction between early Palestinian Christians and later Hellenistic Christians, form critics located the pre-literary history of the gospel tradition in the early Palestinian Christian communities and its eventual textualization in the supposed Hellenistic communities.[16] Importantly, then, form critics argued that, prior to its existence as textualized narratives, the Jesus tradition was neither textualized nor narrativized. The earliest Palestinian Christians were too illiterate and unfamiliar with literary culture to be capable of producing the Gospel narratives, which

method, claiming, "Knowledge and general acceptance of the work of these men is presupposed and necessary for understanding and using the discipline of form criticism" (17). The other two important form-critical studies are Karl Ludwig Schmidt, *Der Rahmen der Geschichte Jesu: Literarkritische Untersuchungen zur ältesten Jesusüberlieferung* (Darmstadt: Wissenschaftliche Buchgesellschaft, 1964); Vincent Taylor, *The Formation of the Gospel Tradition* (2d ed.; London: Macmillan & Co., 1960). Since Dibelius's and Bultmann's "classical form criticism" was most important for the development of the criteria of authenticity, I leave aside more recent developments in form-critical methodology. See, however, Samuel Byrskog, "A Century with the *Sitz im Leben*: From Form-Critical Setting to Gospel Community and Beyond," *ZNW* 98 (2007): 1–27. Elsewhere, Byrskog proposes integrations of newer form-critical approaches, performance criticism, and memory studies (Samuel Byrskog, "The Early Church as a Narrative Fellowship: An Exploratory Study of the Performance of the *Chreia*," *TTKi* 78 [2007]: 223: "We need to show how the study of mnemonic forms and their *Sitz im Leben* provides further sophistication and differentiation in our conceptions of performance and memory"), demonstrating that, among their important differences, form criticism and social memory theory share some common emphases. What follows will further highlight the important similarities and differences. (I thank Professor Byrskog for making his *TTKi* article available to me.)

15. For a helpful introduction to form criticism, see Christopher Tuckett, "Form Criticism," in Kelber and Byrskog, eds., *Jesus in Memory*, 21–38.

16. Rudolf Bultmann, *The History of the Synoptic Tradition* (trans. John Marsh; Peabody: Hendrickson, 1963), 5, claimed the matter of the primitive Palestinian Christians and the later Hellenistic Christians was "the one chief problem of primitive Christianity" and "an essential part of my inquiry." The most considerable blow to this theory was Martin Hengel, *Judaism and Hellenism: Studies in their Encounter in Palestine during the Early Hellenistic Period* (2 vols.; Philadelphia: Fortress, 1974). Larry W. Hurtado, *Lord Jesus Christ: Devotion to Jesus in Earliest Christianity* (Grand Rapids: Eerdmans, 2003), 23–24: "[The] distinction between 'Palestinian' and 'Hellenistic'…has been shown to be simplistic." Similarly, Tuckett, "Form Criticism," 30: "Any distinction between 'Palestinian' and 'Hellenistic' has now been shown to be too crude."

display at least some literary sensibility.[17] Earliest Christians may have encountered the individual units of tradition that comprise the Synoptic Gospels, but not in the arrangement in which one finds them in their written state.[18]

Thus, in order to accomplish their primary task—the writing of the pre-literary history of the Jesus tradition—the form critics had to reconstruct that tradition. Of course, the only evidence with which they could work was the written Gospels as they stand. Form critics therefore had to develop methodological means of identifying oral tradition in written tradition.

1.1.2. *Form Criticism and the Gospel Tradition.* The form-critical means of identifying and extracting pre-literary Jesus traditions from the written Gospels reveal the method's central assumptions about the nature and development of the gospel tradition. First, form criticism asserted that the Synoptic Gospels are a mix of earlier oral traditions and later interpretive traditions of the early Christians, the latter of which are observable through the narrative framework of the written Gospels. One can identify this assumption in the following oft-quoted statement from Bultmann, in which he affirms Wrede and opens the door for redaction criticism: "Mark is the work of an author who is steeped in the theology of the early Church, and who ordered and arranged the traditional material that he received in the light of the faith of the early Church."[19]

The impact of the early Church on the shape of the oral tradition began before it reached Mark, however. "The process of the editing of the material of the tradition was beginning already before it had been fixed in a written form" and the composition of the Gospels "involves nothing in

17.   Martin Dibelius, *From Tradition to Gospel* (trans. Bertram Lee Woolf; SL 124; New York: Charles Scribner's Sons, 1934): "The company of unlettered people which expected the end of the world any day had neither the capacity nor the inclination for the production of books, and we must not predicate a true literary activity in the Christian Church of the first two to three decades. The materials which have been handed down to us in the Gospels lived in these decades an unliterary life or had indeed as yet no life at all" (9); and again, "We must assume unliterary beginnings of a religious unpretentious 'literature'" (39); see also p. 5. In entertaining the idea that the Gospel narratives formed in Aramaic rather than Greek, Dibelius rejects it out of hand on the same grounds: "For in this case we shall have to assume even for the earliest Christian generation a certain literary activity—and that is out of the question" (234).

18.   Ibid., 3: "The position taken by the evangelists in forming the literary character of synoptic tradition is limited…[to] the choice, the limitation, and the final shaping of material, but not with the original moulding."

19.   Bultmann, *History*, 1.

principle new, but only completes what was begun in the oral tradition."[20] These statements reveal a second important assumption of form criticism. The form critics assumed an evolutionary development of the gospel tradition whereby the earliest oral tradition *absorbed* elements of the early Church's faith on an inevitable path towards the tradition's textualization.[21]

Third, as is clear, form criticism assumes that the interpretations of Jesus in the written Jesus tradition came from later Christians, not the earliest stage(s) of oral tradition. This assumption is clear in the quotations from Bultmann above, the aforementioned argument of Dibelius that the earliest Palestinian Christians lacked the literary sensitivity to be responsible for the Gospel narratives, and perhaps most clearly in the crucial role of the early Christian *Sitz im Leben* ("life situation") in the form-critical model. The *Sitz im Leben* was not a historical event per se, but a familiar set of circumstances in early Christian communities that called forth the development of the specific forms.[22] The form critics assumed that, in contrast to the literary goals of the authors of the written Gospels, the impetus for the shaping of the oral Jesus tradition was early Christian existence itself (that is, the life situations) and particularly the missionary activity of preaching.[23] The transmission process thus took the shape of clusters of traditions with similar emphases and themes, organized into/by forms that met different kerygmatic needs in the life of early Christians.[24] In the words of Bultmann, "Every literary category has its 'life situation' (*Sitz im Leben*...) whether it be worship in its different forms, or work, or hunting, or war."[25] Further, "It is only possible to understand [the Synoptic tradition's] forms and categories in connection with their 'life situation', i.e. the influences at work in the life of the community."[26]

20. Ibid., 321 (cf. also p. 163, where he claims the I-sayings "were predominantly the work of the Hellenistic Church, though a beginning had already been made in the Palestinian Church"). Also, Dibelius, *From Tradition*, 3 (quoted in n. 18, above).

21. Similarly, Terence C. Mournet, "The Jesus Tradition as Oral Tradition," in Kelber and Byrskog, eds., *Jesus in Memory*, 47.

22. Bultmann, *History*, 4.

23. Dibelius, *From Tradition*, 13, 37; also p. 8: "The ultimate origin of the Form is primitive Christian life itself." Similarly, and explicitly following Dibelius, Bultmann, *History*, 4.

24. Dibelius, *From Tradition*, 13–14: "Thus the things that were remembered automatically took on a definite form, for it is only when such matters have received a form that they are able to bring about repentance and gain converts."

25. Bultmann, *History*, 4.

26. Ibid.

As a model for the transmission of the Jesus tradition, form criticism depended upon the ability of the form critic to connect Jesus traditions (pericopae, sayings, etc.) in the written Gospels to forms that corresponded to and reflected various *Sitze im Leben*. This process was, of course, inherently circular. One must assume the community needs and life situations a priori in order to conceptualize the forms that then classify the individual units of Jesus tradition; but the forms themselves are the evidence for the life situations that called them forth. This much Bultmann was willing to acknowledge,[27] and the circularity of the method was one of Gerhardsson's major disagreements with it.[28] Significant for present purposes, however, is the assumption that the shape of the Jesus tradition is due to the present theological convictions of the communities. The communities' *Sitze im Leben* influenced both the content of the tradition (individual Jesus traditions) and the means of its delivery (forms) to the extent that the written texts no longer reflected the work of the earliest Palestinian Christians.[29] For Dibelius, this process reached a high point with the writing of the Gospel of John.[30]

Form critics' attempts to connect the individual Jesus traditions of the Gospels to literary forms and *Sitze im Leben*, however, reveal a fourth assumption, which is that scholars are capable of separating the pre-literary oral Jesus tradition from the later interpretive work of the Evangelists and their communities. In light of subsequent Jesus research, it is important to underscore this assumption that, with the right methodological tools, critical scholars could pry earlier oral tradition from later written theology. Bultmann defined this separation of traditions as the very historical task to which form criticism speaks: "The task which follows for historical research is this: to separate the various strata in Mark and to determine which belonged to the original historical tradition and which derived from the author."[31] I will return to this statement of Bultmann.

---

27.   Ibid., 5, 11.

28.   Birger Gerhardsson, *Memory and Manuscript: Oral Tradition and Written Transmission in Rabbinic Judaism and Early Christianity* (trans. Eric J. Sharpe; combined ed. with *Tradition and Transmission in Early Christianity*; BRS; Grand Rapids: Eerdmans, 1998), 9–11. See also Tuckett, "Form Criticism," 34–35.

29.   Thus, Bultmann, *History*, 199, on similitudes: "The original meaning of many similitudes has become irrecoverable in the course of the tradition" (emphasis removed). More extensively, see Dibelius, *From Tradition*, 298.

30.   Dibelius, *From Tradition*, 298.

31.   Bultmann, *History*, 1.

1.1.3. Form Criticism and the Written Jesus Tradition. From a broader perspective, the methodological means of identifying the pre-literary Jesus tradition of the early Palestinian Church—or, more specifically, the means of presenting it in a manner that lent explanatory power to the form-critical method and its hypotheses about early Christianity—consisted of removing individual traditions from their narrative contexts in written texts and reorganizing them under categories of forms. Since form critics assumed that the interpretations of the written Jesus tradition did not represent the earliest stages of the tradition, the path to that earlier stage began by neutralizing the narrative interpretations. Thus, the means of attaining the pre-literary Jesus tradition—that is, getting "through" or "behind" the written text—was through the dissection and re-assignment of the written Jesus tradition.

In view here is Dibelius's and Bultmann's division of their "histories of the Synoptic tradition" principally into chapters on forms.[32] They thereby physically represent the history of the Synoptic Jesus tradition in terms of their schema for its pre-literary existence. The physical organization of their studies (and physical re-organization of the written Jesus tradition) may seem trite. The conceptual framework that it represents, however, has had an important, even era-defining, impact upon subsequent Jesus research. It established for generations of scholars down to today that, when searching for an entity that existed before the written Gospels, the means of attaining that entity is through the division and re-categorization of the written tradition under an alternative schema. This broad method continues to impact scholarship today because the criteria approach inherited it from form criticism.

1.2. The Criteria Approach
As their collective name suggests, the criteria of authenticity were designed as methodological means of identifying "authentic" Jesus tradition and separating it from "inauthentic" Jesus tradition, categories that correspond roughly to the historical Jesus and the Christ of faith.[33]

---

32. Dibelius, *From Tradition*; Bultmann, *History*; also Taylor, *Formation*. Schmidt, *Rahmen*, follows the order of Mark's Gospel.

33. They correspond "roughly" because with, for example, the criterion of dissimilarity, some inauthentic traditions would reflect Second Temple Judaism, not necessarily the Christ of faith. Importantly, the classic expression of the historical Jesus as something other than the Christ of faith, Martin Kähler, *The So-Called Historical Jesus and the Historic Biblical Christ* (trans. Carl E. Braaten; SemEd; Philadelphia: Fortress, 1964), emerged from this same milieu as form criticism, with Bultmann, *History*, 5 n. 3, responding to his own "much criticized skepticism" by sending readers to Kähler.

They thus function as sieves for the Jesus tradition, filters through which scholars can pass the traditions in order to determine whether a saying or deed attributed to Jesus in the Gospels came from the actual past of the historical Jesus or the theological convictions of the early Christians (or elsewhere).[34] As examples, the criterion of dissimilarity passes as authentic any tradition that does not comport with the early Church (or Second Temple Judaism) and the criterion of divergent traditions passes as authentic any tradition that does not help the theological purpose(s) of Gospel authors. The criteria of authenticity do not strictly deny the possibility of traditions that reflect both the historical Jesus *and* early Christian identity, but they do suppress any impact they may have in historical Jesus research by not passing them as authentic.

1.2.1. *Primary Task of the Criteria.* The primary task of the criteria of authenticity, therefore, is to separate the written Gospel texts into two bodies of tradition—one consisting of authentic Jesus tradition; the other consisting of inauthentic Jesus tradition. According to the logic of the criteria, the authentic body of Jesus tradition allows scholars to get "behind" the written Gospel texts with some surety, to glimpse the historical Jesus who existed prior to the interpretations of him reflected in the written narratives. Scholars thus connect portrayals of Jesus in the written Gospels with the historical Jesus only once they have passed through the criteria of authenticity. For example, Evans concludes that the Gospel portrayal of Jesus' subversive usage of Scripture actually represents the "creative, authoritative mind of Jesus" (that is, the histori-cal Jesus) on the basis of the practice's discontinuity with early Christian usage of the Hebrew Bible.[35] Similarly, Hengel affirms Matt 8:22 as historical because the saying "is in fact hardly one that can stem from the tradition either of the Jewish or of the later community."[36]

1.2.2. *The Criteria Approach and the Gospel Tradition.* The primary task of the criteria approach reveals its central assumptions about the gospel tradition. First, the criteria approach fundamentally assumes that the written Gospel tradition consists of a mix of authentic and inauthentic

34. Thus, Schnelle, *Theology*, 68, defines the criteria's task as "to filter out historically authentic sayings of Jesus from the broad stream of tradition, separating them from later interpretations and contemporizing accretions."

35. Craig A. Evans, "'Have You Not Read…?': Jesus' Subversive Interpretation of Scripture," in Charlesworth and Pokorný, eds., *Jesus Research*, 183; quotation from p. 198.

36. Martin Hengel, *The Charismatic Leader and His Followers* (trans. James Greig; New York: Crossroad, 1981), 5.

tradition. Second, it assumes that pristine authentic traditions *absorbed* later inauthentic traditions, "contemporizing accretions" in the words of Schnelle.[37] Third, by attaching authentic tradition to the actual past of Jesus and inauthentic tradition to the theologizing present of the early Church (or Second Temple Judaism, as is the case with the criterion of dissimilarity), the criteria approach assumes that the interpretations of Jesus in the written tradition derive from later early Christian communities or elsewhere, but not from the life of Jesus. This position may not always be explicitly stated as such, but it is certainly implicitly asserted insofar as the criteria of authenticity, particularly the criterion of dissimilarity, pass(es) as authentic only those traditions that can be detached from early Christian (and first-century Jewish) identity.[38] Fourth, the criteria approach assumes that scholars are capable of prying authentic tradition from inauthentic tradition; that is, capable of distinguishing one from another and extracting the necessary authentic tradition.

1.2.3. *The Criteria and the Written Jesus Tradition.* The net effect of the criteria approach is to re-categorize the Jesus traditions in the written Gospels into an alternative schema, namely, authentic and inauthentic bodies of tradition.[39] This schema then dictates the subsequent reconstruction of the historical Jesus based upon authentic tradition.

1.3. *The Historian's Task according to the Criteria Approach and Form Criticism*
According to the criteria approach, therefore, the historian's task is to separate the written Jesus tradition into authentic and inauthentic tradition, after which one can then construct the historical Jesus with the former body of tradition. To quote Schnelle again, the criteria's purpose is "to filter out historically authentic sayings of Jesus…separating them from later interpretations and contemporizing accretions."[40] In this light, it is also worth considering again Bultmann's definition of the historian's task according to form criticism—"to separate the various strata in Mark and to determine which belonged to the original historical tradition and

---

37. Schnelle, *Theology*, 68.
38. On the role of early Christian identity in the criterion of dissimilarity, see Chris Keith with Larry W. Hurtado, "Seeking the Historical Jesus among Friends and Enemies," in *Jesus among Friends and Enemies: A Historical and Literary Introduction to Jesus in the Gospels* (ed. Chris Keith and Larry W. Hurtado; Grand Rapids: Baker Academic, forthcoming 2011), n.p.
39. Funk and the Jesus Seminar, *Acts*, 8, thus speak of "dismantling the written gospels"; see further p. 16.
40. Schnelle, *Theology*, 68.

which derived from the work of the author."[41] The striking similarity is clearest in the respective definitions of the historian's task as beginning with separation of the written tradition. The criteria approach to the historical Jesus mirrors the form-critical approach to the pre-literary Jesus tradition, so much so that the former has simply exchanged "the original historical tradition" in Bultmann's quotation for "the historical Jesus."

1.3.1. *The Substitution of the Historical Jesus for the Pre-Literary Tradition.* The substitution of the historical Jesus for the pre-literary tradition is observable in the historical development of at least one criterion of authenticity, the criterion of dissimilarity.[42] Bultmann first proposed a version of the criterion of dissimilarity as a means to identify similitudes in the state they were in during Jesus' life. After claiming, "The original meaning of many similitudes has become irrecoverable in the course of the tradition," he asserts: "We can only count on possessing a genuine similitude of Jesus where, on the one hand, expression is given to the contrast between Jewish morality and piety and the distinctive eschatological temper which characterized the preaching of Jesus; and where on the other hand we find no specifically Christian features."[43] Porter observes that Bultmann originally made his statement "with regard to only one literary form-critical type, the similitude, [but it] was nevertheless soon made into a more absolute criterion by others who utilized it,"[44] referencing Käsemann, who employed it as a means of recovering "authentic Jesus material,"[45] and Perrin, who advocated the criterion as a way to identify "authentic" tradition that "may be ascribed to Jesus."[46] Porter is correct, but fails to observe the subtle yet important

41. Bultmann, *History*, 1.
42. Stanley E. Porter, "A Dead End or a New Beginning? Examining the Criteria for Authenticity in Light of Albert Schweitzer," in Charlesworth and Pokorný, eds., *Jesus Research*, 25–26, argues that the development of the criterion of dissimilarity in form-critical and redaction-critical scholarship is "a direct response to Schweitzer's challenge for historical method" (25). See Albert Schweitzer, *The Quest of the Historical Jesus: A Critical Study of Its Progress from Reimarus to Wrede* (trans. F. C. Burkitt; Baltimore: The Johns Hopkins University Press, 1998), 10–11. For a full history of this criterion of authenticity, see Theissen and Winter, *Quest*, 27–171.
43. Bultmann, *History*, 199 (emphasis removed), 205, respectively.
44. Porter, *Criteria*, 71–72; also Porter, "Dead End," 26–27.
45. Ernst Käsemann, "The Problem of the Historical Jesus," in *Essays on New Testament Themes* (trans. W. J. Montague; SBT 41; London: SCM, 1964), 36.
46. Norman Perrin, *Rediscovering the Teaching of Jesus* (New York: Harper & Row, 1967), 39; Perrin, *What is Redaction Criticism?* (GBS; Philadelphia: Fortress, 1969), 71, respectively.

shift from form-critical enquiry to historical-Jesus enquiry in the respective formulations of the criterion. Although it is true that Bultmann, Käsemann, and Perrin are all three concerned with connecting Jesus traditions to Jesus himself, and Bultmann (in contrast to Dibelius) did consider pronouncement of historical authenticity part of the form-critical task proper,[47] Bultmann technically forwards his version of the criterion of dissimilarity not as a means of recovering authentic historical Jesus tradition per se but rather as a means of recovering an original meaning as preserved by the similitude form. That is, Bultmann sought the pre-literary *state of the tradition*, not specifically the pre-literary *figure* of the historical Jesus in that tradition, despite the many indivisible conceptual overlaps between the two.[48]

The point of splitting this very fine hair is that, in the transition from Bultmann's usage of the criterion of dissimilarity to attain original traditional material to subsequent usages of it to attain an original historical figure via that material, one observes the criteria approach growing directly from form-critical soil, taking the form of a substitution of the historical Jesus for the pre-literary tradition.[49] The conflation of the criteria approach and form criticism is perhaps most blatant in the Jesus Seminar's *Acts of Jesus* (1998). Subtitled "The Search for the Authentic Deeds of Jesus," and thus reflecting a search for the historical Jesus via authentic tradition, Funk and the Jesus Seminar describe the supposedly necessary critical process of "Dismantling the Gospels" in words Bultmann could have written:

> In order to isolate the lore about Jesus during the oral period, scholars are compelled to dismantle the written gospels and sort the narrative components into two broad categories: (1) basic elements derived from the oral tradition and (2) framing stories and connective tissue used to mold the oral elements into a continuous narrative.[50]

47. Bultmann, *History*, 5.

48. Thus, Haacker, "Moderne," 65, correctly identifies Bultmann's development of the criterion of dissimilarity as "zur Ausschaltung von Fehlerquellen *in der Weitergabe* der Jesusworte" (emphasis added).

49. Insofar as form criticism was concerned with identifying sayings of Jesus that tradition grew around (Dibelius, *From*, 63, 235; Bultmann, *History*, 11), Riesner's introductory comments on the criteria for authenticity likely also reflect the indebtedness of the criteria to form criticism: "Die im foldgenden erörterten Kriterien wurden meist für die Sichtung der Logienüberlieferung entwickelt. Die Merzahl von ihnen kann aber in modifizierter Form auch auf die geschichtlichen Traditionen angewandt werden" (*Jesus*, 87).

50. Funk and the Jesus Seminar, *Acts*, 8; see further p. 16.

They proceed after this statement to present the gospel tradition in classic form-critical literary forms, claiming, "It is to these individual stories that scholars primarily look for historical data."[51] Funk and the Jesus Seminar's approach to the "authentic deeds" of Jesus via literary forms clearly displays the substitution of the historical Jesus for the pre-literary tradition.

As should be clear, the criteria approach's indebtedness to form criticism is also evident in its adoption of the latter's conception of the gospel tradition. Although form criticism and the criteria approach differ as to the past entity being sought—form criticism seeking the pre-literary Jesus tradition and the criteria of authenticity seeking the historical Jesus—the central assumptions about how to recover that-which-existed-before-the-written-texts mirror one another. First, the criteria approach's assumption that the written Jesus tradition is a mix of authentic and inauthentic tradition mirrors form criticism's assumption that the written Jesus tradition is a mix of prior oral traditions and later interpretive categories. Second, the criteria approach's assumption that authentic Jesus traditions absorbed inauthentic traditions in the process of transmission mirrors form criticism's assumption that the earlier Jesus tradition absorbed the later interpretive categories of the early Church in the process of trans-mission. Third, the criteria approach's assumption that inauthentic Jesus tradition represents the theology of the early Church rather than the historical Jesus mirrors form criticism's assumption that the written tradition represents the *Sitz im Leben* in which the tradition was trans-mitted rather than the earliest stages of the oral tradition. Fourth and finally, the criteria approach's assumption that scholars can separate authentic tradition from inauthentic tradition mirrors form criticism's assumption that scholars can separate earlier oral tradition from later written tradition. In other words, *the criteria approach borrows its conception of the gospel tradition from a methodology that New Testament scholarship largely abandoned decades ago.*[52]

1.3.2. *Connecting Jesus Traditions to the Historical Jesus.* It is no surprise, therefore, that the historian's task according to the criteria approach mirrors the historian's task according to form criticism. Both begin with

51. Ibid., 9–16 (quotation p. 9).
52. The exception of the minority Jesus Seminar, discussed above, demonstrates the need to qualify the statement in the main text. Consider, however, Samuel Byrskog, "Introduction," in Kelber and Byrskog, eds., *Jesus in Memory*, 19: "Today form criticism is being challenged on several—if not all—of its basic tenets. Scholars have abandoned it or modified it…"

a distrust of the written tradition's accurate representation of the past (whether past historical figure or past state of tradition). Both proceed to neutralize the interpretations in those narratives by removing individual Jesus traditions from their narrative contexts and aligning them under an alternative framework (whether authentic and inauthentic bodies of tradition or literary forms). And both offer their finished product (whether the historical Jesus or the pre-literary Synoptic tradition) only after applying the alternative framework. Significantly, then, one of form criticism's strongest influences upon historical Jesus research today via the criteria of authenticity is that scholars proceed to connect Jesus traditions in the written Gospels to the historical Jesus *only once the criteria have removed the traditions from the interpretive framework of the Gospel narratives*. I suggest here that the dissatisfactions that have grown in more recent Jesus research over the criteria of authenticity are rejections of this methodological approach to the historical Jesus.

2. *Dissatisfactions with the Criteria of Authenticity*

The challenge to the criteria approach that I offer below, the Jesus-memory approach, falls against the backdrop of prior dissatisfactions with the criteria of authenticity. When Porter published his monograph on the criteria of authenticity in 2000, he noted a rising element of criticism.[53] In some works shortly before his monograph, and certainly in subsequent discussion, there has been a controlled explosion in dissatisfactions with the criteria approach to the historical Jesus. These dissatisfactions are an explosion because of the number of publications and variety of corners of the discipline from which they derive; they are controlled because, despite their insistence and growing decibel, they are still undoubtedly the minority voice in historical Jesus research. Before joining the critical voices, I here briefly consider three prior challenges to the criteria approach: modifications of the criterion of dissimilarity; frank statements of doubt over the criteria; and emphases on the impact of Jesus.

2.1. *Modifications of the Criterion of Dissimilarity*
The criterion of dissimilarity is "the earliest and no doubt most signifi-cant criterion."[54] As discussed above, Bultmann and Käsemann both

---

53. Porter, *Criteria*, 101.

54. Porter, "Dead End," 25. Theissen and Winter, *Quest*, 18, claim the criteria of dissimilarity and coherence are the only "real criteria of authenticity," as opposed to other criteria they consider to be "source-evaluative arguments" that can "only be applied in a negative sense as criteria of *in*authenticity" (emphasis original).

heralded it as the one manner in which scholars could attain firm historical materials.[55] As a result, "In German-speaking scholarship it... attained an almost canonical character."[56] Nevertheless, already in 1972 it was receiving vehement criticism from Hooker, who labeled it "the wrong tool."[57] Eight years later, Stein summarized its status in the academy as such: "Despite the great optimism with which this tool was embraced, there has recently been a heavy barrage of criticism leveled at this tool."[58] The primary criticism of the criterion of dissimilarity has been that its severance of Jesus from Second Temple Judaism and early Christianity produces a patently ahistorical Jesus who could have been neither a Second Temple Jew nor the cause of early Christianity.[59] Despite criticisms, however, the criterion of dissimilarity has remained an important topic in historical Jesus research due to attempts to challenge or correct it, such as those of Wright, Theissen, and Winter.

2.1.1. *The Criterion of Double Similarity/Dissimilarity.* In contrast to the criterion of dissimilarity, Wright proposes the criterion of double similarity/dissimilarity: "When something can be seen to be credible (though perhaps deeply subversive) within first-century Judaism, *and* credible as the implied starting-point (though not exact replica) of something in later Christianity, there is a strong possibility of our being in touch with the genuine history of Jesus."[60] Rather than focusing solely on discontinuity between Jesus and his cultural milieux, then, Wright's criterion also accounts for continuity. Also contrasting the usage of the criterion of dissimilarity, Wright does not intend his criterion as a sieve for isolated Jesus traditions:

---

55. Bultmann, *History*, 205; Käsemann, "Problem," 37.

56. Klaus Haacker, "'What Must I Do to Inherit Eternal Life?' Implicit Christology in Jesus' Sayings about Life and the Kingdom," in Charlesworth and Pokorný, eds., *Jesus Research*, 140.

57. M. D. Hooker, "On Using the Wrong Tool," *Theology* 75 (1972): 574–81. See also her earlier "Christology and Methodology," *NTS* 17, no. 4 (1970): 480–87.

58. Stein, "Criteria," 242.

59. Inter alia, C. Stephen Evans, *The Historical Christ and the Jesus of Faith: The Incarnational Narrative as History* (Oxford: Clarendon, 1996), 328–29; Haacker, "Moderne," 66; Haacker, "What Must I Do?," 140; McKnight, *Jesus*, 44. Theissen and Merz, *Historical*, 115, describe the criterion as "dogmatics disguised."

60. N. T. Wright, *Jesus and the Victory of God* (COQG 2; Minneapolis: Fortress, 1996), 132 (emphasis original).

It does not help very much at all to take each saying, each parable, and work through a multiply hypothetical history of traditions as though aiming thereby to peel the historical onion back to its core.... Such a [method] serves only as a reminder that there is such a thing as serious history, and this is not the way to do it.[61]

In general, Wright is not attempting to eliminate the distinctiveness of Jesus that the criterion of dissimilarity seeks, but is arguing that one must arrive at an understanding of that distinctiveness by placing Jesus back in his socio-historical context and the context of the early Church.

2.1.2. *The Criterion of Plausibility*. After the most thorough critique of the criterion of dissimilarity to date, Theissen and Winter propose in its place the criterion of historical plausibility: "What we know of Jesus as a whole must allow him to be recognized within his contemporary Jewish context and must be compatible with the Christian (canonical and non-canonical) history of his effects."[62] Their criterion has two aspects (or sub-criteria) that replace the criterion of dissimilarity's dual focus on discontinuity—"the criterion of plausibility in the Jewish context, on the one hand, and, on the other hand...the criterion of Christian plausibility of effects."[63] Similar to Wright, Theissen and Winter essentially turn the criterion of dissimilarity upon its head and seek to emphasize continuity with the contexts from which the criterion of dissimilarity severs Jesus. Relevant for the present discussion, they further claim, "Historical research is not faced with the simple alternative 'authentic' or 'inauthentic,' but with the question of how the extant tradition may receive the most satisfactory historical explanation."[64] Elsewhere, Theissen, alongside Merz, is more emphatic: "There are no reliable criteria for separating authentic from inauthentic Jesus tradition."[65]

Subsequent Jesus research claims the criteria of double similarity/dissimilarity and plausibility are not so much challenges to the criterion of dissimilarity as important modifications or shifts of emphasis.[66] Their

---

61. Ibid., 133. See also Theissen and Winter, *Quest*, 10, who claim the historian using the criterion of dissimilarity "distances himself/herself from general historical methodology."

62. Theissen and Winter, *Quest*, 212; also Theissen and Merz, *Historical*, 116–17.

63. Theissen and Winter, *Quest*, 25.

64. Ibid., 204. Cf. their Foreword, however, where they speak of traditions that pass their criterion as "to be considered authentic" (xv).

65. Theissen and Merz, *Historical*, 115 (emphasis removed).

66. Particularly, Porter, *Criteria*, 116–22; Porter, "Dead End," 29, 33; Porter, "Reading the Gospels and the Quest for the Historical Jesus," in *Reading the Gospels*

differences with the criterion of dissimilarity are nevertheless quite
important for the manner in which they have forwarded the discussion.
These criteria both insist that the historical Jesus must be understood in
light of Second Temple Judaism and early Christianity rather than in
contrast to them. This is the case because, for both criteria, searching for
the historical Jesus should not begin by separating the written tradition
into authentic and inauthentic bodies of tradition but rather with the
interpretations of Jesus in the text. I have elsewhere characterized this
shift as a forwarding of the critical discussion by returning to the text, a
"second naiveté" in critical Jesus research.[67] Equally participating in this
"return to the text" are the next trends of dissatisfaction with the criteria
approach.

2.2. *"The Criteria Simply Do Not Work"*

A particularly interesting trend in recent historical Jesus scholarship
is scholars' frank statements that the criteria simply do not work. This
trend is interesting due to its more-or-less autobiographical nature in a
field typically characterized by scholarly rigor, method, and feigning of
objectivity. Although Porter, in an apocalyptic tone, offers his three new
criteria of authenticity "before the entire enterprise is finally abandoned,"
the following indicates that, for some scholars, it already has been.[68]

Perhaps leading the abandonment of the criteria approach to the
historical Jesus is Allison. In his most recent work, *Constructing Jesus*
(2010), he states in the preface: "I learned the discipline during an era
when everyone was taught to employ the so-called criteria of authenticity.... After many years of playing by the rules, however, I have

---

Today (ed. Stanley E. Porter; MNTS; Grand Rapids: Eerdmans, 2004), 52–53. Also
McKnight, *Jesus*, 44: "I am not sure Theissen and Winter's model is actually a
criterion at all. Instead, it is an orientation."

67. Keith with Hurtado, "Seeking," n.p.: "Ricoeur's concept of the second naiveté
is concerned with philosophical, theological, and hermeneutical approaches to
meaning and language as myth (Paul Ricoeur, *The Symbolism of Evil* [trans. Emerson
Buchanan; Boston: Beacon, 1967], 347–57; esp. p. 351). He uses it to propose where
readers (can) go once the introduction of criticism destroys the 'primitive naiveté' of
pre-critical textual encounters. Its relevance in the current discussion is not so much
due to its theological/philosophical import as its description of the critical enterprise.
Jesus studies have paralleled the path Ricoeur describes. After form criticism and the
criteria approach disrupted the narratives of the Gospels and their interpretations of
Jesus in search of 'history,' scholarship has returned to the surface level of the text.
This return, however, is not to the original pre-critical position vis-à-vis the text, but
to a new understanding in light of what the criteria approach has taught scholars."

68. Porter, *Criteria*, 126.

gradually come to abandon them."[69] The cracks in his confidence in criteria of authenticity were already showing over ten years earlier in his widely read *Jesus of Nazareth* (1998):

> We should not deceive ourselves into dreaming that methodological sophistication will ever eventuate either in some sort of unimaginative scientific procedure or in academic concord.... Appeals to shared criteria may, we can pray, assist us in being self-critical, but when all is said and done we look for the historical Jesus with our imaginations—and there too is where we find him, if we find him at all.[70]

He further claims, "Whether or not one shares my misgivings about dissimilarity, coherence, and embarrassment, it is certain that they and other criteria have not led us into the land of scholarly consensus. If our tools were designed to overcome subjectivity and bring order to our discipline, then they have failed."[71] Later, in his *The Historical Christ and the Theological Jesus* (2009), Allison acknowledges that, despite his convictions, he still attempted to rehabilitate the criteria of authenticity in *Jesus of Nazareth*.[72] In this book, like in the subsequent *Constructing Jesus*, his efforts at rehabilitation of the criteria are over.[73] Also, he claims scholars are not left solely with their imaginations, as he earlier intimated, but rather must work with the canonical Gospels.[74] For Allison, we are left with the canonical Gospels not only because "we cannot lay them aside and tell a better story," but because we are not capable of adjudicating between authentic and inauthentic traditions, the first step in telling a story other than the canonical one: "I must confess...that, with every year for further contemplation, I become more uncertain about anyone's ability, including my own, cleanly to extricate Jesus from his interpreters."[75] Importantly, on display in Allison's comments is not

---

69. Allison, *Constructing*, x; see also pp. 460–61.

70. Dale C. Allison, Jr., *Jesus of Nazareth: Millenarian Prophet* (Minneapolis: Fortress, 1998), 7.

71. Ibid., 6. Similarly, Fredriksen, *From Jesus*, 96: "Dispute on the status of individual passages seems virtually endless." Rafael Rodríguez, "Authenticating Criteria: The Use and Misuse of a Critical Method," *JSHJ* 7 (2009): 152–67, suggests that the criteria are actually "vehicles of our subjectivity rather than checks against them" (157; see also p. 167). Hooker, "On Using," 576, had earlier charged similarly.

72. Dale C. Allison, Jr., *The Historical Christ and the Theological Jesus* (Grand Rapids: Eerdmans, 2009), 55.

73. Ibid.: "My question is not Which criteria are good and which bad? or How should we employ the good ones? but rather Should we be using criteria at all? My answer is No."

74. Ibid., 66.

75. Ibid., 23.

simply an abandonment of the criteria approach, but an abandonment of the criteria's inherited form-critical definition of the historian's task as beginning with the separation of the written Jesus tradition. I will return shortly to Allison, since his *Constructing Jesus* aligns with the Jesus-memory approach I propose.

With a similar autobiographical statement, Haacker claims doubts about the criterion of dissimilarity had arisen for him already in his student days at Heidelberg: "I had come to the conclusion that a balanced overall picture of Jesus and his teaching cannot be built on the narrow basis of only those traditions which 'pass the exam' of dissimilarity."[76] Elsewhere, Haacker advocates the return to the text while rejecting current approaches that attempt to identify Jesus solely as an eschatological prophet, charismatic, magician, or Jewish Cynic: "Eine befriedigende Antwort auf die Wer-Frage nach Jesus kann nicht durch das Aufkleben solcher Etiketten erfolgen. Sie ist auf die narrative Redeform angewiesen."[77]

Allison's and Haacker's is not the majority position, but neither is it one of solitude. Several collaborative projects evince similar returns to the written Gospels in search of Jesus. According to the editors of the published results of the Identity of Jesus Project, of which Allison was a member,

> Many scholarly presentations of Jesus operate on assumptions that resemble those of an archaeological expedition. The 'real' Jesus is thought to lie buried beneath historical artifacts—texts and traditions.... The Identity of Jesus Project came to believe that Jesus is best understood not by separating him from canon and creed but by investigating the ways in which the church's canon and creed provide distinctive clarification of his identity.[78]

Similarly, Charlesworth notes in the introduction to the first published results of the Princeton–Prague Symposium, of which Haacker was a member: "The historians in this volume do not imagine that they can find the 'real' Jesus behind the perceptions and theologies of the Evangelists."[79] Several contributors to the Princeton–Prague Symposium

---

76. Haacker, "What Must I Do?," 140.

77. Haacker, "Moderne," 74. Similarly, Toit, "Unähnliche," 125.

78. Beverly Roberts Gaventa and Richard B. Hays, "Seeking the Identity of Jesus," in *Seeking the Identity of Jesus* (ed. Beverly Roberts Gaventa and Richard B. Hays; Grand Rapids: Eerdmans, 2008), 5.

79. James H. Charlesworth, "Introduction: Why Evaluate Twenty-Five Years of Jesus Research?," in Charlesworth and Pokorný, eds., *Jesus Research*, 14. This entire volume is also an excellent example of the criteria approach's stubborn influence. Despite Charlesworth's comment on behalf of all the contributors and at least two

previously contributed essays to *Der historische Jesus: Tendenzen und Perspektiven der gegenwärtigen Forschung*, and in this volume one finds similar opinions.[80] For example, Löhr claims, "Der Versuch, einen historischen Jesus trotz aller Kontextualisierung doch wieder „hinter" den Quellen zu greifen, ist zum Scheitern verurteilt."[81]

In addition to modifications of the criterion of dissimilarity, therefore, these scholars represent a second trend that witnesses a return to the full narratives of the Gospels in order to search for the historical Jesus. Again notable in these scholars' comments is their rejection of the form-critical framework of the criteria approach, either in the rejection of the authentic/inauthentic dichotomy, the dichotomy's dictation of the historian's task beginning with separation of the written tradition, or both.[82]

2.3. *The Impact of Jesus*
A third trend in Jesus studies that demonstrates a return to the written tradition in order to postulate Jesus' identity is scholars who emphasize the impact of Jesus, thus shifting critical discussion away from Jesus' self-understanding and onto others' reception of him. Tilley identifies this

---

contributors questioning the criteria approach (38 [Schröter], 97 [Haacker]), the individual contributions throughout the volume consistently invoke the criteria of authenticity (6, 7, 124, 152 n. 21, 173, 183, 186, 202, 216), including Charlesworth himself, seven pages before making his editorial comment (7).

80. Schröter and Brucker, *Der historische Jesus*. The common contributors are Luz, Pokorný, and Wolter. Dunn, covered immediately below for his emphasis on the impact of Jesus, also contributed a chapter, as did the co-editor of the volume, Schröter, who is covered below in reference to the Jesus-memory approach. Clearly, many of the emphases of these scholars are interrelated.

81. Hermut Löhr, "Jesus und der Nomos aus der Sicht des entstehenden Christentums: Zum Jesus-Bild im ersten Jahrhundert n. Chr. und zu unserem Jesus-Bild," in *Der historische Jesus*, 339. See also Michael Moxter, "Erzählung und Ereignis: Über den Spielraum historischer Repräsentation," in Schröter and Brucker, eds., *Der historische Jesus*, 88; Jens Schröter, "Von der Historizität der Evangelien: Ein Beitrag zur gegenwärtigen Diskussion um den historischen Jesus," in Schröter and Brucker, eds., *Der historische Jesus*, 205–6; repr. in *Von Jesus zum Neuen Testament: Studien zur urchristlichen Theologiegeschichte und zur Entstehung des neutestamentlichen Kanons* (WUNT 204; Tübingen: Mohr Siebeck, 2007), 145–46.

82. For others who reject the inauthentic/authentic dichotomy, see Larry A. Hurtado, "A Taxonomy of Recent Historical-Jesus Work," in *Whose Historical Jesus?* (ed. William E. Arnal and Michel Desjardins; ESCJ 7; Waterloo: Wilfrid Laurier University Press, 1997), 295; Rodríguez, "Authenticating," esp. 156 n. 15; cf. Toit, "Der unähnliche Jesus," 118–22; Richard A. Horsley, *Jesus and Empire: The Kingdom of God and the New World Disorder* (Minneapolis: Fortress, 2003), 8; Richard A. Horsley, "Prominent Patterns in the Social Memory of Jesus and Friends," in Kirk and Thatcher, eds., *Memory*, 62–63.

trend in the work of three scholars, Schüssler Fiorenza, Dunn, and Hurtado, to which one could also now add Bauckham.[83] Although most of these scholars employ memory as an important analytical category, I here describe their research by their common interest in Jesus' historical impact in order to differentiate their methods from formal appropriations of social/cultural memory theory (discussed below).

In re-configuring Jesus scholarship for contexts of ideological struggle, Schüssler Fiorenza argues for a shift from seeking "scientific certainty" to "critical retrieval and articulation of memory."[84] Her program for Jesus research denies the inauthentic/authentic dichotomy of the Jesus tradition that the criteria approach resides upon and also the criterion of dissimilarity particularly.[85] For Schüssler Fiorenza, historical reconstructions of Jesus should focus upon his reception by rememberers.[86]

Dunn finds the criteria inadequate for reconstructing the actual words of Jesus.[87] More importantly, however, Dunn differs from form criticism and the criteria approach in his conception of the gospel tradition. "The Synoptic tradition provides evidence not so much for what Jesus did or said in itself, but for what Jesus was *remembered* as doing or saying by his first disciples, or as we might say, for the *impact* of what he did and said on his first disciples."[88] The Gospels, then, are not collections of things that happened (authentic tradition) and things that did not (inauthentic tradition) but rather "impressions actually made."[89] Further, Dunn locates this impact during the lifetime of Jesus: "We should *not* assume that the impact of Jesus only began with his resurrection, or if you prefer, from the conviction that the crucified Jesus had been raised from the dead."[90] Dunn also dismisses the form-critical and criteria-approach definition for the historian's task as impossible from the outset: "We can never succeed in stripping away that faith from the tradition, as

---

83. Terrence W. Tilley, "Remembering the Historic Jesus—A New Research Program?," *TS* 68 (2007): 3–35; Richard Bauckham, *Jesus and the Eyewitnesses: The Gospels as Eyewitness Testimony* (Grand Rapids: Eerdmans, 2006), respectively.

84. Elisabeth Schüssler Fiorenza, *Jesus and the Politics of Interpretation* (London: Continuum, 2000), 75 (emphasis removed).

85. Ibid., 75, 136.

86. Ibid., 78.

87. Dunn, *Jesus*, 97.

88. Ibid., 130 (emphases original). See also James D. G. Dunn, *A New Perspective on Jesus: What the Quest for the Historical Jesus Missed* (London: SPCK, 2005), 30.

89. Dunn, *New*, 30.

90. James D. G. Dunn, "'All that glisters is not gold': In Quest of the Right Key to Unlock the Way to the Historical Jesus," in Schröter and Brucker, eds., *Der historische Jesus*, 147 (emphasis original).

though to leave a nonfaith core. When we strip away faith, we strip away everything and leave nothing."[91] The remembered Jesus, or more precisely the impact of Jesus upon the rememberers, is the only Jesus historians can hope to grasp.[92]

In a similar vein, according to Hurtado, "The only reasonable factor that accounts for the central place of the figure of *Jesus* in early Christianity is the impact of Jesus' ministry and its consequences, especially for his followers."[93] By emphasizing the impact of Jesus' life, Hurtado establishes a connection between what happened in the actual past of Jesus and the development of the early Church's conceptions of him. Hurtado is most concerned with the polarizing effect of Jesus and not attempting to climb inside Jesus' head and decipher with precision his intentions.[94] He insists rather, like Theissen and Winter, that scholars view the portrayal of Jesus in early Christian literature and practice as a result and effect of Jesus' life.[95] Hurtado thus refuses to sever the faith conceptions of the early Church from considerations of the historical Jesus on the basis that they reflect the beliefs of later Christians.

Bauckham's *Jesus and the Eyewitnesses* (2006) centers on the gospel tradition's status as "testimony" about Jesus in the period between his life and the textualization of the Jesus tradition.[96] With this conception of the Gospels, Bauckham aligns himself, as he has consistently done elsewhere, against form-critical assumptions about the gospel tradition.[97] He rejects the idea that the Gospels are a combination of authentic tradition and inauthentic tradition: "All history…is an inextricable combination of fact and interpretation, the empirically observable and the intuited or constructed meaning."[98] He also rejects the notion that scholars can attain a historical Jesus by going "behind the Evangelists' and the early church's interpretation of Jesus": "We should be under no illusions that,

91. Dunn, *New*, 30. See also James D. G. Dunn, "On History, Memory and Eyewitnesses: In Response to Begt Holmberg and Samuel Byrskog," *JSNT* 26, no. 4 (2004): 479; cf. 478.

92. Dunn, *New*, 31.

93. Hurtado, *Lord*, 53–54 (emphasis original). See further Larry W. Hurtado, "Early Jesus-Devotion and Jesus' Identity" (unpublished paper), 1–16.

94. Hurtado, *Lord*, 54–55.

95. Ibid., 55, 60.

96. Bauckham, *Jesus*, 8.

97. Ibid., 7–8. See also Richard Bauckham, "For Whom Were the Gospels Written," in *The Gospels for All Christians: Rethinking the Gospel Audiences* (ed. Richard Bauckham; Edinburgh: T. & T. Clark, 1998), 18, 23–26; *The Testimony of the Beloved Disciple: Narrative, History, and Theology in the Fourth Gospel* (Grand Rapids: Baker Academic, 2007), 9–12, 18.

98. Bauckham, *Jesus*, 3.

however minimal a Jesus results from the quest, such a historical Jesus is no less a construction than the Jesus of each of the Gospels."[99] Bauckham thus rejects the form-critical and criteria-approach definition of the historian's task: "Testimony is irreducible; we cannot, at least in some of its most distinctive and valuable claims, go behind it and make our own autonomous verification of them."[100] Thus, Bauckham is not interested in getting "behind" the textual traditions but in "imagining how the traditions reached the Gospel writers."[101] Here again one sees an emphasis upon the reception, or impact, of Jesus as revealed in the texts, and a rejection of form-critical categories.

In investigating the historical impact of Jesus—and despite their different research agendas—Schüssler Fiorenza, Dunn, Hurtado, and Bauckham demonstrate a third trend in Jesus studies that rejects the criteria approach to Jesus, as well as its definitions for the gospel tradition and the historian's task in reference to that tradition. Combined with modifications of the criterion of dissimilarity and frank confessions of doubt in the criteria approach, these three trends cumulatively witness a critical return to the text of the Gospel narratives in order to approach the historical Jesus. These prior dissatisfactions with the criteria approach set an immediate backdrop for the remainder of this chapter and entire study, which will forward the Jesus-memory approach to the historical Jesus on the basis of social memory theory.

3. *The Jesus-Memory Approach*

Social memory theory (also known as cultural or collective memory theory)[102] has emerged from the social sciences and marked out its own territory prominently, giving rise to a plethora of interdisciplinary

---

99. Ibid., 4.

100. Ibid., 505.

101. Ibid., 8.

102. "Social memory" or "collective memory" often refers to the work of Maurice Halbwachs while "cultural memory" refers to the work of Jan and Aleida Assmann (see Alan Kirk, "Social and Cultural Memory," in Kirk and Thatcher, eds., *Memory*, 2–6). J. Assmann distinguishes their work from Halbwachs in Jan Assmann, *Religion and Cultural Memory* (trans. Rodney Livingstone; CMP; Stanford: Stanford University Press, 2006), 8–9, with the essential factor being the Assmanns' focus on the transmission of group memories beyond interpersonal interaction or a single generation that writing enables (20–21). The emphasis on the social construction of memory is mutual, however, and thus I will use the terms interchangeably, though generally refer to "social memory."

studies.[103] In the last twenty years, it has also burst onto the scene of New Testament studies. Kirk and Thatcher's co-edited Semeia volume gave a proper introduction of the theory to English-speaking scholarship in 2005,[104] but had antecedents. Keightley's 1987 article on 1 Thessalonians appears to be the first full appearance of social memory theory in New Testament scholarship,[105] although Wilken cited social memory founder Halbwachs (see below) in 1971.[106] Schröter was applying the insights of cultural memory to the sayings tradition in a German monograph in 1997, whose main methodological insights appeared just previously in an English article in 1996.[107] Aguilar employed social memory in a study in 2000 (and 2005); Kirk did in 2001; and Esler did in 2003.[108] Since these

103.   According to Barbie Zelizer, "Reading the Past against the Grain: The Shape of Memory Studies," *Critical Studies in Mass Media* 12 (1995): 216, "The study of collective memory has virtually erased interdisciplinary boundaries." In addition to those studies cited below and inter alia, see Jan Assmann, *Moses the Egyptian: The Memory of Egypt in Western Monotheism* (Cambridge, Mass.: Harvard University Press, 1997); James Fentress and Chris Wickham, *Social Memory* (NPP; Oxford: Blackwell, 1992); Paula Hamilton and Linda Shopes, eds., *Oral History and Public Memories* (CPP; Philadelphia: Temple University Press, 2008); Frigga Haug, ed., *Female Sexualization: A Collective Work of Memory* (trans. Erica Carter; London: Verso, 1987); Jeffrey K. Olick, *In the House of the Hangman: The Agonies of German Defeat, 1943–1949* (Chicago: University of Chicago Press, 2005); Bruce James Smith, *Politics and Remembrance: Republican Themes in Machiavelli, Burke, and Tocqueville* (Princeton: Princeton University Press, 1985); Yosef Hayim Yerushalmi, *Zakhor: Jewish History and Jewish Memory* (New York: Schocken, 1989); Yael Zerubavel, *Recovered Roots: Collective Memory and the Making of Israeli National Tradition* (Chicago: University of Chicago Press, 1995). Cf. also Paul Ricoeur, *Memory, History, Forgetting* (trans. Kathleen Blamey and David Pellauer; Chicago: University of Chicago Press, 2004).
104.   Kirk and Thatcher, eds., *Memory*.
105.   Georgia Masters Keightley, "The Church's Memory of Jesus: A Social Science Analysis of 1 Thessalonians," *BTB* 17 (1987): 149–56. Cf. Anthony Le Donne, *The Historiographical Jesus: Memory, Typology, and the Son of David* (Waco: Baylor University Press, 2009), 13 n. 48. Dennis C. Duling, "Social Memory and Biblical Studies: Theory, Method, and Application," *BTB* 36, no. 1 (2006): 2, fails to mention Keightley.
106.   Robert Wilken, *The Myth of Christian Beginnings* (Notre Dame: University of Notre Dame Press, 1971), 207 n. 7.
107.   Jens Schröter, *Erinnerung an Jesu Worte: Studien zur Rezeption der Logienüberlieferung in Markus, Q und Thomas* (WMANT 76; Neukirchen–Vluyn: Neukirchen Verlag, 1997); Jens Schröter, "The Historical Jesus and the Sayings Tradition: Comments on Current Research," *Neot* 30, no. 1 (1996): 151–68, respectively. See further the essays in Schröter, *Von Jesus*.
108.   Mario I. Aguilar, "Rethinking the Judean Past: Questions of History and a Social Archaeology of Memory in the First Book of the Maccabees," *BTB* 30 (2000):

studies, a host of articles, chapters, essay collections, journal volumes, and books have stressed the significance of social memory for issues in New Testament studies.[109] One may also cite in this context Dunn's tome

58–67; Mario I. Aguilar, "The Archaeology of Memory and the Issue of Colonialism: Mimesis and the Controversial Tribute to Caesar in Mark 12:13–17," *BTB* 35 (2005): 60–66; Alan Kirk, "The Johannine Jesus in the Gospel of Peter: A Social Memory Approach," in *Jesus in Johannine Tradition* (ed. Robert T. Fortna and Tom Thatcher; Louisville: Westminster John Knox, 2001), 313–21; Philip F. Esler, *Conflict and Identity in Romans: The Social Setting of Paul's Letter* (Minneapolis: Fortress, 2003), 174–75, respectively.

109.   Inter alia, see Allison, *Constructing*, 1–30 (esp. 5 n. 30); Markus Bockmuehl, *Seeing the Word: Refocusing New Testament Study* (STI; Grand Rapids: Baker Academic, 2006), 176–77; Byrskog, "Early Church as Narrative Fellowship," 211; Samuel Byrskog, "A New Quest for the *Sitz im Leben*: Social Memory, the Jesus Tradition and the Gospel of Matthew," *NTS* 52 (2006): 319–36; Duling, "Social Memory," 2–3; Philip F. Esler, "Paul's Contestation of Israel's (Ethnic) Memory of Abraham in Galatians 3," *BTB* 36, no. 1 (2006): 23–34; Richard A. Horsley, *Jesus in Context: Power, People, and Performance* (Minneapolis: Fortress, 2008), 14–16, 109–68; Horsley, Draper, and Foley, eds., *Performing the Gospel*; Chris Keith, "The Claim of John 7.15 and the Memory of Jesus' Literacy," *NTS* 56, no. 1 (2010): 55–63; Chris Keith, "A Performance of the Text: The Adulteress's Entrance into John's Gospel," in *The Fourth Gospel in First-Century Media Culture* (ed. Anthony Le Donne and Tom Thatcher; ESCO/LNTS 426; London: T&T Clark, 2011), 49–69; Werner H. Kelber, "The Generative Force of Memory: Early Christian Traditions as Processes of Remembering," *BTB* 36, no. 1 (2006): 15–22; Kelber and Byrskog, eds., *Jesus in Memory*; Jens Schröter, "Geschichte im Licht von Tod und Auferweckung Jesu Christi: Anmerkungen zum Diskurs über Erinnerung und Geschichte aus frühchristlicher Perspektive," in *Von Jesus*, 55–77; repr. from *BTZ* 23 (2006): 3–25; Loren T. Stuckenbruck, Stephen C. Barton, and Benjamin G. Wold, eds., *Memory in the Bible and Antiquity* (WUNT 212; Tübingen: Mohr Siebeck, 2007); Tom Thatcher, "Cain and Abel in Early Christian Memory: A Case Study in 'The Use of the Old Testament in the New,'" *CBQ* 72 (2010): 732–51; Tom Thatcher, *Greater than Caesar: Christology and Empire in the Fourth Gospel* (Minneapolis: Fortress, 2009), 36–41, 88–92; Thatcher, *Jesus*; Tom Thatcher, *Why John Wrote a Gospel: Jesus—Memory—History* (Louisville: Westminster John Knox, 2006); Catrin H. Williams, "Abraham as a Figure of Memory in John 8.31–59," in Le Donne and Thatcher, eds., *Fourth Gospel*, 205–22; Ritva H. Williams, "Social Memory and the DIDACHÉ," *BTB* 36, no. 1 (2006): 35–45; Ruben Zimmermann, "Memory and Form Criticism: The Typicality of Memory as a Bridge between Orality and Literality in the Early Christian Remembering Process," in *The Interface of Orality and Writing: Speaking, Seeing, Writing in the Shaping of New Genres* (ed. Annette Weissenrieder and Robert B. Coote; WUNT 1/260; Tübingen: Mohr Siebeck, 2010), 130–43. My own initial work in social memory theory was Chris Keith, "The Saliency of a Psalm: The Markan Crucifixion as Social Memory" (M.A. thesis, Cincinnati Christian University, 2005), supervised by Tom Thatcher. Some of its main conclusions were

Jesus Remembered (2003). Although not an application of social memory theory (he bases his arguments primarily upon oral hermeneutics),[110] he nevertheless foregrounds the role of memory and arrives at similar conclusions to many of these studies, and in later work has engaged social memory theory.[111] Dunn's final Ph.D. student at the University of Durham, Le Donne, wrote one of two published doctoral theses based on social memory theory, the other being that of Rodríguez.[112] Clearly, Davies is not alone in claiming, "Cultural memory provides a better conceptual tool than history, myth, or tradition for classifying the biblical narratives about the past because it better reflects the ways in which the past was understood and utilized by ancient societies."[113]

As with form criticism and the criteria of authenticity, excellent introductions to social memory theory are readily accessible and so it is not necessary to give a full description of the method here.[114] Rather,

---

later published as Chris Keith, "The Role of the Cross in the Composition of the Markan Crucifixion Narrative," *SCJ* 9, no. 1 (2006): 61–75; cf. Chris Keith and Tom Thatcher, "The Scar of the Cross: The Violence Ratio and the Earliest Christian Memories of Jesus," in Thatcher, ed., *Jesus*, 197–214. James K. Beilby and Paul Rhodes Eddy, "The Quest for the Historical Jesus: An Introduction," in *The Historical Jesus: Five Views* (ed. James K. Beilby and Paul Rhodes Eddy; Downers Grove: IVP Academic, 2009), 44, refer to "social/collective memory studies" alongside orality studies as "one of the most fertile areas of Jesus/Gospels research currently under investigation."

110. For a similar emphasis on memory from the perspective of oral herme-neutics, see Ellen Bradshaw Aitken, *Jesus' Death in Early Christian Memory: The Poetics of the Passion* (NTOA/SUNT 53; Göttingen: Vandenhoeck & Ruprecht, 2004), 14–26.

111. Dunn, "On History," 481–82; Dunn, "Social Memory and the Oral Jesus Tradition," in Stuckenbruck, Barton, and Wold, eds., *Memory in the Bible*, 179–94.

112. Le Donne, *Historiographical*; Rafael Rodríguez, *Structuring Early Christian Memory: Jesus in Tradition, Performance and Text* (ESCO/LNTS 407; London: T&T Clark, 2009).

113. Philip R. Davies, *Memories of Ancient Israel: An Introduction to Biblical History—Ancient and Modern* (Louisville: Westminster John Knox, 2008), 122. Cf. also Jens Schröter, "Konstruktion von Geschichte und die Anfänge des Chris-tentums: Reflexionen zur christlichen Geschichtsdeutung aus neutestamentlicher Perspektive," in *Von Jesus*, 40 n. 17; repr. from *Konstruktion von Wirklichkeit: Beiträge aus geschichtstheoretischer, philosophischer und theologischer Perspektive* (ed. Jens Schröter with Antje Eddelbüttel; TBT 127; Berlin: de Gruyter, 2004), 202–19: "Assmann hat in diesem Sinn die fundierende Funktion von Geschichte als Erin-nerung und Gedächtnis herausgearbeitet.... Für das Christentum, namentlich die Apostelgeschichte des Lukas, ließe sich dies in analoger Weise fruchtbar machen."

114. For general introductions, see Assmann, *Religion*, 1–30; Barbara Misztal, *Theories of Social Remembering* (ThS; Philadelphia: Open University Press, 2003);

what follows will highlight social memory theory's central insights as they relate to the question of historicity. Whereas some scholars view criteria of authenticity as "the wrong tool,"[115] this perspective insists that the Gospels are not the type of ground that can be dug. Therefore, not only do these insights render the criteria approach untenable (buttressing some of the aforementioned dissatisfactions), they require a definition for the Jesus historian's task that differs substantially from the criteria approach.

3.1. *Social Memory Theory—The Present and the Past in Commemorative Activity*

While Dibelius and Bultmann were in Germany emphasizing the role of the Christian *Sitz im Leben* in transmitting the past of Jesus, sociologist Maurice Halbwachs was in France emphasizing the role of the present in all remembrance of the past. Beginning with Halbwachs, the foundational argument of social memory theory is that memory is not a simple act of recall, but rather a complex process whereby the past is reconstructed in light of the needs of the present.[116] In contrast to psychological views of memory as a store-and-retrieve function, he asserts, "No memory is possible outside frameworks used by people living in society to determine and retrieve their recollections."[117] Halbwachs posits that all

Jeffrey K. Olick, "Products, Processes, and Practices: A Non-Reificatory Approach to Collective Memory," *BTB* 36, no. 1 (2006): 5–14; Zelizer, "Reading the Past," 214–39. Related to Biblical Studies, still the best introduction is Kirk, "Social," 1–24. See also Le Donne, *Historiographical*, 41–64. With reference to the Jesus tradition in particular, see Alan Kirk and Tom Thatcher, "Jesus Tradition as Social Memory," in Kirk and Thatcher, eds., *Memory*, 25–42; Horsley, *Jesus in Context*, 109–45.

    115.   Hooker, "On Using," in reference to the criterion of dissimilarity.

    116.   Lewis A. Coser, "Introduction," in *On Collective Memory*, by Maurice Halbwachs (Chicago: University of Chicago Press, 1992), 34: "Halbwachs was without doubt the first sociologist who stressed that our conceptions of the past are affected by the mental images we employ to solve present problems, so that collective memory is essentially a reconstruction of the past in the light of the present." On Halbwach's indebtedness to Henri Bergson and Emile Durkheim, see Coser, "Introduction," 7–13; Mary Douglas, "Introduction," in *The Collective Memory*, by Maurice Halbwachs (New York: Harper Colophon, 1980), 1–19; Olick, "Products," 10–11; cf. also Paula Hamilton and Linda Shopes, "Introduction: Building Partnerships between Oral History and Memory Studies," in Hamilton and Shopes, eds., *Oral History*, x.

    117.   Maurice Halbwachs, "The Social Frameworks of Memory," in *On Collective Memory*, 43.

memory is indeed social because the vehicles that enable memory—
language and the categories that inform thought—are socially formed:
"Individual memory could not function without words and ideas, instruments the individual has not himself invented but appropriated from his
milieu."[118] At the rudimentary level, the accuracy of Halbwachs's observations can be demonstrated by recognizing that when one remembers
statements or phrases, one does so in languages with which one has some
familiarity through cultural experiences; that is, the linguistic shape of
one's memories reveals an inherent debt to social structures. Although
there are certainly individuals, "It is individuals as group members who
remember."[119] In this way, memory is a thoroughly social phenomenon
rather than an individual one.

Stemming from Halbwachs's initial insights, therefore, social memory
theory is essentially concerned with communal commemoration of the
past, whether that be through ritual (festivals, worship, holidays, dances,
etc.), oral tradition (storytelling, songs, etc.), texts (genealogies, written
narratives, textbooks, etc.), monuments (statues, buildings, sacred space,
etc.), or other means. From this perspective, "tradition" refers to any of
these cultural objects that navigate the relationship between the past and
the present,[120] and thus the Assmanns describe "tradition" as *kulturelle
Texte*.[121]

Since he was arguing against the idea that memory functioned like a
file folder into which one placed past experiences, only to recall them in
their original condition when needed, Halbwachs stressed that memory
was not primarily a past-oriented activity. Rather, it was the present that

---

118.   Halbwachs, *The Collective Memory*, 51. Similarly, Halbwachs, "Social
Frameworks," 168: "There are no perceptions that can be called purely exterior, since
when a member of the group perceives an object, he gives it a name and arranges it
into a specific category. In other words, he conforms to the group's conventions
which supply his thought as they supply the thought of others." See also Kirk,
"Social," 2; Olick, "Products," 11.

119.   Halbwachs, *Collective Memory*, 48.

120.   Similarly, Kirk and Thatcher, "Jesus Tradition," 33.

121.   Aleida Assmann, "Was sind kulturelle Texte?," in *Literaturkanon—
Medienereignis—Kultureller Text: Formen interkultureller Kommunikation und
Übersetzung* (ed. Andreas Poltermann; GBIU 10; Berlin: Eric Schmidt, 1995), 232–
44; Jan Assmann, "Cultural Texts Suspended between Writing and Speech," in
Religion, 101–21; repr. and trans. from "Kulturelle Texte im Spannungsfeld von
Mündlichkeit und Schriftlichkeit," in Poltermann, ed., *Literaturkanon*, 270–92. Also,
J. Assmann, *Religion*, ix: "Being that can be remembered is text." Likewise, Alan Kirk,
"Memory," in Kelber and Byrskog, eds., *Jesus in Memory*, 170: "Tradition is the
artifact of memory."

governed memory: "It is one framework that counts—that which is constituted by the commandments of our present society and which necessarily excludes all the others."[122] By focusing upon the *social* formation of
memory in the present, whether that means autobiographical memory
that is socially formed or cultural memory that is autobiographically
appropriated,[123] the primary task of social memory theory is to conceptualize and explain the various manners in which cultures (and individuals as culture-members) appropriate the past in light of, in terms of, and
on behalf of the present.

Although Halbwachs emphasizes the role of the present in the present/
past interplay, he does not altogether deny the existence of the past. In a
footnote, he states:

> Clearly, I do not in any way dispute that our impressions perdure for
> some time, in some cases for a long time, after they have been produced.
> But this 'resonance' of impressions is not to be confused at all with the
> preservation of memories. This resonance varies from individual to
> individual, just as it undoubtedly does from type to type, completely aside
> from social influence. It relates to psycho-physiology, which has its
> domain, just as social psychology has its own.[124]

This *"resonance" des impressions* ("'resonance' of impressions"), a product of what Halbwachs elsewhere calls the *passé réel* ("actual past"),[125] is
thus acknowledged, but located outside the domain of memory proper. It
is "not to be confused at all with the preservation of memories" and

---

122.   Halbwachs, "Social Frameworks," 50.
123.   See Halbwachs's distinction between autobiographical/individual memory
and historical/social memory in *Collective Memory*, 50–55. "Historical memory"
is the major focus of much of the Assmanns' work, though they term it "cultural
memory" in contrast to the "communicative memory" of individuals (see J. Assmann, "Introduction," 3, 24–30). The relationship between individual and collective
memory is one of the most debated issues in the discipline. See, for example,
Ricoeur, *Memory*, 120–24, who insists that individuals' ability to place themselves in
different remembering communities, and thus different social memories, preserves
the distinction of the individual that Halbwachs argues against.
124.   Halbwachs, "Social Frameworks," 40 n. 3. For the French, see Maurice
Halbwachs, *Les cadres sociaux de la mémoire* (ES; New York: Arno, 1975), viii n. 1.
125.   Discussing the appropriation of Christian history by both dogmatics and
mystics in the Catholic Church, Halbwachs, "Social Frameworks," 108, says, "But
nothing proves that [the mystics'] points of view more accurately approached the
actual past [*passé réel*] than did the traditions of the Church." For the French, see
Halbwachs, *Les cadres*, 209. Further on the Gospels and Christian history, see
Maurice Halbwachs, "The Legendary Topography of the Gospels in the Holy Land,"
in *On Collective Memory*, 191–235.

"completely aside from social influence," which, for Halbwachs, is the governing force of memory. The actual past simply has little, perhaps nothing, to do with memory, as Halbwachs even places it outside his academic discipline.

3.1.1. *The Present in the Past (The Presentist Perspective)*. With regard to the respective roles of the present and the past in commemoration, two different trajectories have emerged from Halbwachs's initial insights: the presentist perspective; and the continuity perspective. The presentist perspective, also known as revisionism or constructionism, follows Halbwachs's prioritization of the present in acts of remembrance and is thus highly skeptical about the ability of memory to present historical events in a trustworthy manner. Thus, Bodnar claims regarding public memory: "The *major focus* of this communicative and cognitive process is not the past…but serious matters in the present such as the nature of power and the question of loyalty to both official and vernacular cultures."[126] In fact, the present is so powerful that public memory is not a product of past events; rather "public memory remains a product of elite manipulation, symbolic interaction, and contested discourse."[127] Similarly, according to Gillis, "We are constantly revising our memories to suit our current identities."[128] Not only is the present determinative for "memory work," it is so determinative that the past can be rewritten "constantly" and the socio-cultural matrix of the present is solely responsible for "what is remembered (or forgotten), by whom, and for what end."[129]

3.1.2. *The Past in the Present (The Continuity Perspective)*. Scholars who advocate "the continuity perspective" heavily, and rightly, criticize the presentist perspective.[130] For, "When pushed to the extreme…presentism undermines all historical continuity."[131] Those who express the

---

126.   John Bodnar, *Remaking America: Public Memory, Commemoration, and Patriotism in the Twentieth Century* (Princeton: Princeton University Press, 1992), 15 (emphasis added).

127.   Ibid., 20.

128.   John R. Gillis, "Memory and Identity: The History of a Relationship," in *Commemorations: The Politics of National Identity* (ed. John R. Gillis; Princeton: Princeton University Press, 1994), 3.

129.   Ibid., 3.

130.   Cf. Nachman Ben-Yehuda, *The Masada Myth: Collective Memory and Mythmaking in Israel* (Madison: The University of Wisconsin Press, 1995), 22, on the two models of collective memory. This study employs the term "continuity perspective" in reference to the mediating position of Schwartz (discussed below).

131.   Zelizer, "Reading the Past," 227.

continuity perspective therefore agree with Halbwachs that memory is always formed in, and thus ultimately conditioned by, the present. They disagree, however, with presentism's near complete dismissal of the past from the present's shaping of memory. To the contrary, according to the continuity perspective, it is memory's inherently *social* nature that enables it to preserve the past to an extent by transcending individual existence.[132] Thus, for these scholars, memory is a much more complex social process of mutual influence. The present does not simply run roughshod over the past; the present acts on the past while the past simultaneously acts on the present.

Foremost among social memory theorists who argue for the presence of the past are Schwartz and Schudson. Both argue that the past is malleable in light of the construction of present identity, but only to an extent, and this is precisely why the past is such a contested battleground. Criticizing presentists, Schwartz claims, "To focus solely on memory's contested side is to deny the past's significance as a model for coming to terms with the present."[133] Following Shils,[134] Schwartz insists rather that no society floats in historical midair, detached from that which came before: "The present is constituted by the past, but the past's retention, as well as its reconstruction, must be anchored in the present."[135] Schwartz thus carefully avoids the extremes of presentism and literalism: "In most cases…we find the past to be neither totally precarious nor immutable, but a stable image upon which new elements are intermittently super-imposed."[136]

132.   Edward Shils, *Tradition* (Chicago: University of Chicago Press, 1981), 35: "The past does appear in the present and it does so against the obstacles of death and birth."

133.   Barry Schwartz, *Abraham Lincoln and the Forge of National Memory* (Chicago: University of Chicago Press, 2000), ix. See also his *Abraham Lincoln in the Post-Heroic Era: History and Memory in Late Twentieth-Century America* (Chicago: University of Chicago Press, 2008).

134.   Shils, *Tradition*, 39: "Even if we accept that each generation modifies the beliefs and changes the patterns of action from those which have been presented to it by its predecessors, there is bound always to be a plurality of previously and still espoused beliefs and previously and still enacted patterns of action coexisting with and in particular patterns which are of more recent origin."

135.   Schwartz, *Abraham Lincoln*, 302; see also p. 7.

136.   Ibid., 303. Although Schwartz's primary work is with nineteenth- and twentieth-century figures, his insights maintain relevance for biblical scholars. From a general perspective, the numerous applications of social memory theory to Jewish culture demonstrate its fruitfulness (Ben-Yehuda, *Masada*; Esler, *Conflict*; Kirk and Thatcher, eds., *Memory*; Le Donne, *Historiographical*; Rodríguez, *Structuring*; Zerubavel, *Recovered*, Yerushalmi, *Zakhor*). More specifically, though, Schwartz's

Likewise shifting social memory discussions away from the utter dominance of the present and into considerations of how the present and past mutually inform each other, Schudson emphasizes that the "powers that be" in the present can control the past, but only insofar as society in general accepts that version of the past.[137] Since it is, in the words of Fentress and Wickham, "the remembering community which decides which version is acceptable and which is not," the community itself functions in a role of hermeneutical control.[138] Schudson thus employs the metaphor of sculpting: "The sculptor, and the historian, are at once free and constrained."[139]

Further, in contrast to the presentist perspective, Schudson insists, "The recollection of the past does not always serve present interests. The past is in some respects, and under some conditions, highly resistant to efforts to make it over."[140] To recall the language of Halbwachs, if it is possible for the actual past to leave "impressions" upon collective memory, Schudson points to the fact that some past events leave stronger impressions than others. To this end, Schudson cites several manners in which the past can place constraints on present hermeneutical activity, such as living memory and the existence of multiple versions of the past that create a memory market.[141] These two conditions mean that memory producers must compete against one another for public approval, and in a context where individuals who experienced a past event can function as control mechanisms (thus, for example, the problem that Holocaust survivors present to Holocaust deniers). Schudson also introduces the concept of "the past as scar," which helps explain "the structure of individual choice."[142] In rejecting the notion that rememberers are free to choose any version of the past they desire, Schudson observes that

further research shows that the role of the past is only heightened in more traditional cultures (Tong Zhang and Barry Schwartz, "Confucius and the Cultural Revolution: A Study in Collective Memory," *International Journal of Politics, Culture, and Society* 11, no. 2 [1992]: 189–212). Schwartz addresses Christian origins directly in Barry Schwartz, "Christian Origins: Historical Truth and Social Memory," in Kirk and Thatcher, eds., *Memory*, 43–56.

137. Michael Schudson, "The Present in the Past versus the Past in the Present," *Communication* 11 (1989): 105–13.

138. Fentress and Wickham, *Social Memory*, 74.

139. Michael Schudson, *Watergate in American Memory: How We Remember, Forget, and Reconstruct the Past* (New York: Basic Books, 1992), 219.

140. Schudson, "Present," 107.

141. Schudson, "Present," 112; Schudson, *Watergate*, 207–10. See further Rodríguez, *Structuring*, 59–64.

142. Schudson, "Present," 109–12; Schudson, *Watergate*, 218–19.

traumatic, violent experiences "scar" a culture and thus limit the mal-
leability of that experience: "Not only must Americans confront slavery,
not only must Germans face the Holocaust, but they must do so repeat-
edly, obsessively, necessarily, whether they like it or not."[143] In these
cases, the actual past not only generates commemoration in the present,
it also places constraints upon the present's reconstitution of it, as
present existence can be defined only in terms of the event that threatened group identity. Other scholars have similarly pursued the relationship between violence, group identity, and the role of the past in present
commemoration, confirming that, although violence does not always scar
social memory, it certainly can.[144]

Schwartz and Schudson are by no means the only representatives of
the continuity perspective on social memory theory.[145] Further, one does
not have to accept every aspect of their approach to social memory in
order to recognize the essential correctness of their main point—the
social construction of memory is not a one-way street with the present
being the only contributor to commemorative activity. The present does
provide frameworks for understanding the past, but "the past, itself
constellated by the work of social memory, provides the framework for
cognition, organization, and interpretation of the experiences of the
present."[146]

143.   Schudson, "Present," 110. As with Schwartz, although New Testament and
Jesus scholarship is not Schudson's primary field, his theories' relevance remains
given common concerns. In response to form criticism, Gerhardsson viewed the
apostles' living memory (in their capacity as eyewitnesses) as crucial for the transmission of the gospel tradition (Gerhardsson, *Memory*, 280–88, 329–35; his reference
to memory is on p. 333). More recently, the role of the living memory of the first
generation of Jesus' followers in the shaping of the gospel tradition is foundational
for Bauckham's *Jesus*, esp. 93 (Bauckham discusses Gerhardsson on pp. 249–52).
Further, several New Testament scholars, including the present author, have
demonstrated the importance of the cross as a violent event in affecting its own
interpretation in early Christianity (Keith, "Role"; Keith and Thatcher, "Scar"; Alan
Kirk, "The Memory of Violence and the Death of Jesus in Q," in Kirk and Thatcher,
eds., *Memory*, 191–206).
144.   In particular, see Liisa H. Malkki, *Purity and Exile: Violence, Memory, and
National Cosmology among Hutu Refugees in Tanzania* (Chicago: University of
Chicago Press, 1995); Arthur G. Neal, *National Trauma and Collective Memory*
(Armonk: M. E. Sharpe, 1998).
145.   See also Ben-Yehuda, *Masada*, 22–23; Olick, "Products," 13.
146.   Kirk, "Social," 15. Similarly, Keith, "Claim," 55: "Any act of commemoration…is a complex interworking of the past putting pressure on the present's interpretation of it while the present simultaneously provides the only lens(es) through
which the past can be viewed."

In viewing the written Gospels as Jesus-memory, the present study adopts the continuity perspective and is therefore interested in how early Christians preserved, commemorated, and interpreted the past of Jesus in light of that past and their present. On this account, it is important to underscore that I am not advocating a conservative retreat to a literalist approach to the Gospels as pure images of "what really happened." Rather, I am simply taking seriously that the past is not, in every way, rewriteable and can even, in some cases, set the course for its own commemoration.[147] Therefore, as a research paradigm, the Jesus-memory approach insists that a proper consideration of the transmission of Jesus tradition as the appropriation of collective memory must account not only for the role of the present in shaping the past, but also the role of the past, and past interpretations of the past, in shaping the present.

3.2. *The Jesus-Memory Approach and the Gospel Tradition*
The overall departure from the criteria approach is observable also by contrasting (and comparing) the Jesus-memory approach's assumptions about the nature of the gospel tradition to the aforementioned assumptions of the criteria approach.[148] First, from the perspective of social memory theory, scholars in search of authentic Jesus traditions might as well be in search of unicorns, the lost city of Atlantis, and the pot of gold at the end of the rainbow. Not only are there no longer Jesus traditions that reflect solely the actual past, there never were. In other words, there is no memory, no preserved past, and no access to it, without interpretation. The Jesus-memory approach therefore agrees with the criteria approach that the written Gospels reflect an interpreted past of Jesus; it disagrees, however, with whether there are, in the midst of those interpretations, un-interpreted Jesus traditions that one can separate from the interpretations. The Jesus-memory approach therefore rejects the criteria approach's primary assumption about the gospel tradition: scholars cannot separate Jesus traditions into authentic and inauthentic bodies of tradition because all Jesus tradition (in one form or another) belongs to both categories.

The criteria approach's second assumption about the gospel tradition is that authentic traditions absorbed inauthentic traditions in the process of transmission. In tandem with this assumption, its third assumption is that the interpretations of Jesus in the Gospels are due primarily to those inauthentic traditions and the context that produced them. Whereas the

147.   See also Kirk, "Social," 14.
148.   See above, p. 40.

Jesus-memory approach outright denies the criteria approach's first assumption, its difference with the second and third assumptions is not with their essential thrust but their simplicity. The idea that the transmitters of the tradition left their imprint upon the Jesus tradition, which the criteria approach received from form criticism's emphasis on the *Sitz im Leben*, is correct. How could it be otherwise? Early Christians could think about Jesus and remember him only from their own contexts and with thought categories from that context. If not for those categories in their present, Jesus would not have been remembered at all.[149]

By taking a presentist perspective,[150] however, the question the criteria approach and form criticism fail to answer is—"From where did the present categories for thinking about Jesus derive?" If they appeal in response to social reality vaguely, the *Sitz im Leben*, they simply push the question one step further—"From where did that social reality, and the structures that form it, derive?" In considering the *historical* development of Christianity and the Jesus tradition, however, this is *the* crucial question. In failing to answer it, proponents of the criteria approach and form criticism fail to account for two important factors. First, the broader social memory of first-century Jews provided categories for their initial reception/remembering of Jesus.[151] Thus, the commemorated past was already impacting the first, original interpretations of Jesus by his contemporary audience. Second, initial and subsequent receptions of Jesus' life informed the interpretive categories that gave shape to the narratives of the Gospels. In other words, the development of the Jesus tradition into the written Gospels was not a process whereby inauthentic interpretations were added to an authentic core of historically pristine material until the final product was a mix of both wherein each is identifiable.

---

149.   Anthony Le Donne, "Theological Distortion in the Jesus Tradition: A Study in Social Memory Theory," in Stuckenbruck, Barton, and Wold, eds., *Memory in the Bible*, 166: "Does the localization process have the capacity to distort one's memory? The answer to this is not only yes, but always."

150.   Thus, Schwartz, "Christian Origins," 48–49. He indicts Wilken for claiming that Luke "interpreted the material he had inherited to fit into his scheme" (Wilken, *Myth*, 34) as follows: "Perhaps so, but since no one knows who wrote Luke, Wilken can present no evidence on the author's motives, let alone refute an alternate hypothesis: that the material Luke's author inherited *changed* his scheme" (emphasis original).

151.   For a specific instance of this phenomenon regarding Jesus as "Son of David," see Le Donne, *Historiographical*, 65–189. See also Horsley, *Jesus in Context*, 140–45, and, more generally, Kirk, "Memory," 168–9. Clearly, the socially constructed past of Israel impacted Jesus himself as well. See Kelber, "Work," 204; Mournet, "Jesus Tradition," 58.

Rather, it was a process whereby there were only ever interpretations/ memories of the past to begin with, to which other interpretations—*that grew from, approved of, disagreed with, contradicted, but, in the least, were in dialogue with and thus to some degree constrained by, the earlier interpretations*—were added until the final product was a result of that interpretive activity.[152] Parsing out the respective influences of the present and the past in this process is much more complex than the criteria approach allows. A significant problem with the criteria approach in this respect is that it detaches supposed later, purportedly inauthentic, traditions from the earlier stages of the traditioning process *entirely*, as if those alleged inauthentic traditions appeared out of thin air in the course of history.[153] Showing its form-critical roots, it detaches later Christologies from the historical progression that produced those Christologies, making early Christian communities into beautiful Christologizing castles in the sky. Alleged inauthentic traditions *exist* as historical artifacts, however, and, on that account if no other, demand a historical explanation. Confirming the presence of the present is not equivalent to disconfirming the presence of the past.[154]

Based on the continuity perspective, the Jesus-memory approach instead assumes a connection between earlier and later stages of the traditioning process, a connection between the actual past and how it was remembered, and thus a connection between the historical Jesus and later Christologies. "Portrayals of Jesus, like other historical portrayals, are based on a link between the present and the past, and it is precisely here that they contribute to an understanding of the present as something that has taken shape."[155] Whatever happened in Jesus' life and death, events to

152.   This statement does not imply that the interpretive activity of the present ceased once the traditions were textualized. See Bart D. Ehrman, *The Orthodox Corruption of Scripture: The Effect of Early Christological Controversies on the Text of the New Testament* (New York: Oxford University Press, 1993); Keith, "Performance," 49–69; Alan Kirk, "Manuscript Tradition as a *Tertium Quid*: Orality and Memory in Scribal Practice," in Thatcher, ed., *Jesus*, 215–34. Also, Zimmermann, "Typicality," 140: "The written texts…did not finalize a memory culture so much as set it in motion."

153.   Schwartz, "Christian Origins," 49, in critique of thorough presentists: "Bultmann's and Halbwachs's common failure is their refusal even to ask how pericopae, texts, physical sites reflected what ordinary people of the first century believed." He refers to Halbwachs, "Legendary."

154.   Similarly, Loveday Alexander, "Memory and Tradition in the Hellenistic Schools," in Kelber and Byrskog, eds., *Jesus in Memory*, 152: "The fact that stories are shaped for present needs does not mean they are no use to the historian: the historicality of the material itself has to be assessed on other grounds."

155.   Schröter, "Jesus of Galilee," 38.

which we have no direct access but nevertheless happened, those historical realities set into motion interpretations/memories of him by those who encountered him. The present contexts of the interpreters/remembers, including inherited typologies and categories from the Jewish past, undoubtedly shaped those initial impressions, even for eyewitnesses.[156] The actual past, however, placed some parameters upon those interpretations/memories. At a simplistic level it is safe to say that no one remembered Jesus as a sailor, or as Caesar, or as an astronaut because his actual life did not permit those interpretations; it did not set those interpretations into motion. Equally, it is safe to say that many people remembered Jesus as a first-century Jew who lived in Palestine, taught, healed, and got into trouble with Jewish and Roman authorities because his actual life did permit those interpretations of him; it did set those interpretations into motion.

Importantly, this approach denies neither the inherently hermeneutical production of memories of Jesus' life nor that there are competing memories, or interpretations, of him. Indeed the focus of this book is on two competing, contradictory memories of Jesus that cannot both be true.[157] Early Christians undoubtedly did remember him incorrectly at times. But, as a first level of investigation, one must admit that the *historical* or *earthly* Jesus was a person capable of producing those memories, even the possibly inaccurate ones. Dunn is correct that we are only able to access the remembered Jesus, but *how* Jesus was remembered allows informed speculation about the historical Jesus who produced those memories.[158] In other words, even if a scholar a priori considers a tradition about Jesus to be false, the proper *historical* approach to that tradition is not to ask "*Did* early Christians misremember Jesus?" and dismiss it based on the assumed affirmative answer, but rather to ask "*How* did early Christians misremember Jesus?" and proceed to explain what socio-historical conditions led to the production of that memory.

As should be clear by now, the Jesus-memory approach, as it has been articulated here,[159] also thoroughly rejects the fourth assumption of the

---

156.   Cf. Bauckham, *Jesus*, 9, who follows Samuel Byrskog, *Story as History—History as Story: The Gospel Tradition in the Context of Ancient Oral History* (WUNT 123; Tübingen: Mohr Siebeck, 2000), 28, 165–66, in asserting that eyewitnesses give inherently better testimony to the past.

157.   See Chapter 4's presentation of early Christian memories of Jesus as both a scribal-literate teacher and a scribal-illiterate teacher.

158.   Dunn, *New*, 30–31.

159.   Not all scholars who appeal to social memory theory dismiss the criteria of authenticity entirely. For example, Le Donne, *Historiographical*, appeals consistently

criteria approach—that scholars can separate the Jesus tradition into authentic and inauthentic bodies of tradition. This claim is not, however, the same as claiming that scholars cannot make judgments about which traditions are likely historically accurate and which are not. The point is that such historical judgments cannot proceed under the illusion that scholars can extract un-interpreted material from the Gospels.

3.3. *The Jesus-Memory Approach and the Written Tradition*

In viewing the Gospels as early Christian social memory, the Jesus-memory approach to the historical Jesus differs from the criteria approach's fragmentation of the written tradition in at least two important interrelated respects. First, since the idea that scholars can get "behind" the text to an objective past reality is a façade,[160] the Jesus-memory approach does not remove Jesus traditions from their narrative framework in the written tradition.[161] Second, and strongly related, the Jesus-memory approach does not attempt to neutralize the interpretations of Jesus in that written tradition. More succinctly, scholars affirming the Jesus-memory approach would not *want* to minimize the interpretations of the Gospels even if they could.[162] For, *the interpretations of the past themselves are what preserve any connection to the actual past.* As Kirk observes, "It is only through the transmutation of formative events into transmissible tradition artifacts that the past is preserved at all."[163] Worth repeating once more is that this position is not a denial that scholars can discuss what may have happened in the actual past of Jesus. Rather, it is a denial that one can get closer to that reality by dismissing the interpretations of Jesus in the written tradition.[164]

to the criteria (87–88; 176, 195, 252 n. 107, 265, 267), although he redefines their task since, as he acknowledges, they cannot "verify what 'actually happened'" (87; also 91).

160. Similarly, Allison, *Historical*, 66; Bauckham, *Jesus*, 4; Schröter, "Von der Historizität," 205–6.

161. Also, Horsley, *Jesus and Empire*, 8: "Rather than purposely isolating Jesus-sayings from the only contexts of meaning to which we still have access, that is, the Gospels, we must start from those literary sources"; similarly, Horsley, "Prominent," 62–63.

162. Schwartz, "Christian Origins," 49: "It is not just that localizations distort history; the more they distort the better they work."

163. Kirk, "Memory," 169.

164. Schröter, "Von der Historizität," 205: "Kann…eine gegenwärtigen Jesusdarstellung die narrative Repräsentationen der Person Jesu in den Evangelien nicht einfach beiseite stellen."

3.4. *The Historian's Task according to the Jesus-Memory Approach*
To bring the previous threads of discussion together, according to this approach, the Jesus historian's proper task is to explain the existence of the Jesus-memories in the Gospels. That is, one must quest for the historical Jesus by accounting for the interpretations of the Gospels, not by dismissing them and certainly not by fragmenting them. In the words of Schröter, "Every approach to the historical Jesus behind the Gospels has to explain how these writings could have come into being as the earliest descriptions of this person."[165]

The processes of explaining the existence of Jesus-memory reveal further the Jesus-memory approach's departure with the criteria approach. First, because memory is shaped in the present of the remembering community, the Jesus historian must account for factors within the contexts of remembrance, both earlier and later, that could have affected the shape of the Jesus-memory. Instead of distancing the historical Jesus from first-century Judaism and the early Church, then, as does the criterion of dissimilarity, Jesus historians must place Jesus-memories precisely in these contexts.

Second, in order to explain Jesus-memory, scholars must be astute interpreters in order to know the claims about Jesus that the texts make. The need for proper interpretation of the portrayal of Jesus in the Gospels is another reason for understanding those Jesus-memories in their own historical contexts.[166]

Third, when positing a historical Jesus who produced early Christian Jesus-memories, scholars must temper their claims about their apprehension of the actual past. Scholars must acknowledge that, as I have said elsewhere, "What one may draw from the text with regards to the 'actual past' are indeed *inferences*."[167] On the one hand, the reason we are capable of speculating on the historical Jesus at all is the same reason we do not receive the type of empirical confirmations or disconfirmations we often seek—there is no objective apprehension of past reality. Thus, scholars can speak of what is more or less plausible given the mnemonic evidence and the socio-historical contexts of the historical Jesus and those who remembered him, but not what is definite.[168] On the other

165.   Schröter, "Historical Jesus," 153. Similarly, Le Donne, "Theological Distortion," 165.
166.   See also Schröter, "Jesus of Galilee," 37–38.
167.   Keith, "Claim," 56 (emphasis original).
168.   I borrow the term "mnemonic evidence" from Le Donne, *Historiographical*, 86.

hand, admitting one cannot grasp the historical Jesus in full is not the same as saying one cannot approach him with a degree of confidence; lack of complete access to the past is not the same as a complete lack of access to the past. Jesus historians are warranted in asking "What really happened?" because the actual past *happened* and some of it was preserved through social memory; Jesus historians are warranted in being cautious with their claims because the actual past happened and some of it was preserved *through social memory*.

Cumulatively, then, the Jesus historian must, in light of the various claims about Jesus preserved in early Christian commemoration, posit an actual past that best explains the existence of the Jesus-memories in light of the contexts of remembrance in early Christianity. Le Donne refers to this process as "triangulation," whereby he establishes various interpretive trajectories of an event in Jesus' life: "Triangulation does not pinpoint an exact historical reality; rather it describes the mnemonic sphere that best accounts for the mnemonic evidence. The purpose of triangulation is to establish the most plausible intersection between the established trajectories."[169] Although the term "triangulation" risks simplifying the traditioning process by implying three points and linear relationships between them (a simplification Le Donne's fuller discussion discourages), and I disagree with Le Donne's surprising appeals to criteria of authenticity,[170] he helpfully describes the general historical task of considering what *could* have happened in the past to produce the different interpretive trajectories that exist.

Another analogy may be more helpful. In many respects, the Jesus-memory approach to the historical Jesus provides a means for Jesus historians to approach the actual past in the manner that text critics approach variant readings, by positing as original the reading that best explains the others.[171] After coming to this conclusion some time ago, I discovered that my own *Doktorvater*, Hurtado, had advocated a similar approach already:

---

169.   Ibid. Worth note, however, is that Le Donne is much more interested in the earliest perceptions than the possibilities of the actual past. I return to this difference between his proposal and my method in Chapter 5.

170.   See above n. 159.

171.   Bruce M. Metzger and Bart D. Ehrman, *The Text of the New Testament: Its Transmission, Corruption, and Restoration* (4th ed.; New York: Oxford University Press, 2005), 300, describe this principle as "perhaps the most basic criterion for the evaluation of variant readings."

> In short, I propose that, instead of merely playing off one 'variant' in the
> Jesus tradition against another, we take all these variants as valuable evi-
> dence in the reconstruction effort, and attempt a reconstruction that can
> explain the variants in light of what we know about the transmission
> process, thus producing a proposed reconstruction.[172]

Shortly after Hurtado, Becker made a similar plea (although in conjunction with criteria of authenticity).[173] It does not appear that scholars have
taken up these suggestions with any concentrated effort. This chapter
should provide a fuller methodological basis for approaching the historical Jesus in such a manner.

4. *Conclusions*

This chapter has argued for the Jesus-memory approach to the historical
Jesus, in contrast to the dominant criteria approach. As the previous
discussion demonstrated, rejecting the criteria approach is nothing new;
neither is emphasizing continuity with first-century Judaism and the
early Church; neither is emphasizing the impact of Jesus; neither is
focusing on the finished form of the text in searching for Jesus rather
than fragmenting it; neither is arguing that any historical Jesus must
plausibly explain the mnemonic evidence we have. Appealing to memory
is not completely new in Biblical Studies either, despite social memory
theory's relatively recent arrival on the scene.[174] The strength of the Jesus-
memory approach to the historical Jesus, therefore, is not its innovation.

---

172.   Hurtado, "Taxonomy," 295. Boring, *Continuing*, 193, makes a similar
proposal with his criterion of hermeneutical potential, but as part of the criteria
approach that ultimately seeks authentic tradition; likewise the criterion of traditional continuity proposed by I. Howard Marshall, *I Believe in the Historical Jesus*
(Grand Rapids: Eerdmans, 1977), 207–11. I thank Max Aplin for alerting me to
Marshall's and Becker's (see below) proposals.

173.   Jürgen Becker, *Jesus of Nazareth* (trans. James E. Crouch; Berlin: de
Gruyter, 1998), 14–15. Cf. also Kelber, "Work," 204.

174.   Aitken, *Jesus' Death*; Walter Brueggemann, *Abiding Astonishment: Psalms,
Modernity, and History Making* (Louisville: Westminster John Knox, 1991); Walter
Brueggemann, *David's Truth in Israel's Imagination and Memory* (Philadelphia:
Fortress, 1985); Crossan, *Birth*, esp. 47–93; Nils Alstrup Dahl, *Jesus in the Memory of
the Early Church* (Minneapolis: Augsburg, 1976), esp. 11–29; Burton L. Mack, *A
Myth of Innocence: Mark and Christian Origins* (Philadelphia: Fortress, 1988); Hans-
Ruedi Weber, *The Cross: Tradition and Interpretation* (trans. Elke Jessett; Grand
Rapids: Eerdmans, 1979), esp. 16–29; Wilken, *Myth*, 4–5; Robert L. Wilken,
Remembering the Christian Past (Grand Rapids: Eerdmans, 1995).

One could even argue that it is not necessary to appeal to social memory theory in order to arrive at the conclusions this chapter offers.

Importantly, however, the previous discussion also argued that much prior dissatisfaction with the criteria approach is, more accurately, dissatisfaction with the criteria approach's conception of the Jesus tradition, which it uncritically inherited from form criticism.[175] The strength of the Jesus-memory approach is clearest in this light; for it is a historiographical method based upon a conceptual framework for the nature and development of the Jesus tradition that more accurately reflects the manners in which ancient people appropriated and preserved the past.[176] As a practical advantage, the Jesus-memory approach locates scholarly discussion on the written texts that scholars have instead of hypothetical reconstructed tradition-histories they do not.[177] As a methodological advantage, the Jesus-memory approach avoids the extremes of both Modernity and Postmodernity. It insists that historical portrayals, whether those of the ancients or those of historiographical consciousness, are not the past but *representations* of it.[178] It insists equally, however, in my conception,[179] that scholars nevertheless are warranted to theorize about the actual past based on the commemorations it produced. In this sense, the Jesus-memory approach affirms the best aspect of form criticism and the criteria approach (recognition of early Christian interpretive activity) and addresses their worst aspect (exclusion of the impact of Jesus upon the interpretations of him).

The overall implications of the Jesus-memory approach are significant. They challenge nothing less than the distinction between the historical Jesus and the Christ of faith. The challenge is not so much at the heuristic level, for it is not being denied that there was a Jesus who existed in space and time, whom scholars cannot equate simplistically with the Jesus of the canonical or, for that matter, noncanonical, tradition. The challenge is rather aimed at the cradle of the dichotomy between the two Jesuses, as the Jesus-memory approach denies scholars' abilities to separate cleanly

---

175. Thus, one implication of the present argument is that, in response to Tuckett's observation, "In general terms, the critique of the older form critics' model is probably fully justified, though it is not quite so clear which model might or should replace this" ("Form Criticism," 37), the Jesus-memory approach can stake a claim as a better model for the Jesus tradition.

176. Similarly, Davies, *Memories*, 122.

177. See also Allison, *Jesus*, 27–31.

178. Schröter, "Von der Historizität," 205. See also Ricoeur, *Memory*, 235–38. Cf. McKnight, *Jesus*, 45–46, in reference to modern Jesus scholarship.

179. That is, I do not here claim to speak on behalf of all scholars who employ social memory theory.

the historical Jesus from the Christ of faith and properly returns historical investigation to why early Christians remembered Jesus in the
manners they did. This book will therefore be bold enough to propose an
answer to "What really happened?" with regards to Jesus' literate status
(Chapter 5), but only once the early Christian claims about Jesus' literate
status are appreciated (Chapter 4) in light of the literate landscape of
first-century Judaism (Chapter 3). To that landscape this book now
turns.

Chapter 3

SCRIBAL CULTURE IN THE TIME OF JESUS

*A word should be said about this
loaded concept of "literacy."*[1]

Prior to Chapter 4's presentation of early Christian claims for Jesus'
literate status, this chapter will provide an overview of literacy and scribal
culture in Jesus' socio-historical context.[2] A thorough canvassing of all
aspects of Jewish or early Christian literacy is beyond the scope of the
present study.[3] What follows will thus focus on six characteristics of, or
factors within, Second Temple Palestinian Judaism that are most pertinent to interpreting early Christian portrayals of Jesus' literate status:
widespread illiteracy; widespread textuality; literacy spectrums; scribal
literacy; the acquisition of biblical knowledge; and the perception of
literacy.

Two further remarks are necessary here at the outset. First, the primary purpose of this chapter is to establish an appropriate background
for understanding the diverse *claims* for Jesus' literacy in early Christi-

---

1. Carr, *Writing*, 13.
2. This chapter will focus primarily on literacy in Roman Palestine from ca. first
century C.E., although the next chapter will include evidence from the early Church
up to even the sixth century C.E. Many things changed between the Second Temple
Judaism of Jesus and his disciples and the early Christianity of, for example, Tertullian or Ambrose, but literacy rates generally did not. On the relatively ubiquitous
nature of education and literacy rates in the Greco-Roman world, see Gamble, *Books*,
6–7; Harris, *Ancient*, 280–82; cf. 284; Theresa Morgan, *Literate Education in the
Hellenistic and Roman Worlds* (CCS; Cambridge: Cambridge University Press, 1998),
44–45, 66–67.
3. I offer a detailed analysis of Jewish and early Christian literacy/education in
Keith, *Pericope*, 53–117, and draw on that study here. For the most thorough study of
Jewish literacy, see Hezser, *Jewish*. For the most recent study of Israelite education,
see James L. Crenshaw, *Education in Ancient Israel: Across the Deadening Silence*
(ABRL; New York: Doubleday, 1998).

anity's corporate memory. The primary purpose is not, therefore, to establish a historical context, and a concomitant set of generalizations about that context, that will then be directly applied to Jesus. As Chapter 1 demonstrated, scholars use this particular approach both positively ("most Jewish boys" went to school, *therefore* Jesus did too) and negatively ("most Jewish peasants" were illiterate, *therefore* Jesus was too). Such an approach is too simplistic.

Second, despite many advances in especially the last thirty years, one could fill library upon library with the information scholars do *not* know about the literary culture of first-century Judaism, much less ancient literacy in general.[4] In fact, one could justly describe the current state of discussion as an attempt to decide how best to interpret the paucity of evidence we have in light of the overwhelming amount of evidence we lack. Given the need to avoid claiming more than the evidence can bear, then, in what follows "literate education" will refer to the acquisition of reading and writing skills without implying a formal framework of stages for how that happened, as reflected in later rabbinic tradition.[5] Additionally, although the focus will be on Second Temple Jewish evidence from Roman Palestine, relevant Diasporan and comparative evidence will be included as well.

1. *Widespread Illiteracy*

The first, and most important, characteristic of Jesus' literate landscape is widespread illiteracy. Amid a rapidly growing body of secondary literature on literacy and textuality in first-century Judaism, a majority opinion has emerged concerning the primary sources (texts, inscriptions, abecedaries, etc.): the primary sources do not clearly support theories of widespread literacy because they does not clearly indicate the existence of that which secures widespread literacy; namely, a publicly funded elementary education system. Rather, this evidence explicitly and implicitly attests a lack of widespread literacy.

---

4.   Consider the statement of Crenshaw, *Education*, 4: "What do we really know about education in ancient Israel? Not very much." Similarly, Stuart Weeks, *Early Israelite Wisdom* (OTM; Oxford: Oxford University Press, 1999), 156: "Our ignorance of educational methods in Israel remains profound."

5.   For discussion of the rabbinic descriptions of formal pedagogical stages, see Crenshaw, *Education*, 5–11; Eliezer Ebner, *Elementary Education in Ancient Israel During the Tannaitic Period (10–220 C.E.)* (New York: Bloch, 1956), 69–71. On the unreliability of these texts for pre-70 C.E. Judaism, see Hezser, *Jewish*, 54.

1.1. *Proposed Literacy Percentages*

As reiteration from earlier, Harris asserts a 10 percent literacy rate for the ancient world generally that has been qualified but overwhelmingly affirmed.[6] His widely accepted argument resides on the simple, yet too often overlooked, point that "the vital preconditions for wide diffusion of literacy were always absent in the Graeco-Roman world, and that no positive force ever existed to bring about mass literacy."[7] More specifically, "A pervasive system of schools is a prerequisite for mass literacy," and "what was lacking…in most communities throughout the Greek world was the will to allocate public or philanthropic funds to schooling for the children of the poor," who would have been the majority of the population.[8] Some detractors to Harris's theory have either missed or ignored that he never claims that education *could not* have occurred elsewhere, nor that literacy is always, and *necessarily*, restricted by public elementary school systems.[9] Rather, Harris's argument is that every

---

6. In addition to the affirmations for Harris's study noted in the Introduction and Chapter 1, consider the following comments by specialists in Biblical Studies: "Hardly anyone has questioned his low estimation of the literate rate in the ancient world" (Hezser, *Jewish*, 26); "The conclusions of William V. Harris…were basically confirmed by those who reviewed and supplemented his survey of the limits and uses of literacy in the Roman Empire" (Horsley, Introduction to *Performing the Gospel*, 193 n. 5); "Response to Harris's book seems to be characterized on the whole by acceptance of his basic theory, along with criticism of details of his presentation" (Ian M. Young, "Israelite Literacy: Interpreting the Evidence Part 1," *VT* 48 [1998]: 244). See also Horsley, *Scribes*, 91, 225 n. 6; Karl Allen Kuhn, *Luke: The Elite Evangelist* (PSN; Collegeville: Liturgical, 2010), 17; Mournet, "Jesus Tradition," 51; Susan Niditch, *Oral World and Written Word: Ancient Israelite Literature* (LAI; Louisville: Westminster John Knox, 1996), 39–40, 58–59.

7. Harris, *Ancient*, 12. See also pp. 233–48.

8. Ibid., 233, 245, respectively.

9. Eddy and Boyd, *Jesus*, are an example of this inattention to Harris. The title of their subsection criticizing this aspect of Harris's argument is "Does Literacy Depend upon Public Schools?" (244). Harris, however, never argues that literacy depends upon public schools, but rather quite specifically that "mass literacy" does (Harris, *Ancient*, 233, 327). Furthermore, Eddy and Boyd proceed to accuse Harris of working with a false dichotomy of literate/illiterate and an inattention to semi-literacy (244–45). This accusation on their part is perplexing, not least because of its outright inaccuracy. The index alone shows Harris discusses semi-literates no fewer than ten times (Harris, *Ancient*, 381; there is at least one instance of discussion of semi-literates that is not listed in the index, p. 327) and the first time he discusses semi-literates is on the third page of text, where he says: "We should at least try to avoid an excessively sharp polarity of literacy and illiteracy. At least we must concern ourselves with a category of *semi-literates*, persons who can write slowly or not at all, and who can read without being able to read complex or very lengthy texts" (5;

culture on record that attained *mass literacy* did so via a widely diffused publicly funded elementary education system, and *there is no clear evidence indicating the existence of such a system* that reached a mostly agrarian ancient world.[10]

The significance of Harris's study, and the reason it produced/s so much subsequent work in various fields,[11] is that it requires one to shift his or her default thinking about the ancient world from "widespread literate" to "widespread illiterate." The question, then, for this study is: To what degree did Jesus' specific socio-historical context resemble the general ancient context that Harris presents?

Hezser's extensive study, an explicit focusing of Harris's research topic onto Roman Palestine, answers that question and claims his estimate may in fact be too gracious for the Jewish context.[12] With regard to that context, other scholars offer similar low-literacy percentages; for example, "less than 3 [percent]"[13] or 5 percent.[14] Others still are content with

emphasis original). Also Carol Bakhos, "Orality and Writing," in *The Oxford Handbook of Jewish Daily Life in Roman Palestine* (ed. Catherine Hezser; Oxford: Oxford University Press, 2010), 485: "Although Harris does not delve deeply into the notion of 'semi-literates', he calls our attention to the need to take them into account."

10.   Further, Harris, *Ancient*, 327: "Behind this [lack of symptoms of mass literacy] lie the 'negative' facts about the ancient world: not only the lack of techniques which would have permitted mass diffusion of written texts, and the weakness in antiquity of the ideological notion that all citizens (or all believers) should be able to read and write, but also the slackness of demand for a literate workforce, a demand which, insofar as it existed, was met in good part by slaves."

11.   Beard et al., *Literacy*; Joanna Dewey, "Textuality in an Oral Culture: A Survey of the Pauline Traditions," in Dewey, ed., *Orality*, esp. 39; Hezser, *Jewish*, v.

12.   Hezser, *Jewish*, v (on relation to Harris); 496. Following Hezser is Richard A. Horsley, "Introduction," ix–x, x n. 6; Horsley, *Jesus in Context*, 29; Richard A. Horsley, "Oral Performance and Mark: Some Implications of *The Oral and the Written Gospel*, Twenty-Five Years Later," in Thatcher, ed., *Jesus*, 50; Horsley, *Scribes*, 91, 225 n. 6; Mournet, "Jesus Tradition," 51. Cf., however, Harlow Gregory Snyder, review of Catherine Hezser, *Jewish Literacy in Roman Palestine*, *RBL* 8 (2002), n.p. (cited 14 July 2009). Online: http://www.bookreviews.org/bookdetail. asp?TitleId=1564&CodePage=1564.

13.   Meir Bar-Ilan, "Illiteracy in the Land of Israel in the First Centuries CE," in *Essays in the Social Scientific Study of Judaism and Jewish Society: 2* (ed. Simcha Fishbane, Stuart Schoenfeld, and A. Goldschlaeger; New York: Ktav, 1992), 55. See also Meir Bar-Ilan, "Writing in Ancient Israel and Early Judaism Part Two: Scribes and Books in the Late Second Commonwealth and Rabbinic Period," in *Mikra: Text, Translation, Reading and Interpretation of the Hebrew Bible in Ancient Judaism and Early Christianity* (ed. Martin Jan Mulder; Peabody: Hendrickson, 2004), 33–34.

the general applicability of Harris's 10 percent literacy rate to first-century Palestinian Judaism.[15] Sometimes conceding to the recent waves of studies affirming the lack of widespread literacy, some scholars nevertheless maintain that literacy in Judaism may have been slightly higher than the rest of antiquity, often attributing this to the role of the holy text in Judaism.[16] On the one hand, we will see below that asserting a possible higher level of literacy for Judaism based on its high regard for its Scriptures is to confuse textuality with literacy.[17] On the other hand, whether Judaism at the time of Jesus held a slightly higher or slightly lower literacy rate than 10 percent is irrelevant—slightly higher or lower than 10 percent is still a clear majority of the populace as illiterate.[18]

1.2. *Interpreting the Evidence*

The problem for detractors to the idea of an overwhelmingly illiterate first-century Palestinian Judaism is not necessarily that there is no evidence to which they can point that suggests otherwise. The problem is in demonstrating that such evidence points *conclusively* against the idea of widespread illiteracy and in favor of widespread literacy. The debates concerning this evidence demonstrate the importance of scholars' presuppositions concerning the ancient Jewish literate landscape.[19] Two instructive examples of such debatable evidence are first-century literary attestations and writing exercises.[20]

---

14. Joanna Dewey, "The Gospel of John in Its Oral-Written Media World," in Fortna and Thatcher, eds., *Jesus in Johannine Tradition*, 240; David Rhoads, Joanna Dewey, and Donald Michie, *Mark as Story: An Introduction to the Narrative of a Gospel* (2d ed.; Minneapolis: Fortress, 1999), xii. See also Dewey, "Textuality," 39.

15. Bakhos, "Orality and Writing," 485; Baumgarten, *Flourishing*, 49 n. 36; Boomershine, "Jesus," 21; Jonathan A. Draper, "Vice Catalogues as Oral-Mnemonic Cues: A Comparative Study of the Two-Ways Tradition in the *Didache* and Parallels from the Perspective of Oral Tradition," in Thatcher, ed., *Jesus*, 112; Esler, "Collective Memory," 154; Martin S. Jaffee, *Torah in the Mouth: Writing and Oral Tradition in Palestinian Judaism, 200 BCE–400 CE* (New York: Oxford University Press, 2001), 164 n. 8; Kirk, "Memory," 158; Kuhn, *Luke*, 17, 37, 72; Thatcher, "Beyond," 2; Thatcher, *Why*, 43.

16. Eddy and Boyd, *Jesus*, 245–6; Evans, "Jewish Scripture," 44, 54; Foster, "Educating Jesus," 11–12; Gamble, *Books*, 7; Meier, *Marginal Jew*, 1:274; Millard, *Reading*, 157.

17. See below, p. 87.

18. Similarly, H. Gamble, "Literacy and Book Culture," *DNTB* 645.

19. Likewise, Toorn, *Scribal*, 10.

20. Other examples of evidence that may imply wider literacy—but do not necessarily—are public imperial signage such as seals, coinage, or the *titulus* at Jesus' crucifixion. Cf. Evans, "Jewish Scripture," 43–44 (who suggests the *titulus* may have

1.2.1. *Literary Attestations of Widespread Jewish Literacy.* Josephus and Philo comment on the religious commitment of Jews and, in this context, claim literate education for Jewish children. Josephus notes, for example, "Above all we pride ourselves on the education of our children (παι-δοτροφίαν) and regard as the most essential task in life the observance of our laws and of the pious practices."[21] He claims elsewhere that the law "commanded to teach letters" (γράμματα παιδεύειν ἐκέλευσεν) to children.[22] Similarly, Philo claims Jewish children are "trained…we may say even from the cradle, by parents and tutors and instructors and by the far higher authority of the sacred laws and also the unwritten customs, to acknowledge one God who is Father and Maker of the world."[23] The idea of universal Jewish literacy reflected in these comments, which Carr describes as "new in Judaism,"[24] undergirds Josephus's and Philo's claims that the Jewish people are an especially devout and pious people who, from parents to children, are concerned with knowledge of and adherence to their law.

Thus, one can indeed trace the *idea* that Jewish children in the first century typically received education or training in the law to Jesus' historical context. As a result, some scholars appeal to statements such as these in order to assert a literate and/or Torah-educated Jewish populace, or to argue against an illiterate majority.[25] The problem, however, is in demonstrating convincingly that the *idea* of universal literacy in such statements was reflective of the *reality* of a predominantly agrarian rural Jewish culture; that these statements represent Jewish society as a whole rather than the sliver of society from which the authors derive. The issue is not whether the majority of first-century Jews desired to be able to read Torah and thus follow it more devoutly (assuming dubiously for the

---

been intended to be read by the disciples, among others); Millard, *Reading*, 125–26, 156–57. The interpretation of this evidence is subject to the same sort of criticisms discussed above with regards to literary attestations and writing exercises.

21. Josephus, *Ag. Ap.* 1.12 §60 (Thackeray, LCL).

22. Josephus, *Ag. Ap.* 2.25 §204. Thackeray (LCL) translates "orders that they should be taught to read."

23. Philo, *Legat.* 16.115–16 (Colson, LCL). See also *Legat.* 31.210.

24. Carr, *Writing*, 247.

25. E. Earle Ellis, "The Synoptic Gospels as History," in Chilton and Evans, eds., *Authenticating the Activities of Jesus*, 53–54; repr. from *Crisis in Christology: Essays in Quest of Resolution* (ed. William R. Farmer; Livonia: Dove, 1995), 83–91; Evans, "Jewish Scripture," 44–45; Riesner, *Jesus*, 112–14. Cf. Millard, *Reading*, 157–58; Emil Schürer, *The History of the Jewish People in the Age of Jesus Christ (175 B.C.–A.D. 135)* (trans. and ed. Geza Vermes, Fergus Millar, and Matthew Black; 3 vols.; Edinburgh: T. & T. Clark, 1979), 2:418.

moment that "most Jews" drew a direct line between Torah-observance
and literate skills), but whether the opportunity to do so even existed.
Josephus's father—whom he claims was a reputable Jerusalem priest—
could have taught him.[26] But how many other Jewish children had
priestly fathers who would have had the time, writing materials, and education himself to teach them?[27] Crenshaw rightly observes that Josephus's
"claim can be discounted as exaggerated apologetic."[28] Similarly, Philo
may have been educated "by parents and tutors and instructors" in the
law, but is there any evidence that such training was *typical* for people
outside the privileged class of Philo and Josephus (who, in addition,
resided in urban environments)?[29] As we will see, it is far more likely that
Josephus and Philo reflect only the status of the privileged few such as
themselves, and universal literacy was nowhere near a reality for Second
Temple Judaism as a whole. (According to later rabbinic texts, it appears
that the idea of universal literacy would not even have been fully reflective of the priesthood, as *m. Yoma* 1:3 and 1:6 entertain the possibility of
a priest who cannot read.)

1.2.2. *Writing Exercises.* Similar to literary attestations like those of
Josephus and Philo, writing exercises from Roman Palestine have the
capacity to suggest a broader literate state but fall far short of providing
conclusive evidence. These writing exercises include abecedaries written
on ostraca, parchment, or even in funerary contexts such as ossuaries and
catacombs, as well as inscriptions.[30] Some previous scholars have cited

26.   Josephus, *Life* 1–2 §1–7. Similarly, Carr, *Writing*, 247.
27.   According to Luke 1:8, 63, John the Baptist did. On this text, see below,
p. 80.
28.   Crenshaw, *Education*, 6. He continues, "Moreover, it may refer to knowledge
acquired from hearing the Torah recited in the synagogue rather than from studying
a written text." Similarly, Millard, *Reading*, 157–58, regarding Josephus's and Philo's
claims, and *y. Ket.* 32c (8:11): "How widely that was in force is unknown and it is
likely that many who learnt to read the Scriptures learnt by heart and never read any
other book." This statement is an example of the shift in the tone of Millard's argument, as his earlier research argued more forcefully for widespread literacy rather
than knowledge of/about writing. On this shift in Millard's research, see Young,
"Israelite Literacy," 241 n. 12; cf. Hezser, *Jewish*, 28–33.
29.   On the connection between urbanism and literacy rates, see Bar-Ilan, "Illiteracy," 48–50; Baumgarten, *Flourishing*, 137 (following Bar-Ilan); Harris, *Ancient*,
17; Hezser, *Jewish*, 496. Cf. Nicholas Everett, *Literacy in Lombard Italy, c. 568–774*
(Cambridge: Cambridge University Press, 2003), 12–13, who is unpersuasive in light
of the plethora of evidence demonstrating a connection between urbanism and
literacy.
30.   See discussion in Hezser, *Jewish*, 85–89.

such evidence as the work of schoolboys and thus as evidence for the existence of a Jewish elementary school system that included instruction in writing.[31] Haran refers to this thesis, which is particularly (though not exclusively) associated with the work of Lemaire,[32] as the "abecedary-school connection."[33] Other scholars note this evidence in their arguments for a widespread Israelite literacy. For example, with regards to ancient Israel, Mazar claims, "The ostraca and simple inscriptions on potsherds and pottery jars as well as the abundance of seals are evidence that, at least during the last two centuries of the Monarchy, the knowledge of writing was widespread."[34]

Apart from the ambivalent phrase "knowledge of writing," to which I will return, there are problems for this interpretation of the evidence. First, the contexts of some of the abecedaries, especially the funerary ones, make clear that some were not school exercises, unless one is to imagine the instruction of young children taking place among rotting corpses.[35] Second, the ostraca or parchments that admittedly could be the work of an illiterate just learning to write are nonetheless open to various other interpretations as well, such as the testing of writing implements by a practiced scribe.[36] Furthermore, it is not clear that these were the work

---

31. Wilhelm Bacher, "Das altjüdische Schulwesen," *Jahrbuch für jüdische Geschichte und Literatur* 6 (1903): 66; Nathan Drazin, *History of Jewish Education from 515 BCE to 220 CE* (Baltimore: The Johns Hopkins University Press, 1963), 85; André Lemaire, *Les Ecoles et la Formation de la Bible dans l'Ancien Israël* (OBO 39; Fribourg: Editions Universitaires, 1981), 7–33. Cf. Ebner, *Elementary*, 76, who describes the process of writing instruction based on rabbinic evidence.

32. Lemaire, *Ecoles*, 7–33.

33. Menahem Haran, "On the Diffusion of Literacy and Schools in Ancient Israel," in *Congress Volume: Jerusalem 1986* (ed. J. A. Emerton; Leiden: Brill, 1988), 88.

34. Amihai Mazar, *Archaeology of the Land of the Bible, 10,000–586 B.C.E.* (ABRL; New York: Doubleday, 1990), 515. See also his "The Iron Age I," in *The Archaeology of Ancient Israel* (ed. Amnon Ben-Tor; trans. R. Greenberg; New Haven: Yale University Press, 1992), 299–300; and Gabriel Barkay, "The Iron Age II–III," in Ben-Tor, ed., *Archaeology of Ancient Israel*, 349; Richard S. Hess, "Literacy in Iron Age Israel," in *Windows into Old Testament History: Evidence, Argument, and the Crisis of "Biblical Israel"* (ed. V. Philips Long, David W. Baker, and Gordon J. Wenham; Grand Rapids: Eerdmans, 2002), 82–102. Cf. Niditch, *Oral World*, 39.

35. Haran, "On the Diffusion," 87–91; Hezser, *Jewish*, 85; Weeks, *Early Israelite Wisdom*, 144, 150–51. Also, Crenshaw, *Education*, 102, in reference to an abecedary in a single dwelling remote location accessible only by rope ladder. Cf., however, the cautious statement of Carr, *Writing*, 123, on "contemporary assumptions about where education could and could not take place."

36. Crenshaw, *Education*, 62–63; Hezser, *Jewish*, 87–88. David Toshio Tsumura, "'Misspellings' in Cuneiform Alphabetic Texts from Ugarit: Some Cases of Loss or Addition of Signs," in *Writing and Ancient Near Eastern Society: Papers in Honor*

of young schoolboys rather than adult scribes, or even possibly adults at a remedial stage of scribal training. "There is probably no single interpretation to be put on all the abecedaries which have been recovered, and the automatic association of abecedaries with the learning or writing, let alone with schools, is to be regarded with profound suspicion."[37]

A number of more recent scholars, therefore, have argued insistently against the abecedary-school connection and, concomitantly, against the idea of a widespread Jewish education system and thus against widespread Jewish literacy.[38] Regarding the Second Temple period, Haran even concludes, "The fact is that in Second Temple times there is virtually no proof of a connection between abecedaries and schools, while there are proofs of the absence of any such connection."[39] The problem is not a dearth of evidence, but a dearth of evidence that points decidedly in favor of widespread literacy.

The relationship between arguments and evidence is circular on both sides of this debate. Whether one thinks writing exercises point to a general elementary school system that taught writing will likely be determined by whether one thinks there were such schools in place to produce the evidence; and vice versa for those who see the abecedaries as the work of a minority scribal elite produced in their specialized scribal education or, in the least, produced as a result of it. The evidence has the capacity to support—though not prove—either theory.

---

of Alan R. Millard (ed. Piotr Bienkowski, Christopher Mee, and Elizabeth Slater; JSOTSup 426; London: T&T Clark, 2005), 143–51, raises another possibility when he suggests that some Ugaritic abecedaries contain phonetic spellings rather than "misspellings" that point to an unpracticed or unlearned writer.

37. Weeks, *Early Israelite Wisdom*, 151.

38. Crenshaw, *Education*, 62–63, 100–108; Haran, "On the Diffusion," 85–91; Hezser, *Jewish*, 85–89; Horsley, *Scribes*, 92; Emile Puech, "Les Ecoles dans l'Israël Préexilique: Données Epigraphiques," in Emerton, ed., *Congress Volume: Jerusalem 1986*, 189–96, and esp. 202–3; Christopher A. Rollston, "The Phoenician Script of the Tel Zayit Abecedary and Putative Evidence for Israelite Literacy," in *Literate Culture and Tenth-Century Canaan: The Tel Zayit Abecedary in Context* (ed. Ron Tappy and P. Kyle McCarter; Winona Lake: Eisenbrauns: 2008), 70–72; Christopher A. Rollston, "Scribal Education in Ancient Israel: The Old Hebrew Epigraphic Evidence," *BASOR* 344 (2006): 47–50, 67; repr. in *Writing*, 91–113; Weeks, *Early Israelite Wisdom*, 137–56 (who is less certain about the issue of literacy, pp. 152–53). See also Samuel Byrskog, *Jesus the Only Teacher: Didactic Authority and Transmission in Ancient Israel, Ancient Judaism and the Matthean Community* (ConBNT 24; Stockholm: Almqvist & Wiksell, 1994), 66. Cf., however, Emanuel Tov, *Scribal Practices and Approaches Reflected in the Texts Found in the Judean Desert* (STDJ 54; Leiden: Brill, 2004), 13–14.

39. Haran, "On the Diffusion," 88.

An example from the New Testament illustrates how these matters impact the interpretation of narrative claims. Luke 1:63 portrays John the Baptist's priestly (1:8) father Zechariah as writing "His name is John" on a wax tablet (πινακίδιον) and that, upon his writing, those who came to circumcise the infant Baptist were amazed. Assuming its historical accuracy for the moment, one is nevertheless left with a plethora of questions regarding its significance for understanding the literate landscape. Does it demonstrate that even in the Judean hill country (1:39) people could read and write? Or does it demonstrate that one person could write and a few could read? Could Zechariah's fellow hill-country dwellers write like him? Or was Zechariah, as perhaps the lone priestly representative in the village, also the sole local grapho-literate? Was his status as a lone grapho-literate related to his status as a lone priest? Alternatively, were those performing the circumcision (1:59), who were amazed at what he wrote, also priests? If so, does this text suggest that literate skills were restricted to the priesthood in the Judean hill country? Was Zechariah's audience amazed because they read what he wrote (possible but not narrated) or because someone capable of reading told them what he wrote (also possible but not narrated) or because they could figure out what he meant without having to read what he wrote (again, possible but not narrated)? Did the phrase "His name is John" encapsulate Zechariah's writing abilities? Did reading that simple phrase encapsulate his audience's reading abilities? Or was he capable of more advanced compositional abilities, and they capable of more advanced reading abilities?

The sole claim of Luke 1:63 is that Zechariah wrote a short phrase on a wax tablet and those around him were amazed. As the questions above demonstrate, entirely unaddressed are the extent of his abilities and how representative they were for his friends, family, fellow priests, or even himself. In assimilating such a reference to a larger image of Jesus' literate landscape, therefore, a scholar's preconceived notions will almost inevitably fill the gaps and influence whether he or she sees Zechariah as an example of widespread majority Jewish literacy (that reached even into the hill country) or as an example of minority literacy (associated with the Jerusalem aristocracy and its functionaries)—to cite only two possible interpretations of many.

Others have also stressed the tendentious nature of the evidence and the role of scholarly preconceptions. With regard to evidence such as seal impressions containing alphabetic letters, for example, Haran states, "They can bear various explanations and much depends on the question [of] how the concept of literacy itself is understood."[40] With regard to

40.   Ibid., 85; cf. 82, 85 n. 8.

preconceptions, Niditch says, "One might well ask why Israelite society should have been so much more literate than all other ancient societies or than many modern traditional societies in today's Third World."[41] Niditch's comment forces scholars to make explicit their point of reference for their assumptions and theories about Jewish education and literacy, and likely implicitly notes that scholars often approach the evidence with the mindset of the industrialized modern West. In a similar vein, Young highlights the importance of allowing comparative evidence from antiquity to alter expectations:

> All that we have learned from the comparative method, and from Harris's discussion of the classical world leads us to *expect* that Israelite literacy was fairly limited. Contrary to modern western society where the question of the extent of literacy would look for who cannot read, it seems more prudent to approach an ancient society with the question reversed.[42]

Given the importance of preconceptions in interpreting the evidence, then, scholars must approach the evidence for Jewish literacy in the first century C.E. by adjusting their expectations from a modern Western context with publicly funded elementary education systems that teach reading and writing (and thus illiteracy is the social abnormality) to a pre-Gutenberg predominantly rural culture with no centralized publicly funded education system (and thus literacy is the social abnormality). Two further considerations demonstrate the types of adjusted expectations that are required and support the thesis that Jesus' literate landscape was characterized by widespread illiteracy: religious devotion did not require literate education; and literate education was not practical in an agrarian culture.

1.3. *Religious Devotion Did Not Require Literate Education*

With regard to a presumed connection between literacy and religious devotion, Bar-Ilan observes, "According to the Torah, there is no need to read or write, except for writing the *Mezuza*, *Tefilin*, and the Torah itself. However, for these purposes there was always a scribe, so a Jew in antiquity could fulfill the commandments of the Torah while being illiterate."[43] Although it may appear that Bar-Ilan underestimates the religious expectation of the biblical texts, this is unlikely in light of the semantic

---

41. Niditch, *Oral World*, 38.

42. Young, "Israelite Literacy," 244–45 (emphasis added). He continues, "We cannot assume that anyone except professional scribes was able to read and write unless the evidence points strongly to the literacy of another group" (245).

43. Bar-Ilan, "Illiteracy," 55.

range for the verbs used for reading and writing. Throughout the Hebrew Bible קָרָא ("to read") and כָּתַב ("to write") could and often did mean that someone else would actually be performing the literate tasks for the person of higher status, who are, nonetheless, the subjects of the verbs.[44] Second Kings 22:16 has the prophetess Huldah refer to the recently discovered book of the law that Josiah read (קָרָא; LXX ἀνέγνω), despite the fact that 22:10 specifies that actually his scribe "Shaphan…read (וַיִּקְרָאֵהוּ; LXX ἀνέγνω) it out loud to the king." With regard to writing, God commands that Jeremiah "take a scroll and write (וְכָתַבְתָּ; LXX γράψον) on it all the words that I have spoken" in Jer 36:2 (LXX 43:2). Two verses later, however, the narrative clarifies that Jeremiah's method of obeying God's command did not include *his* usage of the skill of writing at all: "Then Jeremiah called Baruch son of Neriah, and Baruch wrote (וַיִּכְתֹּב; LXX ἔγραψεν) on a scroll at Jeremiah's dictation all the words of the Lord that he had spoken to him" (Jer 36:4; LXX 43:4).[45] Another example is when God claims, "I will write" (וְכָתַבְתִּי; LXX γράψω) the words from the first tablets onto the second set in Exod 34:1, although he commands Moses to write (כְּתָב; LXX γράψον) the words for him in 34:27.

When considering passages where Israel collectively is the subject of verbs for reading and writing that presumably demonstrate their religious commitments (such as Deut 6:9; 11:20, and 27:3, 8), then, one must remember that the semantic range of each of those verbs includes meanings that do not attribute literate skills directly to all Israel or even to the subject(s) of the verb(s).[46] These texts are, therefore, not evidence that the literate skills of reading and writing were widespread. Bar-Ilan is correct in his assertion that illiteracy did not bar Jews from participation in the religious heritage of Israel.

1.4. *Literate Education Was Not Practical*
In terms of the practicality of literate education, "It is plain that rural patterns of living are inimical to the spread of literacy."[47] Since education was not publicly funded, possibilities for acquisition of literate skills resided on the literate education of the parents (both their own attainment of it and their leisure/availability to teach their children) and/or the

---

44. Young, "Israelite Literacy," 248–53; also Horsley, *Scribes*, 92.
45. Young, "Israelite Literacy," 248. He also cites Esth 8:8–9.
46. Ibid., 249–50.
47. Harris, *Ancient*, 17.

family's wealth as a means of securing a child's education through public education (if available),[48] a private tutor, or apprenticeship.[49]

The acquisition of literate skills for free children was thus a realistic possibility only for those who had wealth and/or leisure time in which to pursue it.[50] (Slaves trained as copyists would obviously have been educated, but this only further demonstrates the connection between household wealth and education.[51]) Moore thus observes that the Jewish ideal that the father was responsible for providing education (reflected in, for example, *Jub* 8:2, 11:16; *4 Macc.* 18:10; *L.A.B.* 22:5; *b. B. Bat.* 21a) "restricted education in general to the children of parents who were able to teach them or to pay for having them taught, and had the interest to do it."[52] Extending the implications of a predominantly illiterate agrarian culture further, then, Bar-Ilan asks poignantly, "Why should a farmer send his son to learn how to read when it entails a waste of working time (= money)?"[53] Drawing these threads together, Hezser observes the restricted nature of Jewish education in the time of Jesus:

> Since only fathers who knew letters and were knowledgeable of the Torah themselves would have been able to teach Torah to their children, in the first two centuries, when few opportunities for an elementary education outside the home existed, children's basic instruction in the Torah would have been restricted to certain educated circles.[54]

Clearly, such observations do not demonstrate that an interested agrarian child or adult could not have sought out a literate education if so desired,

---

48. The availability of a literate education was predominantly impacted by proximity to an urban environment. See Bar-Ilan, "Illiteracy," 48–50; Baumgarten, *Flourishing*, 135; Harris, *Ancient*, 17; Hezser, *Jewish*, 496.

49. One example of apprenticeship in the Greco-Roman milieu is P.Oxy. 724, a contract for a slave to learn shorthand. Cf. also, Sir 51:23. Quintilian (first century C.E.), *Inst.* 1.2.1, describes the decision between public and private education for his son.

50. Consider also Origen, *Cels.* 1.29, who refers to noble men who receive "an upbringing at the hands of wealthy people who are able to spend money on the education of their son" (Chadwick).

51. On the education of slaves, see A. D. Booth, "The Schooling of Slaves in First-Century Rome," *TAPA* 109 (1979): 11–19; Harris, *Ancient*, 247–48, 255–59; S. L. Mohler, "Slave Education in the Roman Empire," *TAPA* 71 (1940): 262–80.

52. George Foot Moore, *Judaism in the First Centuries of the Christian Era: The Age of the Tannaim* (3 vols.; Cambridge, Mass.: Harvard University Press, 1927–30), 1:316. Also, Baumgarten, *Flourishing*, 117.

53. Bar-Ilan, "Illiteracy," 55. Similarly, Crenshaw, *Education*, 39; Poirier, "Linguistic Situation," 79, 90.

54. Hezser, *Jewish*, 69.

assuming he or she lived in close enough proximity to a teacher. But they do provide a decisive check against automatic assumptions that one was readily available and attainable by the majority of the population in a culture where most were manual laborers, there was little financial incentive to acquire literate skills, and ambitions of "upward mobility" (in the modern sense) are an anachronism.[55] Scholars cannot, and should not, assume that Second Temple Jewish society required literate skills religiously and supported their acquisition geographically and financially on a large scale.

Indeed, according to the lauded scribe in Sirach (second century B.C.E.),[56] the position of the literate scribe in the Second Temple period is directly related to the ability to avoid manual labor:

> The wisdom of the scribe (γραμματέως) depends on the opportunity of leisure; only the one who has little business can become wise. How can one become wise who handles the plow, and who glories in the shaft of a goad, who drives oxen and is occupied with their work, and whose talk is about bulls?… So it is with every artisan (πᾶς τέκτων)[57] and master artisan (ἀρχιτέκτων) who labors by night as well as by day…. So it is with the smith, sitting by the anvil…. So it is with the potter sitting at his work and turning the wheel with his feet…. All these rely on their hands, and all are skillful in their own work…. Yet they are not sought out for the council of the people, nor do they attain eminence in the public assembly. They do not sit in the judge's seat, nor do they understand the decisions of the courts; they cannot expound discipline or judgment, and they are not found among the rulers…. But they maintain the fabric of the world, and their concern is for the exercise of their trade. *How different the one who devotes himself to the study of the law of the Most High!*[58]

According to the scribe of Sir 38, the largest cross-section of Jewish culture in the Second Temple period, despite being responsible for the majority of societal tasks and "maintain[ing] the fabric of the world" (38:34), were not able to study the Torah in a focused manner because of

55.   Cf., however, the study on Roman scribal culture by Nicholas Purcell, "The *Apparitores*: A Study in Social Mobility," *PBSR* 51 (1983): 125–73.

56.   M. Gilbert, "Wisdom Literature," in *Jewish Writings of the Second Temple Period: Apocrypha, Pseudepigrapha, Qumran Sectarian Writings, Philo, Josephus* (ed. Michael E. Stone; CRINT 2.2; Philadelphia: Fortress, 1984), 291, dates the writing of Sirach to 190 B.C.E. and the Greek translation to 132 B.C.E.

57.   Note that Mark 6:3 identifies Jesus as ὁ τέκτων. See discussion in Chapter 4.

58.   Sir 38:24–34 (emphasis added). Similarly, in *PHerc.* 1005 16.17–18, the Epicurean Philodemus (first century B.C.E.) refers to "manual laborers/servants" (οἱ δουλεύσαντες) as those "who have not learned letters" (γράμματα μὴ μαθόντες). For the text, see Anna Angeli, *Agli amici di scuola* (PHerc. *1005*) (LSE 7; Naples: Bibliopolis, 1988), 181.

their location in the social grid.[59] Especially in the wake of Harris's sustained argument that the ancient world lacked the social, financial, political, and organizational ability to support widespread literacy, the author of Sirach is likely more forthcoming about the historical reality of the general availability of literate education and its benefits than are the comments of Philo and Josephus.

For these reasons, one cannot uncritically take the written material that remains from first-century Judaism as evidence for widespread literacy. Again, the point is not that a lack of public education necessarily prohibited interested individuals from attaining literate skills, but that there are no grounds upon which one can describe such attainment as *typical* for Jews in Jesus' time. Although the profound amount of information we do not know about Jewish education should cause scholars to hold their convictions about precise literacy rates, and so on, with a large dose of humility, there is certainly not enough evidence to overturn the majority conviction that, like the rest of the ancient world, Second Temple Judaism was profoundly illiterate.[60]

2. Widespread Textuality

That widespread illiteracy characterized Jesus' Judaism should not lead scholars to conclude that it was therefore unfamiliar with texts or their effects.[61] Thus, when Roberts claims, "The world into which Christianity was born was, if not literary, literate to a remarkable degree," one must ask further what he means by "literate to a remarkable degree."[62] If

59. Note also the optimum conditions, including leisure, necessary for Josephus to pen his history of the Jewish war: "Then, in the leisure which Rome afforded me, with all my materials in readiness, and with the aid of some assistants for the sake of the Greek, at last I committed to writing my narrative of the events" (*Ag. Ap.* 1.9 §50; Thackeray, LCL).

60. In addition to Harris, for comparative evidence, see John Baines, "Literacy (Ancient Near East)," *ABD* 4:333–37; John Baines, "Literacy and Ancient Egyptian Society," *Man* 18 (1983): 572–99; Carr, *Writing*, 17–109; Crenshaw, *Education*, 15–27, 40–49; Toorn, *Scribal Culture*, 51–73.

61. Some scholars who stress (appropriately) that the Jewish and early Christian cultures were oral/aural unfortunately press this matter too far in their descriptions of this oral/aural environment as something antithetical to textuality. See further Keith, "Performance," 54–61.

62. C. H. Roberts, "Books in the Graeco-Roman World and in the New Testament," in *The Cambridge History of the Bible.* Vol. 1, *From the Beginnings to Jerome* (ed. P. R. Ackroyd and C. F. Evans; Cambridge: Cambridge University Press, 1970), 48. John Sawyer, *Sacred Languages and Sacred Texts* (RFCC; New York: Routledge, 1999), 44, cites Roberts approvingly. Similarly ambiguous is Hurtado, "Greco-

Roberts means that, although an oral/aural culture, Second Temple Judaism was also inundated with texts and writing—marriage contracts, land contracts, censuses, tax receipts, holy texts, imperial markings on coins, and so on—he is correct.[63] For, "Even the most remote peasant farmer would know that the black marks on papyrus rolls or the scratches on waxed tablets spelled out their fate," and "even illiterate Jews from Palestine…recognized the roll of writing in the systems of political and religious power that dominated their lives."[64] The Babatha cache, consisting of documents that Babatha could not sign herself, demonstrates conclusively that profoundly textual Roman Palestinian Jews could also be profoundly lacking in nascent literate skills.[65] It is certain, then, that almost every Jew in Roman Palestine was no stranger to texts and, in this sense, the culture was "literate to a remarkable degree."

This does not appear to be Roberts's meaning, however. He continues, "In the Near East in the first century of our era writing was an essential accompaniment of life at almost all levels to an extent without parallel in living memory."[66] If Roberts is claiming that writing ability was widespread in "almost all levels" of the social order, he is incorrect. The skill of writing was even more rare than reading and there is no incontrovertible evidence that writing was even taught in first-century Jewish literate education.[67] Most Jews, however, could neither read nor write to a significant degree. This observation, again, is not to denigrate their intelligence but rather to observe that their lives did not require literate skills, and certainly not advanced literate skills.[68] The presence of texts in

Roman Textuality," 95: "Especially in Jewish society, literacy was a valued and widely shared competence and that writing, reading, and hearing of texts had deeply and widely affected the populace for centuries."

63. Bar-Ilan, "Writing," 37; R. A. Derrenbacker, Jr., *Ancient Compositional Practices and the Synoptic Problem* (BETL 186; Leuven: Peeters, 2005), 29–30; Jaffee, *Torah*, 15; Millard, *Reading*, 156–57, 170; A. R. Millard, "Literacy (Israel)," *ABD* 4:338–39. Similarly, regarding the Greco-Roman context, D. M. Scholer, "Writing and Literature: Greco-Roman," *DNTB* 1283.

64. Millard, *Reading*, 170; Thatcher, *Why*, 43, respectively. E. G. Turner, *Greek Papyri: An Introduction* (Oxford: Clarendon, 1968), 83, presents a farmer who could not write but kept an archive. In the fourth century C.E., Lactantius describes Roman census-takers gathering both the *urbanae ac rusticae plebes* ("urban and rustic population," *Mort.* 23.2; McDonald, FC).

65. See further below, p. 91.

66. Roberts, "Books," 48.

67. See especially Hezser, *Jewish*, 88. The next section will address reading and writing gradations.

68. Bar-Ilan, "Illiteracy," 55; Dewey, "Textuality," 41; Harris, *Ancient*, 30; Hezser, *Jewish*, 496; Millard, *Reading*, 154.

Roman Palestine does not require that all members of that culture were able to access them (read, write, understand, etc.) on their own.

Roberts's mistake, and others' who take a similar position and cite the presence of texts as direct or indirect evidence for the presence of many readers/writers of those texts, seems to derive from a confusion of literacy and textuality. Literacy, in its most simple definition of consisting of the skills of reading and writing in various shades,[69] concerns personal ability to access the content of texts for oneself. The usages of texts, however, are not limited to their content and the users of texts are not limited to those who can access that content personally. In some cases, the primary usage of texts derives from the social circumstances surrounding the text rather than its content, circumstances in which the users of texts may not have even been able to read them. This is particularly the case with Jewish and Christian magical texts and/or texts used as amulets, which "generally had either an apotropaic or a curative function."[70] As Gamble observes regarding early Christian magical texts, "In a society in which few could read, texts were esoteric objects to many, and if spoken words were powerful, so were inscribed words, for they had the advantage of duration and secrecy."[71] Sometimes, then, the importance of a text derives from the absence of a widespread readership rather its presence.

In contrast to literacy, textuality is the knowledge, usage, and appreciation of texts regardless of individual or majority ability to create or access them via literate skills. Textuality, that is, focuses on the social and rhetorical functions of texts apart from, or in addition to, the content. Literacy and textuality often have a symbiotic relationship, but,

69.   David E. Aune, "Literacy," in *The Westminster Dictionary of New Testament and Early Christian Literature and Rhetoric* (Louisville: Westminster John Knox, 2003), 275.

70.   Tommy Wasserman, *The Epistle of Jude: Its Text and Transmission* (ConBNT 43; Stockholm: Almqvist & Wiksell, 2006), 64. See also Sawyer, *Sacred*, 122–24. Other forms of texts, such as opisthographs, likely reflect the primary importance of the content, rather than the form, of the text and could have been personal copies not meant for public display. See further Larry W. Hurtado, *The Earliest Christian Artifacts: Manuscripts and Christian Origins* (Grand Rapids: Eerdmans, 2006), 57 n. 49; Larry W. Hurtado and Chris Keith, "Book Writing and Production in the Hellenistic and Roman Era," in *The New Cambridge History of the Bible* (ed. James Carleton Paget and Joachim Schaper; Cambridge: Cambridge University Press, forthcoming), n.p. The Jewish and Christian practice of bibliomancy combined an emphasis on the text as a numinous object and the text's content. See P. W. van der Horst, "Bibliomancy," *DNTB* 165–67.

71.   Gamble, *Books*, 237. See further E. A. Judge, "The Magical Use of Scripture in the Papyri," in *Perspectives on Language and Text* (ed. Edgar W. Conrad and Edward G. Newing; Winona Lake: Eisenbrauns, 1987), 339–49.

significantly, they are different phenomena. "Literacy is not textuality. One can be literate without the overt use of texts, and one can use texts extensively without evidencing genuine literacy."[72] For this reason, Harris notes that the presence of an extensive "written culture" in Rome and Italy does not require extensive literacy, contrary to those who have argued otherwise.[73] Similarly, Hurtado observes, "Suffice it to say that the extent of literacy does not determine the extent of the appreciation for and influence of texts. Even illiterates can admire and appreciate texts and be influenced by them through hearing them read."[74] In fact, in some contexts, textuality and literacy can be diametrically opposed, as the quotation from Gamble above regarding magical texts observes.

There are two important matters for this study in light of the difference(s) between literacy and textuality. First, arguments that first-century Palestinian Judaism *must* have been literate, or at least more literate than the rest of the ancient world, due to its religious commitment to sacred texts, must be rejected. To state again, the importance of texts, reading, and writing does not necessarily relate directly to the number of individuals capable of those literate skills.[75] Attainment of literate skills in Jesus' Judaism was almost always a function of wealth and status, whether one's own, that of a patron, or (in the frequent case of literate slaves) that of an owner, not religious commitment.[76] To put forward arguments to the contrary confuses literacy and textuality.

Second, the simultaneous existence of widespread illiteracy and widespread textuality did contribute heavily to the social order in Second Temple Judaism. Specifically, the importance of reading and readers related directly to the tremendous amount of social esteem held by the relatively small slice of the population capable of reading and copying the holy Scriptures for everyone else. I will return to the important issue of scribal literacy, the form of literacy this state of affairs enables, after addressing a third characteristic of Jesus' literate landscape—literacy spectrums.

72. Stock, *Implications*, 7. For an application of Stock's model to Second Temple Judaism, see Tom Thatcher, "Literacy, Textual Communities, and Josephus' *Jewish War*," *JSJ* 29 (1998): 123–42.
73. Harris, *Ancient*, 259.
74. Hurtado, *Earliest*, 25 n. 59.
75. Thus, Kirk, "Memory," 158–59, appropriately claims: "Literate education was the preserve of elites.... The fact that Palestinian Judaism was a Torah-centered religion is not incongruous with this scenario. Written Torah would have been appropriated by the nonliterate population orally and aurally."
76. On the later development among Christian ascetics of literate education as part of religious devotion, see Hurtado and Keith, "Book Writing," n.p.

3. *Literacy Spectrums*

As Harris notes, "There are infinite gradations of literacy for any written language."[77] This reality ultimately makes the dichotomy literate/illiterate false. Truer to the ancient reality, including Second Temple Judaism, is the notion of literacy spectrums that consisted of different literate skills, different languages, and different social/professional manifestations of those skills.

3.1. *A Spectrum of Literate Skills*
Literacy is not a monolithic entity but rather a spectrum, running from simple skills like signing one's name to advanced skills like composing intricate texts.[78] Despite the fact that the lines between various points on this spectrum are blurry rather than well-defined,[79] some of the locations on this literacy spectrum are observable.

3.1.1. *Semi-Literacy.* One well-attested gradation of literacy in Greek documentary papyri that demonstrates the falsity of the literate/illiterate dichotomy is "semi-literacy." Many lower-level bureaucrats in the Greco-Roman world held this status, which is closer to illiteracy than literacy. Harris defines such individuals as "persons who can write slowly or not at all, and who can read without being able to read complex or very lengthy texts."[80] That is, semi-literates possess literate skills, but those skills do not extend beyond the earliest stages of literate education. Youtie places "slow writers" such as the now-famous late second-century C.E. village scribe (κωμογραμματεύς) Petaus, who was barely capable of producing his name and formula for document reception, in the same category, "between literacy and illiteracy."[81] Such individuals were "slow writers" because they had to reproduce words letter for letter without

---

77.   Harris, *Ancient*, 5.

78.   Aune, "Literacy," 275–76; Gamble, "Literacy," 644; Derrenbacker, *Ancient*, 22; Kirk, "Memory," 158; John S. Kloppenborg Verbin, *Excavating Q: The History and Setting of the Sayings Gospel* (Edinburgh: T. & T. Clark, 2000), 167; Rafael Rodríguez, "Reading and Hearing in Ancient Contexts," *JSNT* 32, no. 2 (2009): 154–56.

79.   Haran, "On the Diffusion," 83.

80.   Harris, *Ancient*, 5.

81.   Herbert C. Youtie, "Βραδέως γράφων: Between Literacy and Illiteracy," in *Scriptiunculae II* (Amsterdam: Adolf M. Hakkert, 1973), 629–51; repr. from *GRBS* 12, no. 2 (1971): 239–61. Ann Ellis Hanson, "Ancient Illiteracy," in Beard et al., *Literacy*, 172, claims low-level officials like Petaus who "did not know letters" proliferated after his time.

being able to recognize the larger language units (words, sentences, etc.) they formed. While practicing his formula, Petaus does not recognize that he makes a mistake by omitting a vowel and repeats it subsequently because he is mechanically copying the preceding line.[82]

3.1.2. *Signature Literacy.* Petaus could at least produce a short formula in addition to his name, even if imperfectly. Many other ancients' literate skills did not extend beyond writing his or her name.[83] Moving even closer to the illiterate end of the literacy spectrum, this literate skill is thus designated "signature literacy."

Cribiore's research into the Egyptian Greco-Roman school papyri reveals that one of the main pedagogical aims of education at this time was simply to get students to the level of signature literacy. Since most students would not continue beyond initial alphabetic instruction,[84] attainment of signature literacy was crucial for the individual to be able to participate in literate culture, even if marginally by signing documents for him- or herself:

---

82. Petaus's imperfect practicing of the formula Πεταῦς κωμογρα(μματεύς) ἐπιδέδωκα ("I, Petaus, village scribe, have received") occurs on *P.Petaus* 121 (P.Köln inv. 328). A convenient image of *P.Petaus* 121 appears on Roger S. Bagnall, *Reading Papyri, Writing Ancient History* (AAW; New York: Routledge, 1995), xiii. Thomas J. Kraus, "(Il)literacy in Non-literary Papyri from Graeco-Roman Egypt: Further Aspects to the Educational Ideal in Ancient Literary Sources and Modern Times," in *Ad fontes: Original Manuscripts and Their Significance for Studying Early Christianity—Selected Essays* (TENTS 3; Leiden: Brill, 2007), 118–20; repr. from *Mnemosyne* 53 (2000): 322–42, discusses mistakes on the papyrus other than Petaus's repeated omission of the initial verbal *epsilon.*

83. Female education was less common than the education of males or even slaves, but not unknown. Origen, for example, employed female calligraphers (Eusebius, *Hist. eccl.* 6.23.1–2). On female literacy/education, see further Lynn H. Cohick, *Women in the World of the Earliest Christians: Illuminating Ancient Ways of Life* (Grand Rapids: Baker Academic, 2009), 45–46, 55–56, 144, 206–9, 242–54; Bakhos, "Orality," 491–92; Eldon Jay Epp, "The Oxyrhynchus Papyri: 'Not without honor except in their hometown'?," in *Perspectives*, 772–77; repr. from *JBL* 123 (2004): 5–55; Kim Haines-Eitzen, *Guardians of Letters: Literacy, Power, and the Transmitters of Early Christian Literature* (New York: Oxford University Press, 2000), 41–52; Ross S. Kraemer, "Women's Authorship of Jewish and Christian Literature in the Greco-Roman Period," in *"Women Like This": New Perspectives on Jewish Women in the Greco-Roman World* (ed. Amy-Jill Levine; Atlanta: Scholars Press, 1991), 221–42.

84. Carr, *Writing*, 183, 187, 192, too notes that few made it through the entire pedagogical process.

There can be no doubt that inhabitants of Graeco-Roman Egypt preferred to sign documents and letters in their clumsy, belabored characters rather than be considered among illiterates. It was better to possess and exhibit the skill in limited and imperfect degree, however difficult and unpleasant to the eye their efforts.[85]

Thus, as soon as students began learning letters they also began learning to write their names, as teachers maximized what time they had with students.[86] Cribiore points to a Roman period ostracon, where a student named Kametis writes his name and then practices the first letters of the Greek alphabet imperfectly, as evidence of this pedagogical method in practice.[87] Lemaire claims that average ancient Israelite villagers' literate skills would not have extended beyond "the ability to write their own names."[88]

3.1.3. *Illiterate yet Textual.* Despite the importance of signature literacy, and possibly challenging Lemaire's claim that an "average" ancient Israelite villager would have attained it, the documentary papyri preserve a wealth of comparative evidence demonstrating that many in the Roman Empire had not attained even signature literacy. The papyri contain

85. Raffaella Cribiore, *Writing, Teachers, and Students in Graeco-Roman Egypt* (ASP 36; Atlanta: Scholars Press, 1996), 10. I have elsewhere suggested that the importance of using what literate skills one has is the proper background against which to view Paul's utilization of his own grapho-literate skills in Greek (Chris Keith, "'In My Own Hand': Grapho-Literacy and the Apostle Paul," *Bib* 89 [2008]: 39–58).

86. Raffaella Cribiore, *Gymnastics of the Mind: Greek Education in Hellenistic and Roman Egypt* (Princeton: Princeton University Press, 2001), 167.

87. See ibid., 168, for an image and discussion. This ostracon is a good example of the tricky interpretation of writing exercises (see above, pp. 75–81). Cribiore plausibly interprets the sequence ΑΒΓΔΒΤΑ as a failed attempt to write the first four letters of the alphabet frontward and backward, ΑΒΓΔ-ΔΓΒΑ, where the *delta* has been traced over at least twice (as indicated by its darker appearance) and the Τ is a deformed Γ. (Her paleographical analysis is on Cribiore, *Writing*, 185, no. 51.) Perhaps inspiring caution, the boy does not appear to write the letters of his name with error, although they are in "large clumsy capitals" (*Writing*, 51). For Cribiore, *Gymnastics*, 168, this indicates "that pupils combined somewhat mechanically the letters that formed their names when they still had only a shaky grasp of them." That is, she takes the failed writing exercise and oversized capital letters as indicative of the fact that Kametis had only a "shaky grasp" of how to write his name. If this is not a *failed* attempt to write the sequence Cribiore (again, very plausibly) proposes, which is possible, Kametis's supposed shaky grasp of his name is much less obvious.

88. André Lemaire, "Writing and Writing Materials," *ABD* 6:1005. He continues, "The average villager probably would have had a difficult time composing a letter and probably did not have the technical skill to draft a will or a contract."

extremely common formulae noting that one individual (typically a scribe) signed a document on behalf of another on account of the latter's illiteracy. In 1950, Calderini published a study on 1,738 Greco-Roman Egyptian individuals identified with such illiteracy formulae (1,365 men and 373 women).[89] Kraus groups the formulae into three main types and provides examples of each, the last of which shows that even slow writers sometimes needed someone to add a subscription for them: ἔγραψα ὑπὲρ αὐτοῦ μὴ εἰδότος γράμματα; ἔγραψα ὑπὲρ αὐτοῦ ἀγραμμάτου (ὄντος); and ἔγραψα ὑπὲρ αὐτοῦ βραδέως γράφοντος.[90] These formulae, the papyri upon which they occur, and the illiterate owners of the contracts provide further conclusive evidence that lack of literate skills did not translate into lack of participation in literate culture. Such individuals were illiterate, yet also very textual.

Jewish evidence attests the presence of illiterate-yet-textual individuals in ancient Israel and Roman Palestine. In the former context, Isa 29:12 portrays a text coming before אֲשֶׁר לֹא־יָדַע סֵפֶר (literally "one who does not know a book"; NRSV "who cannot read") with the illiterate individual responding: לֹא יָדַעְתִּי סֵפֶר (literally "I do not know a book"; NRSV "cannot read"). In the latter context, Babatha's documents from the Bar Kokhba period often include statements noting her own lack of signature literacy. For example, P. Yadin 22.34 claims the Aramaic scribe כתבת על פום בבתא ("wrote by order of Babatha"); P. Yadin 16.35 states that the scribe Judanes ἔγραψα ὑπὲρ αὐτῆς ("wrote for her"); and P. Yadin 15.35–36 explains thoroughly that an Eleazar had to write for Babatha διὰ τὸ αὐτῆς εἰδέναι γράμματα ("on account of her not knowing letters").[91] In attesting Babatha's lack of signature literacy, these documents witness the social lacuna that even a meager and brief literate education could fill, and thus why the teachers whom Cribiore studied in Greco-Roman Egypt were anxious to teach their students at least this skill.

89. Rita Calderini, "Gli ἀγράμματοι nell'Egitto greco-romano," *Aeg* 30 (1950): 14–41 (esp. 22–23).

90. Kraus, "(Il)literacy," 110–11.

91. For the texts, see Naphtali Lewis et al., eds., *The Documents from the Bar Kokhba Period in the Cave of Letters: Greek Papyri* (JDS; Jerusalem: Israel Exploration Society, 1989), 99, 67, 60, respectively. Prior to the publication of the full Babatha cache, Joseph A. Fitzmyer, "The Languages of Palestine in the First Century A.D.," *CBQ* 32 (1970): 523; repr. in his *A Wandering Aramean: Collected Aramaic Essays* (combined ed., incorporating *The Semitic Background of the New Testament*; BRS; Grand Rapids: Eerdmans, 1997), 29–56, thought it "scarcely credible that she would have legal and financial documents drawn up for her in a language that she did not understand or read." As is now clear, this was exactly the case.

3.1.4. *Illiterate and Non-textual.* The Jewish evidence may challenge Lemaire's aforementioned assertion that an "average" Israelite villager would have attained signature literacy because they emerge from a class above average Israelite villagers. Of course, one cannot base conceptions of a whole society upon one person; but if Babatha, a twice-married land owner who thus had at least some wealth,[92] had not gained signature literacy, it is a very safe assumption that many non-land-owning Jews had not as well. The difference between Babatha and these Jews was that she could afford to have scribes like Judanes and Eleazar write for her. The majority of the Jewish population mirrored Babatha's lack of literate skills but likely were incapable of hiring a private scribe or supporting a literate household slave. Since these Jews, who were nonetheless aware of texts, letters on coinage, signage, and so on, could thus not participate in literate culture even at a degree of remove, one can describe them as illiterate and non-textual.

3.1.5. *Those Who Know* γράμματα. Turning toward the opposite end of the literacy spectrum, and on the other side of semi-literacy, literate skills varied also among those capable of reading and writing.

    3.1.5.1. *Reading and writing as separate skills.* Of first importance, reading and writing were separately taught and acquired skills, and ability in one did not necessarily imply ability in the other.[93] Previous scholars have thought differently, as exemplified by Marrou in his classic *History of Education in the Ancient World*: "Writing was taught in the same way as reading."[94] In the ancient context, however, reading and writing appeared at different stages of the educational process. Signature

---

    92. Lewis et al., *Documents*, 24.

    93. Cribiore, *Gymnastics*, 177; Cribiore, *Writing*, 9–10, 148; Alfred Edersheim, *Sketches of Jewish Social Life* (updated ed.; Peabody: Hendrickson, 1994), 111–12, 122; Everett, *Literacy*, 6; Goodman, "Texts," 99–100; M. C. A. Macdonald, "Literacy in an Oral Environment," in Bienkowski, Mee, and Slater, eds., *Writing*, 52–56, 65; Millard, *Reading*, 154; Peter Müller, *"Verstehst du auch, was du liest?": Lesen und Verstehen im Neuen Testament* (Darmstadt: Wissenschaftliche, 1994), 169 n. 86 (see further next footnote); Rodríguez, "Reading," 154–56.

    94. H. I. Marrou, *A History of Education in Antiquity* (trans. George Lamb; London: Sheed & Ward, 1956), 155. See also, Müller, *Verstehst*, 169 n. 86, who, after stating correctly, "Man muß aber zwischen Lesen und Schreiben unterscheiden…so daß nicht jeder, der lesen konnte, automatisch auch schrieb," goes on to claim curiously: "Für das erste christliche Jahrhundert wird man aber davon ausgehen können, daß Lesen- und Schreiben-Lernen Hand in Hand gingen." For the latter statement, Müller cites Riesner, *Jesus*, 191–93, whose argument is built heavily upon anachronistic rabbinic material.

literacy and other forms of rote copying (writing) were present at the initial stages of alphabetic instruction and letter recognition (reading).[95] These nascent writing skills are quite different, however, from the ability to compose a personal letter or, indeed, a philosophical treatise. Advanced compositional ability only appeared after reading skills had been mastered. Dionysius of Halicarnassus (first century C.E.) says,

> When we are taught to read, first we learn by heart the names of the letters, then their shapes and their values, then, in the same way, the syllables and their effects, and finally words and their properties.... And when we have acquired knowledge of these things, we begin to write and read, syllable by syllable and slowly at first. It is only when a considerable lapse of time has implanted firmly in our minds the forms of the words that we execute them with the utmost ease, and we read through any book that is given to us unfalteringly and with incredible confidence and speed. It must be assumed that something of this kind happens with accomplished professional writers when they come to deal with literary composition and the harmonious arrangement of clauses.[96]

Importantly, Dionysius claims that advanced writing ability is something accomplished by professionals and comes at the very end of the process he narrates. Again, length of education directly impacted the literate skills one attained and the degree to which one attained them, explaining how someone like Petaus could write a short phrase but not read enough to correct his own mistake. In signing his name and copying by rote a one-word formula, Petaus is maximizing his literate abilities. Cribiore observes concerning the evidence of the Egyptian Greco-Roman school papyri generally:

> The assumption that the two skills [reading and writing] were attained at the same time and according to the same pedagogical principles is unwarranted.... To be sure, both skills belong in school contexts, yet only the privileged few progressed through all education levels [and] the majority who had any education at all attained only minimal ability from limited schooling.[97]

Although modern scholars may hesitate to affirm these conclusions, it should take little reflection upon their own acquisition of research languages (ancient or modern) to demonstrate that the time one is able to spend learning a language will determine the degree of familiarity one has with it. Since only those who pursued the furthest stages of literate

---

95. Quintilian, *Inst.* 1.1.27; Seneca, *Ep.* 94.15.
96. Dionysius of Halicarnassus, *On Literary Composition* (Usher, LCL). This reference is from 2.229 of the Loeb edition. Cf. Manilius, *Astronomica* 2.755–61.
97. Cribiore, *Writing*, 9–10.

education learned advanced writing, compositional writing was a more advanced literate skill than reading (or signature literacy).

3.1.5.2. *"Knowing γράμματα" in Jewish tradition.* Second, focusing upon Jesus' own context, it is not clear that writing was even part of the curriculum for those few first-century Jews who received a literate education. Lacking direct unambiguous evidence for the precise contours of first-century Jewish literate education, scholars are again dependent upon glimpses from literary attestations. Several texts mention reading and writing explicitly. Cumulatively, however, the texts are ambiguous regarding writing or are unhelpful for understanding typical literate education.

Josephus claims the law commands parents to teach children γράμματα ("letters").[98] In addition to the fact that no one passage in the Mosaic Law requires literate education for children and the established unlikelihood that Josephus's claim reflected reality for all first-century Palestinian Jews, Josephus's claim is difficult because "knowing letters" is a notoriously vague phrase in Greek and Latin.[99] Remaining within Jewish Greek literature (although the comparative evidence is the same), sometimes "knowing γράμματα" refers clearly to reading, as in LXX Isa 29:12 where the illiterate responds to the unambiguous instruction ἀνάγνωθι τοῦτο ("read this") with οὐκ ἐπίσταμαι γράμματα ("I do not know letters"). "Knowing γράμματα" can also refer clearly to writing, however, as above in *P. Yadin* 15.35–36 where Babatha's "not knowing γράμματα" means Eleazar had to write for her. Thus, both ἀναγινώσκω and γράφω fall within the semantic range of "knowing γράμματα," although one cannot automatically assume that any one reference has the other skill also in mind. Josephus's statement should likely be translated neutrally as "teach letters" given its lack of clarifying context.[100] In the least, it does not clearly indicate that writing appeared in the education of children, even the education of the children Josephus has in mind.

Turning to texts that Jews read or knew in the first century C.E. that reference reading and writing abilities, Deut 6:9 and 11:20 instruct the Exodus generation to write God's words on their doorposts, while Deut 27:3, 8 require those crossing the Jordan River to write God's words on stones. As was seen, however, one cannot assume that such instructions were directly applicable to every individual Jew (and thus evidence of

---

98. Josephus, *Ag. Ap.* 2.25 §204.

99. Harris, *Ancient*, 6: "Such expressions have to be interpreted case by case." See further Keith, "Claim," 51–53.

100. In LCL, Thackeray translates γράμματα παιδεύειν in *Ag. Ap.* 2.25 as "taught to read." Hezser, *Jewish*, 68, also seems to take it as a reference to reading.

typical grapho-literate education) in light of the semantic range of the verb כָּתַב in the Hebrew Scriptures.[101] More likely is that designated, qualified individuals would do the writing on behalf of the population.

According to *Jub.* 4:17–18, Enoch was "the first who learned writing… who wrote in a book…[and] first wrote a testimony."[102] The medieval Greek fragment of this text from George Cedrenus's *Historium Compendium*, the only surviving Greek fragment of this verse, uses γράμματα in translating the first phrase as "first to learn and teach letters" (πρῶτος γράμματα μανθάνει καὶ διδάσκει).[103] Since the context of *Jubilees* makes clear that writing skills are in view for Enoch, this text is—if the fragment accurately represents the Greek original—a Second Temple text where "knowing γράμματα" means specifically knowing how to write.

Writing may appear again in *Jub.* 8:2; 11:16, and 19:14. *Jubilees* 8:2 and 11:16 refer respectively to Cainan (Noah's great-grandson) and Abraham with the phrase, "And his father taught him writing."[104] *Jubilees* 19:14 claims one of Abraham's grandsons was literate while the other was not: "And the youths grew up and Jacob learned writing, but Esau did not learn because he was a rustic man and a hunter."[105] No Greek fragments survive for *Jub.* 8:2 and 19:14, and the one that does for 11:16 does not contain the reference to Abraham's literate instruction from his father.[106] The surviving Latin for *Jub.* 19:14 ambiguously refers to Jacob learning "letters": *et didicit Jacob litteras et Esau non didicit.*[107] Only the context of *Jub.* 8:2 offers clarification of which literate skills are in view, although it ultimately attributes to Cainan both reading *and* writing/copying (8:3–4)

101.   See above, pp. 82–83.
102.   Wintermute, *OTP*.
103.   *Jubilees* is dated to the second century B.C.E. (*OTP* 2:43–44) and survives as a complete text only in Ethiopic, from which most English translations derive. Hebrew fragments and references were discovered at Qumran (1QS 8.5; 4Q180; 4Q227; 4Q270 [*Damascus Document* 16.3]; 4Q364; 4Q369; 4Q384; 4Q510–511; 11Q19) and Masada (see Shemaryahu Talmon, "Hebrew Written Fragments from Masada," *DSD* 3, no. 2 [1996]: 168–77, who notes that the three fragments could be from manuscripts brought from Qumran). None preserves the texts under discussion. Later writers preserve Greek fragments, which Albert-Marie Denis, *Fragmenta Pseudepigraphorum Quae Supersunt Graeca* (PVTG 3; Leiden: Brill, 1970), 70–104, presents. R. H. Charles, *The Ethiopic Version of the Hebrew Book of Jubilees* (AO; Oxford: Clarendon, 1895), presents the Ethiopic and surviving Latin, which does not begin until ch. 13, side-by-side. For the Greek fragment of *Jub.* 4:17–18, see Denis, *Fragmenta*, 83.
104.   Wintermute, *OTP*.
105.   Ibid.
106.   See Denis, *Fragmenta*, 85 (8.2), 91 (11.16), 95 (19.14).
107.   For the text, see Charles, *Ethiopic*, 69.

activity. Abraham, however, turns immediately to agricultural interests and manual labor (*Jub.* 11:18–24) and the context of *Jub.* 19:14 does not portray Jacob's usage of the literate skill(s) he learned. The narrative is thus not clear enough for certainty. Nevertheless, if one can suppose that a reference to γράμματα underlies the Ethiopic in *Jub.* 8:2 and 19:14, which is possible in light of the surviving fragment of *Jub.* 4:17–18 and the Latin of *Jub.* 19:14, then these verses could be further references to writing being included in literate education. Importantly, however, although these texts from *Jubilees* present (grapho-)literate education, none references a process that is typical (see further below).

Whereas *Jub.* 4:17–18 may be a clear example of "knowing γράμματα" being a reference to writing, the second-century B.C.E. *Testament of Levi* provides a clear Second Temple example of "knowing γράμματα" referencing specifically reading ability.[108] Furthermore, it is the closest to a clear reference to expectations for a literate class that we have. *Testament of Levi* 13:2 portrays Levi as instructing his priestly sons:

δίδαξατε δὲ καὶ ὑμεῖς τὰ τέκνα ὑμῶν γράμματα
ἵνα ἔχωσι σύνεσιν ἐν πάσῃ τῇ ζωῇ αὐτῶν
ἀναγινώσκοντες ἀδιαλείπτως τὸν νόμον τοῦ θεοῦ

Teach also your children letters,
that they have understanding in all their life,
reading unceasingly the law of God.

Similar to my translation here, Kee translates the first line of instruction neutrally as, "Teach your children letters," while Baumgarten, Schams, and Horsley assume that reading and writing are in view.[109] In this text, however, the direct purpose and result of Levi's children teaching their children γράμματα, communicated by the ἵνα clause and the circumstantial participle ἀναγινώσκοντες[110] is that they gain understanding by

---

108.   On the date of the *Testament of the Twelve Patriarchs*, see Robert Henry Charles, *The Greek Versions of the Testaments of the Twelve Patriarchs* (Oxford: Oxford University Press, 1966), ix; H. C. Kee, "Introduction," to "The Testaments of the Twelve Patriarchs," *OTP* 1:777–78.

109.   Kee, *OTP* 1:792; Baumgarten, *Flourishing*, 121, 124; Christine Schams, *Jewish Scribes in the Second Temple Period* (JSOTSup 291; Sheffield: Sheffield Academic, 1998), 86; Horsley, *Scribes*, 80, respectively.

110.   Following the majority of manuscripts and critical texts of Charles, *Greek Versions*, 53; M. de Jonge, *The Testaments of the Twelve Patriarchs* (PVTG 1/2; Leiden: Brill, 1978), 40. Two manuscripts preserve variants that replace ἀναγινώσκω ("read") with γινώσκω ("know"): Vatican Library Greek 1238 (twelfth/thirteenth century); Mount Athos 39 (tenth/eleventh century). For description of the texts, see Charles, *Greek Versions*, x–xi; Jonge, *Testaments*, xv–xvii.

being able to *read* the law. García Martínez and Tigchelaar translate
4Q213 (4QAramaic Levi[a]), which underlies *T. Levi* 13,[111] with a similar
emphasis on reading: "But now, reading (ספר) and instruction and wisdom [teach them to your sons.... See then, my sons, [my brother Joseph
who taught reading (ספר), and instruct]ion of wisdom."[112]

   Therefore, references to teaching and knowing γράμματα in Second
Temple literature (or texts read during that time period) indicate reading
(*T. Levi* 13:2), writing (*Jub.* 4:17–18, possibly 8:2; 11:16, and 19:14), or fail
to specify (Josephus). That both literate skills fall within the semantic
range of γράμματα does not negate the earlier argument that reading and
writing should not be viewed as a package set. Rather, it reflects the fact
those who held any substantive literate skills—regardless of which and to
what degree—could be described as knowing γράμματα in contrast to an
ἀγράμματος who received no literate education.

   None of these texts, however, constitutes clear evidence that first-
century Jewish literate education typically included writing. Josephus is
ambiguous. *Jubilees* discusses four literate founding figures. One is—
importantly—responsible for writing "the teaching of the Watchers"
(Cainan);[113] another is the quintessential patriarch who received the
covenant (Abraham); a third is father of the twelve tribes (Jacob); and the
fourth (Enoch) is the first to attain a writing ability that was previously
non-existent among God's people. Categorically, then, none of *Jubilees*'s
grapho-literates is "typical," and all have likely absorbed the literate
characteristics of the literate author(s) memorializing them.[114]

   The closest one gets to a reference to a typical literate education of a
literate class is the clear instruction for the sons of Levi to teach reading
in *T. Levi* 13:2. Even this text, however, portrays Levi the *priest* giving
instructions on literate education to his *priestly* children. That is, *T. Levi*
13:2 may give the only fragile indication of literate education among a
group, but also restricts it to a privileged priestly minority. "The author
of the Testament of the Twelve Patriarchs...does not place similar
recommendations in the mouths of the other sons of Jacob."[115] *Jubilees*,

---

111.   Robert A. Kugler, *From Patriarch to Priest: The Levi-Priestly Tradition from
Aramaic Levi to Testament of Levi* (SBLEJL 9; Atlanta: Scholars, 1996), 130–31,
211–12.
112.   4Q213 = 4QAramaic Levi[a] 1.1.9, 12 (García Martínez and Tigchelaar).
Kugler, *From*, 120, translates ספר as "reading and writing," and is followed by Carr,
Writing, 205–6.
113.   *Jub.* 8:3–4.
114.   Thus, Hengel, *Judaism*, 1:82, in reference to *Jub.* 19:14: "The book of
Jubilees also stresses the great value of education, transferring it to the past."
115.   Baumgarten, *Flourishing*, 117.

too, preserves the connection between Levi and his descendents and teaching/instruction when it identifies Levi as the inheritor of Jacob's library (45:15). Indeed, "Within [*Jubilees*'s] narrative world, all literate figures up to and including Jacob are priests, while—of the descendents of Jacob—it is the descendents of Levi who are especially learned in the textual world created by Jubilees."[116] Along a similar line, Sir 45:17 portrays the priest Aaron as responsible for teaching the law, Neh 8:3–8 portrays Ezra the priest and scribe (8:9) reading the law publicly, and Philo describes priests (and elders) performing the reading of the law in the synagogue.[117] Additionally, the *Damascus Document* requires knowledge of the law and the ability to read it well publicly from the community's priestly leader.[118] And one should not forget that Josephus, who makes the claim for universal literacy for Jews, also claimed to be a priest.[119] Far from portraying a typical process, these Second Temple texts attest the connection between wealth, social privilege, and the priesthood on the one hand, and literate education on the other hand. They thus set an important backdrop for the discussion of scribal literacy below.

The argument here is not that writing was not taught in the Second Temple period. It clearly was; a fact to which the manuscripts, texts, and possibly some ostraca from this period concretely bear witness.[120] Rather, the argument is that it does not appear to have been a common practice in literate education generally, remembering that "common" and "generally" here refer to the privileged minority that gained a literate education of any consequence in the first place. Writing seems to have occurred as part of a specialized scribal training to which a select few progressed after having mastered reading in the Hebrew Torah.[121] This stage of

116.   Carr, *Writing*, 204–5. Cf. Baumgarten, *Flourishing*, 117; Hezser, *Jewish*, 75.

117.   Philo, *Hypoth.* 7.12–13. This work of Philo survives only in quotations in Eusebius's *Praeparatio evangelica*.

118.   4QD[a] 14.6–8.

119.   Josephus, *Life* 1 §1–6.

120.   Carr, *Writing*, 220–21, argues that some of the ostraca at Qumran were elementary writing exercises. Qumran was, however, likely the exact type of specialized scribal community, albeit with a sectarian bent, where grapho-literate education occurred. Carr even claims, "The community thus defined represents an important extension of priestly learning beyond that of the priests alone" (220). He claims later than many of the texts found at Qumran may have even come from the Jerusalem temple (233).

121.   Affirming that writing was taught in a specialized scribal education are Bar-Ilan, "Writing," 22; Aaron Demsky, "Writing in Ancient Israel and Ancient Judaism Part One: The Biblical Period," in Mulder, ed., *Mikra*, 13; Gamble, *Books*, 7; Goodman, "Texts," 100; Hezser, *Jewish*, 500; Nathan Morris, *The Jewish School: An Introduction to the History of Jewish Education* (London: Eyre & Spottiswoode,

(grapho-)literate education included training in the material matters of the scribal craft, skills that were useless for anyone outside the scribal guild and underscore this pedagogical rung's specialized nature.[122] "As far as the instruction of writing in Jewish elementary schools is concerned, the material evidence concurs well with the evidence from Josephus and rabbinic documents, then: there is no unambiguous evidence that it ever took place."[123] The earliest even possible evidence that writing had a home in general Jewish elementary education is not until the Palestinian Talmud (ca. 400 C.E.) with *y. Ta'an* 69a (4:8).[124]

3.1.6. *Gradations of Reading Skills.* The pedagogical focus of literate education, therefore, appears to have been on learning to *read* the Torah, and this focus "seems to have been customary at least since the last centuries of the Second Temple."[125] Scholars are more certain of reading's presence in first-century Jewish literate education because of the liturgical significance of reading the Torah. "There can be little question that scriptural readings constituted the core of contemporary [Second Temple] Jewish worship in the synagogue."[126] Among those Jews who knew

1937), 55, 81–81; Schmuel Safrai, "Elementary Education, Its Religious and Social Significance in the Talmudic Period," *Cahiers d'Histoire Mondiale* 11 (1968): 154. Cf. Crenshaw, "Education," 605–6, 614; Haran, "On the Diffusion," 92.

122. Tov, *Scribal*, 13: "Scribes were introduced to their trade during the course of a training period, in which they learned writing and the various scribal procedures connected with it (such as writing at a fixed distance below ruled lines and in columns; the division of a composition into sense units; the treatment of the divine names; the correction of mistakes, etc.). Furthermore, scribes had to master various technical skills relating to the material on which they wrote, the use of writing implements, and the preparation of ink." Likewise, Bar-Ilan, "Writing," 22; Demsky, "Writing," 13.

123. Hezser, *Jewish*, 88. Cf. Carr, *Writing*, 242 n. 5.

124. This clearly legendary text, which claims there were 500 schools in Bethar with no fewer than 500 students, all of whom were burned in their Torah scrolls except a lone survivor, describes writing instruments as possible weapons. Ebner, *Elementary*, 108, describes the passage as "the only direct reference that writing was taught in the elementary school."

125. Hezser, *Jewish*, 68. Also Bakhos, "Orality," 487. Carr, *Writing*, 206–12, argues that other Hebrew Scriptures outside the Torah were used in educational context, and that the shift toward Torah dominance occurs in Sirach. Müller, *Verstehst*, 38, also notes the centrality of Torah in reading instruction.

126. Lee I. Levine, *The Ancient Synagogue: The First Thousand Years* (2d ed.; New Haven: Yale University Press, 2005), 150. Levine later identifies Torah reading as the "one worship element that was carried over from the pre-70 worship context"

γράμματα, not all were expected to be scribes or copyists of the holy text, but all should be able to read it to some degree. And "one must remember…that there are varying degrees of competence in reading as in writing: reading ability can range from the recognition of one or more words to the comprehension of a whole text."[127]

Several first-century texts highlight the importance of reading the Torah, and among them some also reveal gradations of reading ability among literate Second Temple Jews. These gradations appear because reading aloud was the normative practice (although there is no longer any reason to believe that silent reading was unknown in the ancient world).[128] Anyone who overheard a reader, then, could assess the degree of proficiency that person had achieved. Such a context revealed the difference between those who could stumble their way through a Torah scroll and those who could read eloquently. Due to the holiness of the Torah and desire to avoid disparaging it,[129] public reading of Torah without errors was a particularly coveted reading skill.

The best example of the importance of public reading is from the Qumran community. The *Community Rule* instructs members of the community: "And in the place in which the Ten assemble there should not be missing a man to interpret the law day and night, always, one relieving another. And the Many shall be on watch together for a third of each night of the year in order to read the book, explain the regulation, and bless together."[130] So important was reading from the law to the identity of the community that those who inexpertly read it were not permitted to read (presumably publicly) according to the *Damascus Document*:

> [And anyone who is not quick to under]stand, and anyone w[ho speaks weakly or staccato], [with]out separating his words to make [his voice] heard, [such men should not read in the book of] [the Torah], so that he will not lead to error in a capital matter [...] [...] his brothers, the priests, in service.[131]

(536). See also Stephen K. Catto, *Reconstructing the First-Century Synagogue: A Critical Analysis of Current Research* (LNTS 363; London: T&T Clark, 2007), 116.

127. Cribiore, *Writing*, 151.

128. Hurtado and Keith, "Writing and Book Production," n.p.

129. Levine, *Ancient*, 146: "By the first century C.E., the Torah had become the holiest object in Judaism outside the Temple itself and its appurtenances."

130. 1QS 6.6–8 (García Martínez and Tigchelaar).

131. 4Q266 5.2.1–4 (García Martínez and Tigchelaar). Alternatively: "Whoever speaks too fast (or: too quietly, lit. swift or light with his tongue) or with a staccato voice and does not split his words to make [his voice] heard, no one from among

The offensive error to which 4Q266 refers is the inability to identify quickly the constituent syllables of words in Hebrew script and mentally combine them in order to read them as separate words. If incapable of doing so, the reader would have to sound out the individual syllables, thus reading/speaking "staccato."[132] He would have to "sound it out." In contrast, the *Damascus Document* establishes higher expectations for the group's leader: "And the priest who is named ‹at the head› of the Many will be between thirty and sixty years old, learned in the book of H[A]GY and in all the regulations of the law, to formulate them in accordance with their regulations."[133] Vermes, as well as Wise, Abegg, and Cook, take the correct "formulation" this text requires as a reference to pronunciation; the former translating it as "so as to pronounce them correctly" and the latter as "speaking them in the proper way."[134] This text therefore reveals at least two gradations of reading ability—staccato reading and eloquent/error-free reading.

As a gradation below the imperfect public readers at Qumran, one may cite the early Christian author of the *Shepherd of Hermas*. This author was commanded to copy a little book (βιβλιδίου).[135] In his claim that he succeeded, he reveals that he, like Petaus, was a slow writer: "I copied it all, letter by letter, for I could not make out the syllables."[136] Despite being able to copy a small book, this author claims he cannot read enough to recognize syllables. Perhaps this is why, when commanded to read a book, he must do so "along with the elders who preside over the church."[137] Cribiore discusses a school papyrus of Euripides's *Phoenissae* that assisted a reader such as Hermas by dividing the words into syllables.[138]

---

these shall read the Book of [the] La[w] that he may not misguide someone in a capital matter" (Vermes).

132.   This text thus suggests against arguments that the commitment of texts to heart (Prov 3:3; 7:3) "was probably not the result of physically reading a written copy of the book" (Horsley, *Scribes*, 104). In at least some cases, that is precisely how one gained knowledge of a text.

133.   4QD[a] 14.6–8 (García Martínez and Tigchelaar).

134.   Geza Vermes, trans., *The Complete Dead Sea Scrolls in English* (New York: Penguin, 1997), 143; Michael Wise, Martin Abegg, Jr., and Edward Cook, trans., *The Dead Sea Scrolls: A New Translation* (San Francisco: HarperSanFrancisco, 1996), 72.

135.   Herm., *Vis.* 2.1.3–4.

136.   Herm., *Vis.* 2.1.4 (Holmes).

137.   Herm., *Vis.* 2.4.3 (Holmes).

138.   Rafaella Cribiore, "The Grammarian's Choice: The Popularity of Euripides' *Phoenissae* in Hellenistic and Roman Education," in *Education in Greek and Roman Antiquity* (ed. Yun Lee Too; Leiden: Brill, 2001), 251.

Returning to the Jewish context, the ability to read Torah without errors was thus a privileged accomplishment of literate education, of which not even all those among the educated were capable. Further evidence for the importance of this literate skill in Jesus' Judaism comes from first-century discussions of the public reading of the law in synagogues. I underscore here that these descriptions of synagogues services are indispensable for understanding the Synoptic debate over Jesus as a synagogue teacher, discussed in the next chapter.

Josephus claims: "He appointed the Law to be the most excellent and necessary form of instruction, ordaining, not that it should be heard once for all or twice or on several occasions, but that every week men should desert their other occupations and assemble to listen to the Law and to obtain a thorough and accurate knowledge of it."[139] Significantly, these men are not described as studying the law the rest of the week, and indeed when they do pause from their occupations, their active engagement with the text is limited to listening. Luke too affirms, via Paul's speech, that Moses is proclaimed weekly on the Sabbath in synagogues, not through study per se, but through public reading (ἀναγινωσκόμενος; Acts 15:21). Likewise, the Theodotus inscription from pre-70 C.E. Jerusalem claims the synagogue was constructed "for the reading of the Law and the teaching of the commandments" (εἰς ἀνάγνωσιν νόμου καὶ εἰς διδαχὴν ἐντολῶν).[140] Josephus is thus here likely closer to the reality of Second Temple Judaism than some of his other comments—most could not afford the time to study the text or gain literate education that would enable detailed study. When they did "study," someone else read the text for them.

Similarly, Philo claims that the Palestinian Essenes gathered to hear the text read on the Sabbath:

> In these [the laws of their fathers, 12:80] they are instructed at all other times, but particularly on the seventh days. For that day has been set apart to be kept holy and on it they abstain from all other work and proceed to sacred spots which they call synagogues. There, arranged in rows according to their ages, the younger below the elder, they sit decorously as befits the occasion with attentive ears. Then one takes the books and reads aloud and another of especial proficiency comes forward and expounds what is not understood.[141]

139.   Josephus, *Ag. Ap.* 2.17 §175 (Thackeray, LCL); cf. *Ant.* 16.2.4 §43.

140.   See further Catto, *Reconstructing*, 120; Charles Perrot, "The Reading of the Bible in the Ancient Synagogue," in *Mikra*, 137.

141.   Philo, *Prob.* 12.81–82 (Colson, LCL). Elsewhere, Philo presents the Essenes as a group of manual laborers (*Hypoth.* 11.6–9).

Although Philo notes that the interpreter, who allegorizes the text, is of "especial proficiency" (ἐμπειροτάτων), there is no reason to think that the reader was not also esteemed.[142] This notion is supported not only by the Qumran instructions discussed earlier, but also because elsewhere Philo describes the reader in a Sabbath gathering (in Alexandria?) as a textual authority:

> He [the lawgiver] required them to assemble in the same place on these seventh days, and sitting together in a respectful and orderly manner hear the laws read so that none should be ignorant of them.... But some priest who is present or one of the elders (τῶν γερόντων) reads the holy laws to them and expounds them point by point till about the late afternoon, when they depart having gained both expert knowledge of the holy laws and considerable advance in piety.[143]

In summary, reading was likely much more common than writing among Second Temple literates, although not all readers had the same level of proficiency. Some Jewish readers, similar to the early Christian Hermas, could not read syllables well or at all. Other readers, like those whom 4Q266 prohibits from reading, could read syllables but not identify them collectively as words quickly enough to read the Torah smoothly. Others, like those permitted to read publicly in Qumran or in the synagogue services described by Josephus, Luke, and Philo, had reached a higher level of reading proficiency. Their reading skills were advanced enough that they did not risk dishonoring the holy text while reading it before fellow worshippers in one of the most central practices to the construction of first-century Jewish identity.

3.1.7. *Gradations of Writing Skills.* Like reading, writing often played a religious role in Second Temple Judaism. Although not all Jewish scribes were Torah authorities, the canonical Gospels and Second Temple literature make clear that some scribes, as practitioners of the craft of writing, used their grapho-literacy in order to attain positions as authoritative interpreters.[144] Such authority was likely based on the presumed high degree of familiarity with the written holy text that the guild of copyists for that Hebrew-language text possessed. According to *Jub.* 12:25–27, Abram is able "to know everything which he was unable (to understand)" only once he can study his father's books after having

---

142. *Pace* Catto, *Reconstructing*, 124.
143. Philo, *Hypoth.* 7.12–13 (Colson, LCL).
144. On the variety of social positions for Second Temple Jewish scribes, see esp. Schams, *Jewish*, 36–273.

copied them in Hebrew.[145] Also relevant, in reference to the law, Philo claims that he who "write[s] with his own hand…wishes to have the ordinances cemented to his soul."[146] It is thus no surprise at all that grapho-literate Torah interpreters were highly esteemed, as later *b. Soṭah* 20a even describes copying the law as divine work.

Copyists of the holy text were also highly esteemed because copying intricate texts like the Mosaic Law and other Hebrew Scriptures was an advanced writing skill. We have already seen that signature literacy was a nascent grapho-literate skill. Between this early accomplishment of literate education and professional writers like those whom Dionysius of Halicarnassus mentions were other gradations of grapho-literacy. Copying full texts in an aesthetically pleasing and clear script was an ability held only by an accomplished scribe, whose abilities were inferior only to those capable of compositional writing. As Cribiore observes, "Writing is a multifaceted activity, involving many levels of competence ranging from the ability to trace a few characters or copy a text to the capacity to engage in literary composition."[147] She further identifies four levels of writing ability in the Greco-Roman Egyptian context: tracing words; copying or taking dictation; crafting rhetorical units; and authoring an original text.[148]

Greco-Roman literary evidence supports Cribiore's statement. For example, Cicero describes his scribe Spintharo as capable of taking dictation syllable-by-syllable, and compares him to another scribe, Tiro, who can follow whole sentences.[149] Tiro likely was capable of shorthand, an important skill for a household scribe. Indeed, in a passage describing various grapho-literate competencies, Quintilian claims members of the aristocracy should not disparage the skill of shorthand and, ideally, possess it themselves:

> The art of writing well and quickly is not unimportant for our purpose, though it is generally disregarded by persons of quality. Writing is of the utmost importance…and by its means alone can true and deeply rooted proficiency be obtained. But a sluggish pen delays our thoughts, while an unformed and illiterate hand cannot be deciphered, a circumstance which necessitates another wearisome task, namely the dictation of what we

---

145. Wintermute, *OTP*. On this text, see further John C. Poirier, *The Tongues of Angels: The Concept of Angelic Languages in Classical Jewish and Christian Texts* (WUNT 2/278; Tübingen: Mohr Siebeck, 2010), 12–14.

146. Philo, *Spec. Laws* 4.32 §160 (Colson, LCL; more fully, see §160–64).

147. Cribiore, *Writing*, 10.

148. Ibid., 69.

149. Cicero, *Att.* 13.25.

have written to a copyist. We shall therefore at all times and in all places, and above all when we are writing private letters to our friends, find a gratification in the thought that we have not neglected even this accomplishment.[150]

Quintilian's statement reveals that the well-born of Roman society ("persons of quality") may need to dictate to a scribe based on their own limited writing skills. The ideal for Quintilian, however, is that one should be capable of composing personal correspondence him- or herself.

Quintilian's statement also reveals, along with the disparagement of rote copying in the *Rhetorica ad Herennium* (first century B.C.E.),[151] that one mark of high culture was the possession of literate skills *and* the ability to avoid their usage by having someone write on one's behalf. Attainment of literate skills was a product of wealth, as was the ability to educate slaves in order to avoid writing or reading when desired.[152] In this sense, "One might almost say that there was a direct correlation between the social standing that guaranteed literacy and the means to avoid writing."[153] These social realities were no less true in Jewish and Christian contexts. Paul, though a trained Pharisee (Acts 22:3; Phil 3:5), used an amanuensis.[154] Origen had at his disposal scribes of varying grapho-literate abilities. According to Eusebius and Jerome, Ambrose provided Origen with short-hand writers, copyists, and calligraphers, implicitly revealing also the various stages in the production of Origen's writings.[155] Eusebius even portrays Origen as the ringmaster of a scriptorium, keeping busy seven of the shorthand writers, seven of the copyists, as well as the calligraphers, simultaneously.

The strong correlation between the possession of literate abilities and the ability to avoid using them will be important in the next chapter, as early Christian sources from the first century to the fourth century, and spread across (what would become) orthodox, apocryphal, and heretical sources portray an "epistolary Jesus" who dictates letters. Some of these texts attribute literate skills to him directly and some do not. Regardless,

---

150.   Quintilian, *Inst.* 1.1.28–29 (Butler, LCL). See also Libanius, *Or.* 18.158, who acknowledges some provincial governors' shorthand abilities while scorning them scathingly.

151.   *Rhet. Her.* 4.4.6.

152.   Cicero, *Att.* 13.25; Pliny the Younger, *Epistulae* 3.5.

153.   Bagnall, *Reading*, 25. Also, Derrenbacker, *Ancient*, 24.

154.   On Paul's usage of amanuenses, see E. Randolph Richards, *The Secretary in the Letters of Paul* (WUNT 2/42; Tübingen: Mohr Siebeck, 1991).

155.   Eusebius, *Hist. eccl.* 6.23; Jerome, *Vir. ill.* 61. Similarly, Augustine composed by dictation; see *Retract.* prol. 2.

though, the very image they employ implicitly places Jesus in a class associated with literate education.

On the safe assumption that the Second Temple Jewish context was, with regard to varying gradations of grapho-literacy, similar to the rest of antiquity, two more important implications emerge. First, even among the literate who were capable of reading Torah, scribes capable of copying it were even more advanced. Since advanced writing and copying skills were even rarer than reading skills,[156] among the scribal-literate Pharisees, priests, Sadducees, et al., the γραμματεῖς were more familiar with the holy γράμματα due to their specialized training.

Second, this further scribal education translated into an increased authority in Torah interpretation.[157] In passages where the Gospels claim that Jesus bested a Jewish leadership consisting of scribes (as in, for example, John 8:5), the claim is that Jesus not only defeated the authoritative interpreters, but also the most educated interpreters. Scribal authority is also an important background for claims that Jesus' pedagogical activity located him outside the class of scribes (Mark 1:22; Matt 7:29).

Jesus' literate landscape was therefore one in which "literacy" consisted of various degrees of literate skills and included gradations of literacy, such as semi-literacy, that seemingly held literacy and illiteracy together simultaneously. Almost all first-century Palestinian Jews were textual, but the majority were illiterate or semi-literate, possessing signature literacy at best. The ability to read the Torah proficiently was the possession of a minority educated elite, among whom further educated scribes were capable of advanced grapho-literate skills such as copying and compositional writing.

3.2. *A Spectrum of Languages*
In addition to Jesus' literate landscape consisting of a spectrum of literate skills, it also consisted of a spectrum of languages.[158] At least five languages were present in Palestine—Greek, Aramaic, Hebrew, Latin, and Nabatean. The first three are most important for understanding Jesus'

---

156.   Similarly, Goodman, "Texts," 99–100; Gerhardsson, *Memory*, 61–66.

157.   See further Keith, *Pericope*, 104–15.

158.   In addition to the standard of Fitzmyer, "Languages," 501–31, see also Bar-Ilan, "Writing," 32; Matthew Black, "Language and Script: The Biblical Languages," in Ackroyd and Evans, eds., *Cambridge History of the Bible*, 1:1–11; Shaye J. D. Cohen, *From the Maccabees to the Mishnah* (2d ed.; Louisville: Westminster John Knox, 2006), 30–32; Harris, *Ancient*, 188–90; Meier, *Marginal Jew*, 1:253–68; Millard, *Reading*, 84–153; Schürer, *History*, 2:20–28; and Sawyer, *Sacred*, 9–22, who catalogues a greater linguistic variety. The most recent treatment is that of Poirier, "Linguistic Situation," 55–134.

context, as Latin was mainly restricted to imperial administration and the evidence for Nabatean in Palestine is slight.[159]

Although scholars agree that Aramaic, Greek, and Hebrew were in use in Palestine in the first century C.E., the degrees to which each was used, and by whom, have been heavily debated. In 1970, Fitzmyer provided a thorough summary of the evidence and prior discussion, eventually concluding that Aramaic was "the most common language in Palestine" in the first century C.E.[160] More recently, Poirier's comprehensive essay provides a needed update to Fitzmyer and comes largely to the same conclusion.[161] His concluding statement also provides a helpful description of the complexity of the matter:

> The questions involved are not always easily answered, but a judicious arrangement of the thousands of pieces to the puzzle, to my mind, supports a sort of trilingualism of Aramaic, Hebrew, and Greek, but one very noticeably tilted toward Aramaic…. Aramaic certainly possesses more right than either Greek or Hebrew to be called a common vernacular for Jewish Palestine in the first through the third centuries C.E., and for some time after that.[162]

Thus, although there will likely never be a consensus in this discussion, whether in grand theories or in details, there is nevertheless considerable agreement that Aramaic was the most common language of first-century Jews. Hebrew, the traditional and ancient language of the Israelites, and Greek, the *lingua franca* of the Empire that was the language of Diasporan Jews such as Philo and was possibly being used in a few Greek-speaking Palestinian synagogues,[163] were less common but also present to varying degrees.

This multilingual context means that first-century Jews could hold different literate skills in different languages. Hezser observes:

> A center-and-periphery model of concentric circles may be applied to Jewish reading practices in Roman Palestine: At the center one has to imagine a very small number of highly literate people who could read literary texts

---

159.   On Nabatean, see Fitzmyer, "Languages," 523, 527; Millard, *Reading*, 95, 100–101.

160.   Fitzmyer, "Languages," 531. Affirming Fitzmyer is Bruce D. Chilton, *A Galilean Rabbi and His Bible: Jesus' Use of the Interpreted Scripture of His Time* (GNS 8; Wilmington: Michael Glazier, 1984), 38–39.

161.   Poirier, "Linguistic Situation," 55–134.

162.   Ibid., 133–34.

163.   Catto, *Reconstructing*, 120–121; Perrot, "Reading," 155. Cf., however, Lee I. Levine, *Judaism and Hellenism in Antiquity: Conflict or Confluence?* (Peabody: Hendrickson, 1998), 161–62. On Greek in Palestine, see further Porter, *Criteria*, 126–80.

in both Hebrew/Aramaic and Greek. Then there was another, slightly broader circle of those who could read literary texts in either Hebrew/ Aramaic or Greek only. They were surrounded by people who could not read literary texts but only short letters, lists, and accounts. A broader proportion of the population may have been able to merely identify individual letters, names, and labels. They as well as the vast majority of their entirely illiterate contemporaries had access to text through intermediaries only.[164]

Hezser's comments on diverse skills focus upon reading ability, but apply equally to writing skills, as well as conversational skills in other languages gained outside literate education (that is, as a by-product of living in a multilingual culture).

Knowledge of Hebrew was not entirely limited to scribal circles. Ossuary inscriptions and masonry markings, for example, demonstrate that Hebrew had made inroads to at least a limited degree in the population at large.[165] In terms of literary works, however, Hebrew was almost exclusively found in scribal and/or liturgical circles where it "remained the primary language of literary expression."[166] In other words, Hebrew was the language of educated Palestinian Jews, the scribal elite responsible for transmitting and teaching the Hebrew Scriptures, as well as producing other literary texts. Hebrew texts, for example, clearly dominated the Qumran community's library, as one estimate places over 82 percent of the Qumran cache in Hebrew.[167] In light of Aramaic being the vernacular language of most Palestinian Jews, first-century Palestinian synagogues were likely already finding the need to provide Aramaic translations of the holy text pressing.[168] In such an Aramaic-dominated

---

164.   Hezser, *Jewish*, 473. Similarly Gamble, *Books*, 3; Haines-Eitzen, *Guardians*, 10.

165.   See Millard, *Reading*, 123–25, and images on previous pages.

166.   Cohen, *From the Maccabees*, 32. Also, Poirier, "Linguistic Situation," 78: "Outside of synagogues and the Temple, there is little in the way of inscriptions to suggest that Hebrew was known at all." Carr, *Writing*, 253–72, argues that Hebrew "education-enculturation" experienced a renaissance among elite Jews during the Hasmonean period as a resistant response to Hellenism. Consider the legendary "revival" of Hebrew in *Jub.* 12:25–27.

167.   Poirier, "Linguistic Situation," 69. Poirier notes further that the Hebrew percentage is 79 percent "when we bracket the biblical scrolls" (69 n. 47). On the Hebrew dominance in the Qumran cache, see Wise, Abegg, Jr., and Cook, *Dead Sea Scrolls*, 9; Eileen Schuller, *The Dead Sea Scrolls: What Have We Learned 50 Years On?* (London: SCM, 2006), 3; Vermes, *Dead Sea Scrolls*, 10.

168.   The only first-century *targumim* are a Job targum and Leviticus targum from Qumran. Poirier, "Linguistic Situation," 64–110, however, persuasively argues for the "linguistic necessity" of providing Aramaic translations/interpretations for a

context, however, Hebrew manuscripts' significance as "numinous links of Israelites to the divine and to an otherwise inaccessible past" only increased.[169]

Not only, therefore, could someone in Jesus' literate landscape hold different levels of literate skills, an individual could also hold different levels of literate skills in (at least) three different languages. Most important for the present study, though, the power of scribal literacy in Palestine emanated foremost from Hebrew, the holy texts that it transmitted, and the fact that few could read it.

4. Scribal Literacy and Craftsman's Literacy

Further demonstrating the complexity of the first-century Palestinian Jewish literate landscape of Jesus is the difference between scribal literacy and craftsman's literacy. Distinguishing these forms of literacy were not necessarily the different skills employed (although that is part of their difference), but rather the different social and professional contexts in which those skills were employed. In short, first-century Palestinian Jews typically gained and used what literate skills their position in life required of them. Being an authoritative interpreter required different, and more, literate abilities than being a craftsman.

4.1. Scribal Literacy

In text-centered communities, "scribal literacy" refers to literate skills that allow some educated individuals to function as authoritative interpreters of texts. Although these could be bureaucratic scribes associated with the necessary written documentation of civil government,[170] scribal literacy can also refer to religious authorities who are experts in texts that are determinative for the group's identity. Thus, some scholars also speak of "sacred literacy," "high literacy," or "religious literacy."[171] With regard to the first-century Palestinian Jewish context, scribal literacy and its benefits belonged to socially recognized authoritative readers, copyists,

---

Jewish population that increasingly did not understand Hebrew in the first century C.E. See also Chilton, *Galilean Rabbi*, 38–39; Fitzmyer, "Languages," 525; Timothy H. Lim, *The Dead Sea Scrolls* (VSI 143; Oxford: Oxford University Press, 2005), 69–71.

169. Carr, *Writing*, 169; see also p. 158. Similarly, Snyder, *Teachers*, 186–87. On the rising importance of Hebrew as one moves toward the rabbinic period, see Poirier, *Tongues*, 8–30.

170. Harris, *Ancient*, 7–8.

171. Fox, "Literacy," 129; Toorn, *Scribal*, 11; Jack Goody, *The Interface between the Written and the Oral* (SLFCS; Cambridge: Cambridge University Press, 1987), 139, respectively.

and teachers of the law, in contrast to other literates who were responsible for writing marriage contracts, land deeds, or bills of sale, and so on.

Several Second Temple texts, already discussed, reveal scribal literates and the power associated with their literacy. In the second century B.C.E., Sirach draws a clear distinction between manual laborers and those who have the leisure time to study the holy text in Sir 38:24–34.[172] The former must concentrate on their trades while the laudatory latter are those who are able to gain expertise in "the law of the Most High God" (38:34). At Qumran, he who reads the Torah publicly must be literate enough to do so with eloquence and unbroken pronunciation. Similarly, according to Philo, the Palestinian Essenes listen to the holy texts and its exposition by an authoritative interpreter.[173] Philo also claims that it is priests and elders who perform the reading and interpreting of the law in the synagogue.[174]

Similarly, when Josephus recalls—with no small amount of hubris—the effort he exerted in learning Greek, he describes it as particularly praiseworthy because Jews privilege first and foremost training in their own holy texts, revealing implicitly the esteem for interpreters:

> For my compatriots admit that in our Jewish learning I far excel them. I have also labored strenuously to partake of the realm of Greek prose and poetry, after having gained a knowledge of Greek grammar (γραμμάτων) and poetry, although the habitual use of my native tongue has prevented my attaining precision in the pronunciation. For our people do not favour those persons who have mastered the speech of many nations, or adorn their style with smoothness of diction, because they consider that not only is such skill common to ordinary freemen but that even slaves who so choose may acquire it. But they give credit for wisdom to those alone who have an exact knowledge of the law and who are capable of interpreting the meaning of the Holy Scriptures (γραμμάτων).[175]

According to Josephus, first-century Jews are much less impressed with the ability to speak in other languages than they are with knowledge of the sacred writings. He, in fact, contrasts the Greek γράμματα with the holy γράμματα, implicitly acknowledging the social prestige afforded those who had mastered the latter.

172. See above, p. 84.
173. Philo, *Prob.* 12.81–82.
174. Philo, *Hypoth.* 7.13.
175. Josephus, *Ant.* 20.12.1 §263–65 (Feldman, LCL). Below I will note that one cannot always assume in Josephus and Philo that attributions of "knowledge of the law" refer to scribal literacy. Since, however, Josephus is here describing an educational endeavor, it is likely that he is referring to scribal literates who "acquire an exact knowledge of the Law."

In addition to these texts, New Testament tradition also reveals the social authority of scribal literates. Here, as elsewhere, scribes, Pharisees, Sadducees, priests, and the like function as authoritative text-brokers of the Hebrew Scriptures. *Scribes* and *chief priests* inform Herod of the birthplace of the Messiah based on the Scriptures (Matt 2:4). *Scribes* hold official opinion on Elijah and the Messiah (Mark 9:11//Matt 17:10; Mark 12:35). "The *scribes* and the *Pharisees* sit on Moses' seat" (Matt 23:2, emphasis added) and have "the best seats in the synagogues" (Mark 12:39//Matt 23:6//Luke 20:46).[176] A *scribe* debates Jesus about the greatest commandment (Mark 12:28–34). The *Sadducees* question Jesus regarding Moses' teaching on levirate marriage, and when Jesus responds, a *scribe* commends his exegetical savvy (Luke 20:27–40). The *scribes* and the *Pharisees* test Jesus over the requirements of the Mosaic law (John 8:5). In one of the clearest images of scribal literacy in the New Testament, one to which the next chapter will give further attention, the *chief priests* and *Pharisees* of John 7:45 denigrate the crowd and its opinions of Jesus based on their lack of knowledge of the law (7:49) and inability to search it (7:52).

Millard observes that this separation between scribal literates and everyone else in John 7 applies to the Synoptics as well.[177] Jesus asks "Have you not read?" to Pharisees (e.g. Matt 12:3, 5), Sadducees (e.g. Mark 12:26), a lawyer (e.g. Luke 10:26), and chief priests and scribes (e.g. Matt 21:16). He addresses "the crowds" of Matt 5:1, however, by referencing not what they have read but what they "have heard that it was said" in the Mosaic Law (Matt 5:21, 27, 31, 33, 38, 43; cf. 2 Cor 3:15).

Portrayals of the first-century Palestinian Jewish landscape from within the New Testament and broader tradition, as well as Philo's description of the (Alexandrian?) synagogue, thus demonstrate the significant social prestige afforded those minority individuals, who, based on their education and literate skills (and in the case of formal scribes, extended grapho-literate education), functioned as authoritative text-brokers of the Hebrew holy texts.[178]

4.2. *Craftsman's Literacy*
Not to be a scribal literate, however, was not necessarily to be completely illiterate. In fact, one can define scribal literacy in contrast to another professional/social manifestation of literate skills—craftsman's literacy.

---

176.   Mark 12:39 and Luke 20:46 mention only the scribes.
177.   Millard, *Reading*, 158.
178.   On textual authority residing among the elite few, see Horsley, *Scribes*, 91; Jaffee, *Torah*, 15; Kirk, "Memory," 158; Kuhn, *Luke*, 23–29; Mournet, "Jesus Tradition," 50–51; Schwartz, *Imperialism*, 74; Snyder, *Teachers*, 221.

Harris defines craftsman's literacy as "the condition in which the majority, or a near-majority, of skilled craftsmen are literate, while women and unskilled labourers and peasants are mainly not."[179] Significant for present purposes, this form of literacy is not organized around a body of literature and its social power, as is scribal literacy, but rather around the craftsman's trade. Thus, it would be entirely right to think of first-century Jewish artisans whose native tongue is Aramaic gaining enough literate skills in Greek in order to work or trade. Petaus's ability to reproduce his formula and sign his name in Greek, however imperfectly, is a form of craftsman's literacy. He attained the literate skills necessary to function as a κωμογραμματεύς. The Hebrew letters and numerals instructing builders at Masada on how to construct a column similarly demonstrate that these craftsmen, too, knew at least enough Hebrew to follow them.[180]

Because the literate skills required of an artisan would have varied from trade to trade, and further from one geographical locale to another, it is extremely difficult to determine how literate an average craftsman in the ancient world would have been. In fact, Harris claims, "It is craftsmen and shopkeepers…who are the most difficult to be sure about. They had been a partly literate, partly semi-literate, partly illiterate social stratum in the high Empire."[181]

Despite whatever literate skills an artisan attained, however, there remained a stark difference between those skills and the literate skills of a scribal-literate teacher of the law. To repeat again, Sir 38:24–34 contrasts specifically the the τέκτων and ἀρχιτέκτων with the γραμματεύς. Haran similarly contrasts craftsmen with scribes:

> Even though artisans, potters and engravers, and sometimes ordinary local folk, managed to employ alphabetic writing, the difference between their knowledge and the training acquired by scribes must be pointed out. Craftsmen of various kinds could gain facility in using the alphabet even without being fully adept or literate. The scribes, who had undergone years of discipline with ethical and civil education and were counted among the wise men, could be at the peak of the erudition of their time…. The practical acquaintance with writing possessed by artisans could have been acquired at a mature age and for specific applications only. Scribes, by contrast, were required to master reading and writing as schoolchildren…and for them this was only the beginning of a long course of study, education and training.[182]

179. Harris, *Ancient*, 8; also p. 328.
180. Images appear on Millard, *Reading*, 122, discussion on p. 125.
181. Harris, *Ancient*, 315. See also Gamble, *Books*, 5, 248 n. 14, who cites Harris. Cf. also Demsky, "Writing," 15.
182. Haran, "On the Diffusion," 92.

More succinctly, Crenshaw states, "A huge chasm separated the professional scribe from persons whose knowledge of writing was only superficial."[183]

4.3. *Implications of Scribal Literacy and Craftsman's Literacy for Jesus' Literacy*

The importance of the difference between scribal literacy and craftsman's literacy in first-century Palestine for the present argument is difficult to overestimate, not least because, as the next chapter will demonstrate, early Christians remembered Jesus as both a scribal-literate teacher and as an artisan/craftsman. Several clarifying points and criticisms of earlier studies of Jesus' literacy are thus necessary.

First, to state explicitly what may be obvious by now, the real question with regard to Jesus' literacy is not whether he was a literate teacher but whether he was a scribal-literate teacher. I am not concerned with whether Jesus, as a first-century Galilean Jew, could read or write anything at all in any language. For, Jesus' primary opponents in the canonical Gospels—the scribal-literate Jewish leadership—were not concerned about Jesus' ability to sign his name, read directional signs, or follow instructional alphabetic or numeric indicators in a construction project. Rather, they were concerned quite specifically with whether his teachings on God, the kingdom, and especially Moses and Torah, were backed by a scribal-literate education that enabled him to be an authoritative teacher worthy of the social authority that the Gospels claim he attained among some of his audiences. This concern on their part is especially the case in scenes where Jesus teaches in or near the temple in Jerusalem and during a Jewish festival (e.g. Matt 22:34–40).

Second, since the main question with which the present study is concerned is Jesus' scribal-literate status, it is not necessary to determine the language(s) Jesus spoke.[184] Indeed, I regard it as relatively impossible to affirm anything regarding Jesus' native language beyond generalities. Given that he was a Palestinian Jew of the first century C.E., it is safe to assume that Jesus spoke Aramaic and may have spoken Greek and/or Hebrew to more limited degrees. Assertions beyond these generalities, however, must necessarily enter a cul-de-sac and devolve into debates about what an "average" first-century Palestinian Jew could or could not do and then further into debates about the various degrees to which

---

183. Crenshaw, *Education*, 36.

184. Harris Birkeland, *The Language of Jesus* (SNVA 1; Oslo: Jacob Dybwad, 1954), 9, states that the matter of Jesus' native tongue is "of the greatest importance for the reconstruction of the sayings of Jesus." This statement reflects the confidence that source and form criticism could mine the tradition for Jesus' sayings.

Jesus would fit the category of "average."[185] Regardless of the outcome of such discussions, the ability to speak a language does not necessarily enable reading and writing skills and thus settling the matter of Jesus' language would have no direct bearing upon his scribal literacy/authority. Further, whereas the Gospel tradition provides no firm indication of Jesus' spoken language(s) beyond occasionally quoting him in Aramaic (Mark 5:41; 7:34), it provides multiple indications of his scribal literacy or lack thereof.[186]

Third, the previous discussion highlights the inadequacy of some of the previous arguments over Jesus' literacy that Chapter 1 rehearsed. One such argument is that of (inter alia) Crossan, who believes Jesus' identity as a τέκτων guarantees that he was illiterate.[187] In light of the complex gradations of literacy in Second Temple Judaism, and particularly the presence of craftsman's literacy, one should not be so quick to identify artisanship with utter illiteracy. Chapter 4 will return to Mark 6:3's identification of Jesus as a τέκτων.

Another argument that underestimates the complexity of Jesus' literate landscape and the functions of literacy therein is that of (again, inter alia) Meier and Evans, who believe that Jesus was not formally educated but could, nevertheless, read the Hebrew Scriptures.[188] In fact, although he concedes that John 7:15 indicates a lack of formal education for Jesus, Meier attributes scribal literacy to him.[189] As the above discussion demonstrates, however, the ability to read the Hebrew Scriptures was one acquired in literate education, an education that the vast majority of individuals in Jesus' context did not receive. Further, Sirach, Josephus, Philo, the Synoptic Gospels, the Gospel of John, and later Jewish tradition[190] all maintain a distinction between those who study, read, and personally access the text on one hand, and those who break from their labor for Sabbath readings of the text and/or gain knowledge of their contents without explicit(ly-attributed) literate access to them.

---

185.   Consider Ehrman, *Jesus*, 100: "We might assume that he had a normal childhood—but unfortunately we aren't even sure what a 'normal' childhood would have been like in rural Galilee."

186.   See Chapter 4.

187.   Crossan, *Jesus*, 23–26.

188.   Meier, *Marginal Jew*, 1:278; Evans, "Context," 21; Evans, *Fabricating*, 39; Evans, "Jewish Scripture," 51. See also Ulrich Luz, "Founding Christianity: Comparing Jesus and Japanese 'New Religions'," in Charlesworth and Pokorný, eds., *Jesus Research*, 240.

189.   Meier, *Marginal Jew*, 1:269, 278.

190.   See the description of the Alexandrian synagogue, where craftsmen sit together in *y. Sukkah* 55a–b (5:1); *t. Sukkah* 4:6.

Therefore, the ideas that Jesus (1) was not formally educated but (2) still attained scribal literacy are mutually exclusive at worst and an aberration demanding explanation at best. As in other points in history, it seems safe to assume that those who were formally educated could also perform manual labor. The apostle Paul, despite having studied under Gamaliel (Acts 22:3) and being a scribal-literate Pharisee (Phil 3:5), was also a manual laborer (1 Thess 2:9; Acts 18:3; cf. 20:34). *Jubilees* portrays Abraham as a recipient of literate education who then turns to perform manual labor (*Jub.* 11:16–24). Other Jewish sages are also described as performing manual labor.[191] A claim in the opposite direction, however— that someone remembered as a τέκτων (Mark 6:3), his son (Matt 13:55), "not like the scribes" (Mark 1:22//Matt 7:29), or simply as someone who was not exposed to scribal education (Origen, *Cels.* 1.29) had nonetheless attained scribal literacy—is a different matter.[192] Once Meier and Evans (and Riesner, see below) acknowledge that Jesus was not formally educated, they also leave any firm grounds for asserting his attainment of scribal literacy. Appealing to a presumed "high degree of natural talent— perhaps even genius—that more than compensated for the low level of Jesus' formal education" will not suffice for explaining *how* Jesus obtained the ability to read the Hebrew Scriptures.[193] All the talent and genius in the world do not by-pass the process to which those imperfect readers at Qumran were subjected before being allowed to read the holy text publicly. Similarly, one cannot assume without further information that Joseph, if a τέκτων himself (Matt 13:55), provided Jesus with enough literate education to enable him to read manuscripts of Hebrew holy texts.

5. *The Acquisition of Biblical Knowledge*

Two further matters require discussion prior to proceeding to early Christian portrayals of Jesus' scribal-literate status: the acquisition of biblical knowledge; and the perception of literate skills.

Texts such as John 7:42—where the crowd asks, "Has not the scripture said that the Messiah is descended from David and comes from

---

191.   Maccoby, *Jesus the Pharisee*, 181, on Shammai and Hillel. See also *m. 'Abot* 2.2.

192.   *Contra* D. Strauss, *Life*, 201, who claims that Matt 7:29's distancing of Jesus from scribal pedagogy is irrelevant for whether he "enjoyed the education of a scribe" (emphasis removed).

193.   Meier, *Marginal Jew*, 1:278. Similarly, *pace* Foster, "Educating," 14, who follows Meier, "being raised in the milieu of a pious Jewish family, and demonstrating a fascination with the scriptures" does not automatically increase "the probability that Jesus was able to read."

Bethlehem?"—raise an obvious question: How did non-scribal Jews gain knowledge of what "Scripture says" given that they were likely incapable of accessing it themselves? There were at least two certain contexts in which non-scribal Jews could regularly learn the biblical text in first-century Palestine: the home and the synagogue. (One should also assume that, like in the synagogue, a first-century Jew could hear the text read and exposited in Jerusalem at festivals.) As has already been seen, however, the first-century evidence for such biblical acquisition preserves a distinction between general biblical knowledge and scribal literacy.

5.1. *The Home*
In light of the common instruction for parents to impart knowledge of the law to their children in Jewish tradition,[194] it is safe to assume that at least some Jewish parents carried out such tasks. The degree of knowledge of the law a given parent was capable of passing to his or her child, however, was, like the degree of literate education a parent was capable of passing to his or her child, dependent upon his or her own knowledge. Here one must again keep in mind the implications of first-century Palestine being a primarily agrarian culture where most of the population did not receive a formal education. Whatever knowledge of the law a parent was able to pass to a child likely came from the parent's own synagogue attendance.

5.2. *The Synagogue*
In addition to New Testament texts such as Acts 15:21, which describes the synagogue as a place where the law is read, Josephus claims that, by "desert[ing] their other occupations and assembl[ing] to listen to the Law" in the synagogue, Jews "obtain a thorough and accurate knowledge of it."[195] Philo also describes those who assemble in the synagogue as sitting together to "hear the laws read so that none should be ignorant of them."[196]

Two interrelated matters from these first-century texts are important for the present argument. First, none of these authors describes literate education as part of the teaching that occurs.[197] Quite to the contrary,

---

194.   Deut 6:2, 7; *4 Macc.* 18:10; *Jub.* 8:2; 11:16; Philo, *Hypoth.* 7.14; *L.A.B.* 22.5; *b. B. Bat.* 21a.

195.   Josephus, *Ag. Ap.* 2.17 §175; cf. *Ant.* 16.2.4 §43.

196.   Philo, *Hypoth.* 7.13; cf. *Prob.* 12.81–82.

197.   *y. Meg.* 73d (3:1) places 480 synagogues in Jerusalem in the general time of Jesus (see the reference to Vespasian), each with a *bet sefer* and *bet midrash*. Hengel, *Judaism*, 1:82, correctly labels this as "late and certainly exaggerated"; see also Toorn, *Scribal*, 24. On the unreliability of rabbinic tradition for pre-70 C.E. Jewish education and literacy, and specifically mentioning *y. Meg.* 73d (3:1) as an example, see Hezser,

and as observed above, Josephus and Philo both state explicitly that the Sabbath is the one day a week in which the synagogue audience stops their weekly work, and also both describe those who stop their weekly work as those who listen to the text read aloud by others.[198]

The second important matter is that both Josephus and Philo describe the synagogue attendees' passive role as hearers of the text as nevertheless sufficing for perfect knowledge of the law. Josephus claims synagogue attendance gives "thorough and accurate knowledge" of the law and Philo claims that reading of the laws aloud ensures "that none should be ignorant of them" and that "they depart having gained expert knowledge of the holy laws."[199] Philo, in fact, claims more: "And so they do not resort to persons learned in the law with questions as to what they should do or not do, nor yet by keeping independent transgress in ignorance of the law, but any one of them whom you attack with inquiries about their ancestral institutions can answer you readily and easily."[200] Since Philo has just described the actual reading and interpretation of the law being done by a priest or elder, his claim of lack of submission to textual authorities is likely overstated rhetoric. Both authors are, of course, polemically presenting an ideal reverent Jewish culture. But it is significant that in doing so both assume that even non-scribal manual laborers can acquire a sufficient amount of biblical knowledge simply by attending synagogue once a week and hearing the text read aloud. To reiterate an earlier point, illiteracy did not bar one from participation in Israel's religious heritage via its holy texts.

Therefore, first-century Palestinian Jews could acquire biblical knowledge in the home and the synagogue. One cannot, however, assume without further mitigating factors (and evidence of those factors) that a devout home context or synagogue attendance alone could vault an individual from illiteracy, semi-literacy, or craftsman's literacy to scribal literacy, from listener in a synagogue to reader and/or teacher.[201]

Jewish, 46–54. On p. 54, Hezser notes that synagogues in the amoraic period (third–fourth centuries C.E.) could be the appropriate location for reading instruction: "The increase of references to 'schools' and elementary teaching in amoraic texts may therefore be directly connected with the emergence and spread of synagogues especially in the Galilee at that time."

198.   Josephus, *Ag. Ap.* 2.17 §175; Philo, *Prob.* 12.81; Philo, *Hypoth.* 7.10–20. See also the words of the synagogue leader in Luke 13:14.

199.   Josephus, *Ag. Ap.* 2.17 §175; Philo, *Hypoth.* 7.13 (Colson, LCL).

200.   Philo, *Hypoth.* 7.14 (Colson, LCL).

201.   One group that presents the possibility to move from craftsman's literacy to scribal literacy is the Essenes. Philo describes them as manual laborers in *Hypoth.* 11.6–9. If the Qumran community consisted of Essenes, however, as seems likely

The relevance of these two matters is clear when considering Riesner's argument that Jesus' home life and synagogue attendance are "die beiden stärksten Argumente für eine Elementarschulbildung" for him.[202] He is undoubtedly correct that Jesus' home (which he presumes was pious), synagogue attendance, and festival attendance gained him biblical knowledge (*biblischem Wissen*).[203] The correlation between that biblical knowledge and Jesus' *Elementarschulbildung*, however, remains problematic. Like Meier and Evans, Riesner claims, "Jesus hat keine 'höhere' schriftgelehrte Ausbildung absolviert."[204] In support of an elementary education for Jesus, however, he appeals to synagogue attendance and a supposed popular education system in the synagogue,[205] for which there is no clear first-century evidence. He further argues that a synagogue attendant could have functioned as an elementary educator (*Elementarlehrer*), but bases this argument anachronistically on rabbinic tradition.[206] In addition, Riesner asserts that "many men could read and write and were used to memorizing and expounding the Scriptures,"[207] and that Jesus learned in his home "davidische und priesterliche Traditionen."[208] In assessing these claims, it is important to bear in mind that Riesner wrote prior to the explosion of literacy and scribal culture studies following Harris's *Ancient Literacy*, which has forced scholars to re-evaluate the evidence. From the perspective these studies provide, however, Riesner's argument(s) claim much, much more than the evidence for Jesus' literate landscape can support and confuses, at several stages, scribal literacy and passive auditory acquisition of knowledge of the Hebrew Scriptures. Jesus, like other Jews, could "presuppose a knowledge of the Old Testament," but that does not solve the matter of whether that knowledge came from listening or literacy.[209]

How much knowledge of the Hebrew Scriptures is required before a given scholar sees Jesus as a scribal-literate teacher rather than a craftsman is crucial to how one interprets the canonical tradition, and thus is

(Vermes, *Dead Sea Scrolls*, 46–48), they clearly had a scribal-literate wing of the movement, although it is not clear whether or how easily an individual Essene could move between two such communities. Regardless, one certainly cannot take the Essenes as indicative of first-century Jewish culture as a whole.

202. Riesner, *Jesus*, 232.
203. Ibid., 244.
204. Ibid.
205. Ibid., 191.
206. Riesner, "Jüdische," 31.
207. Riesner, "Jesus," 191.
208. Riesner, *Jesus*, 244.
209. Riesner, "Jesus," 191.

crucial to the topic of this book. The evidence for Jesus' literate landscape does not permit scholars to assume that Jesus' knowledge of an Old Testament text indicates his ability to read that text from a manuscript anymore than one can assume that an average church or synagogue attendee's biblical knowledge today indicates an ability to read the texts in the original languages. Even in today's highly literate cultures, Biblical Studies as an academic discipline sets apart those with authoritative knowledge of the text (with concomitant ability to read the original languages) from those with passing knowledge of the text from repetitious familiarity via personal or liturgical reading in native languages! John 7's portrayal of scribal authority corroborates Josephus's and Philo's portrayals of acquisition of biblical knowledge—knowledge of what the text says (7:42) does not constitute authoritative knowledge of the text (7:49) that derives from an ability to search it for oneself (7:52).

6. *The Perception of Literacy*

The final pertinent factor from Jesus' literate landscape is perhaps also the most important and overlooked—the perception of literacy. Attributions such as "literate," "illiterate," "slow writer," or "scribal literate" were ultimately the perceptions of individuals and groups who judged whether one belonged in any or none of those categories. Furthermore, the literate status of the judge(s) of literacy impacted the perception of both literate skills and the social status associated with a particular set of skills.

One of the clearest examples of the role of perception in attributions of literate status is Petaus, the village scribe whom I have already discussed as a slow writer whose literate skills did not extend beyond the ability to sign his name and copy by rote (and imperfectly at that) his formula for document reception.[210] Interestingly, one of Petaus's colleagues, a certain Ischyrion, was accused of being illiterate (ἀγράμματος). In coming to Ischyrion's defense, Petaus claimed that he was obviously literate because he had signed the documents. In the words of Youtie, "He was in effect offering a defence not only of Ischyrion, against whom the accusation had been directed, but also of himself and his own procedure."[211] In other words, Ischyrion's limited literate skills were capable of garnering simultaneously the accusation of "illiterate" from his accuser and the defense of "literate" from Petaus. Petaus's own limited literate skills undoubtedly impacted his assessment of Ischyrion's literate status.

---

210. See above, p. 89.
211. Youtie, "Βραδέως," 240.

In addition to the initial attribution of literate skills, an individual or group's perception also played a significant role in placing those skills against a broader socio-cultural matrix. Petaus was quick to defend Ischyrion because he knew that, if the charge of illiteracy were accepted, the stigma of falling outside the literate class would apply to him as well. As it were, village scribes were already among the lower rungs of literate society and not particularly honorable in the eyes of the elite. Demonstrating the relevance of Petaus's example for the Jewish context, Josephus too discusses the literate skills of village scribes and their connection to status. He reports that, according to Salome's daughter, Alexander and Aristobulus had threatened, upon ascedency, "to set the mothers of their other brothers to work at the loom along with the slave-girls, and to make the princes themselves village scribes (κωμῶν γραμματεῖς), sarcastically referring to the careful education (πεπαιδευμένος ἐπιμελῶς) they had received."[212] Josephus does not contradict that the education level of village scribes is open to mockery by those truly educated.[213] Thus, although a completely illiterate farmer would likely have considered Petaus's semi-literacy as evidence that he was among the literate and thus a socially significant individual (or, in the least, an individual who was more socially significant than himself), a truly literate member of elite culture such as Josephus has no qualms with a claim that a village scribe did not receive a proper education.[214] Not only were literate skills subject to perception, then, so were attributions of the social significance of those skills and, by extension, the social significance of that individual.

Like the difference between scribal literacy and craftsman's literacy, the significance of the social perception of literate skills is difficult to overestimate for this study. First, texts such as Mark 1:22//Matt 7:29 and John 7:15 claim that Jesus' contemporaries *did* assess his teaching authority by comparison with and contrast to scribal-literate individuals. In considering how the various early Christian memories of Jesus' literate

---

212.   Josephus, *J. W.* 1.24.3 §479 (Thackeray, LCL).

213.   Although one should not assume that Petaus, Ischyrion, and the village scribes whom Josephus references are fully representative of all ancient village scribes, their examples nevertheless present considerable difficulty for the suggestion of William E. Arnal, *Jesus and the Village Scribes: Galilean Conflicts and the Setting of Q* (Minneapolis: Fortress, 2001), 170, that Q[1] or Q was the product of village scribes who were "relatively proficient at the production (composition, authorship) of texts, and literary texts at that."

214.   See also Libanius's criticism of provincial governors who had the ability to write shorthand (οἳ γράφοντες μὲν σὺν τάχει), undoubtedly a product of elite education and esteemed by illiterates, of having no knowledge (νοῦν δὲ οὐκ ἔχοντες) (Libanius, *Or.* 18.158).

status emerged in early Christianity, then, it is important to remember that different cross-sections of first-century Palestinian Judaism may have remembered Jesus' scribal status differently.

Second, the perception of literacy shows how society at large viewed scribal literates as authoritative interpreters regardless of the literate status of any one member of the group. That is, some members of a scribal-literate group could have, in reality, been semi-literate or even illiterate.[215] Nevertheless, most first-century Jews would still attribute scribal-literate authority to all members of the group, since the group as a whole would have been overwhelmingly more literate than the majority of the population. Schwartz thus appropriately highlights the role of public perception in attributions of scribal literacy and authority for members of the group: "Local judges, teachers, scribes, and so on, *who were as far as most Judeans were concerned the representatives of Torah, whether or not they were learned men who had studied the Pentateuch and learned how to interpret it…*"[216] That is, the attribution of scribal authority both was and was not dependent upon the possession and utilization of scribal-literate skills. It was dependent upon the well-established and correct assumption that groups such as priests, Pharisees, and scribes consisted predominantly of interpreters with a scribal-literate education in the Hebrew texts. The essential correctness of this assumption, however, did not dictate that every individual group member had to read Torah publicly before the majority of the populace would attribute scribal authority to the group member.

Third, the role of authoritative interpreters in first-century Jewish society, the perception of their authority, and the concomitant assumptions regarding their scribal literacy would have created expectations for Torah teachers.[217] In such a context, the rhetorical deployment of scribal literacy (or skills or positions assumed to be dependent upon scribal literacy) was crucial to interpretive authority in order to meet the audience's expectation. Public displays, ranging from reading in a synagogue to teaching in the temple to interpretive duels with known scribal-literate authorities, were opportunities for a teacher to gain or lose the public's perception of him as a scribal-literate person with scribal authority. The perception of scribal literacy, therefore, is crucial to interpreting the controversy narratives that portray Jesus battling recognized scribal literates over interpretative matters.

215.   *m. Yoma* 1.3 and 1.6 suggest the possibility of a high priest who could not read. Snyder, *Teachers*, 58–59, notes illiterate and less-literate Epicureans. Cf. also the פתי ("simpleton," García Martínez and Tigchelaar) priest in 4QDa 13.6.

216.   Schwartz, *Imperialism*, 68 (emphasis added). See also Carr, *Writing*, 288.

217.   See further Chapter 5.

7. *Summary and Conclusions*

Jesus' literate landscape was complex. Although almost all first-century Palestinian Jews were aware of texts and their power, and indeed organized their identity around (holy) texts, illiteracy was the rule of the day. There is no concrete evidence that literate education was typical for first-century Palestinian Jews (or the rest of antiquity). For those Jews who did receive an education, Torah reading was a prime focus, with writing instruction being reserved for later specialized scribal training. The various gradations of literacy, as well as the multilingual context, reveal literacy spectrums where a single person could hold different literate competencies in different languages. Importantly, however, scribal literacy in Palestine was based upon knowledge of the Hebrew holy texts. Craftsmen too may have been functionally literate, as were other bureaucratic scribes. But for those literates who specialized in transmitting and interpreting the Hebrew Scriptures, their literacy—scribal literacy—translated into significant scribal authority. Undoubtedly, manual laborers and others could acquire knowledge of the Scriptures, but that knowledge was not comparable to scribal literacy/authority. Furthermore, one must be aware of the manners in which these differing sections of Jesus' literate landscape could have perceived the rhetorical deployment of literate skills in an interpretive situation—a single pedagogical event could suffice for convincing some audience members of one's (scribal-)literate status (and thus authority) while also convincing other members of one's lack of (scribal-)literate status (and thus lack of authority).

With this multifaceted literate landscape for Jesus' preaching and teaching ministry established, the current study now proceeds to early Christian memories of Jesus' scribal-literate status. Interestingly, early Christian memory is corporately confused as to whether Jesus was a scribal-literate teacher.

Chapter 4

Jesus' Scribal-Literate Status in Early Christianity

> *Scholars are divided on this question*
> *because the evidence is somewhat*
> *ambiguous.*[1]

This chapter will argue that two streams of social memory concerning Jesus' scribal-literate status co-existed in early Christianity, occasionally contradicting each other or intertwining.[2] In both streams, Christians remember Jesus as a powerful teacher capable of astounding his audiences. One stream denies or questions his scribal literacy, however, while the other affirms it. A main point of the following discussion, then, exceedingly simple but curiously overlooked, is that Jesus' scribal-literate status *was* a debated issue among early Christians.

What follows will trace the contours of this debate by focusing upon Gospel traditions (Jesus-memories) from the first century that most directly assert, deny, or comment otherwise upon Jesus' scribal-literate status, as well as their reception-histories. I will first address the Synoptic debate over Jesus as a synagogue teacher, then the explicit questioning of Jesus' scribal-literate status in John's Gospel. A third section will demonstrate the eventual predominance of the scribal-literate image of Jesus in orthodox, apocryphal, and heretical tradition in the second to sixth centuries C.E.

In light of my focus on Jesus' scribal-literate status, texts that may indicate a functional level of literacy for Jesus, such as the claim that Jesus knew (possibly read) what was engraved upon a coin (Mark 12:16//

---

1. Evans, *Fabricating*, 35.
2. I use the default phrase "scribal-literate status" in order to indicate neutrally the existence of the debate over Jesus in these texts rather than "scribal literacy" or "scribal illiteracy," each of which signals one side of the debate.

Matt 22:20), will not be included here;[3] neither will texts that deal with the scribal-literate status of his followers (Acts 4:13; Origen, *Cels.* 1.62). Also not included in this chapter are texts that imply Jesus' knowledge of the content of Hebrew Scriptures, particularly texts where Jesus asks his opponents, "Have you never read?..."[4] To reiterate from the previous chapter, knowledge of what the texts say, even intricate knowledge, does not necessitate the ability to read them for oneself.[5] Undoubtedly, Jesus' ability to debate recognized scribal-literate teachers successfully, which these texts portray, and even his ability to refer to Scripture in those debates, would have contributed to his contemporaries' opinions about his own scribal-literate status. This is an important point and I will return to it in the next chapter. But the focus of this chapter is not upon *how* early Christians likely came to remember Jesus in particular ways (that is, the historical events and social conditions that contributed to the shape of the memory), but rather *what* those memories are. To the earliest of those memories we now turn.

1. *Jesus as a Synagogue Teacher in the Synoptic Gospels*

The Synoptic Gospels contain an intra-Christian debate over Jesus' proper location in a synagogue service, a debate into which the subsequent handlers of that tradition frequently entered.[6] The authors agree that Jesus frequently taught (as well as preached, healed, and performed exorcisms) in synagogues, an opinion they collectively share with the Gospel of John.[7] This claim alone is significant for the issue of Jesus' scribal-literate status. As Chapter 3 presented, in Second Temple synagogue services the social/authoritative division between scribal-literate

---

3. Harris, *Ancient*, 213, and Millard, *Reading*, 156, cite coinage as evidence that even those who could not read and write were aware of the purposes and power of writing.

4. Mark 2:25//Matt 12:3//Luke 6:3; Mark 12:10//Matt 21:42; Mark 12:26//Matt 22:31; Matt 12:5; 19:4–5; Luke 10:26; cf. Mark 12:24; Luke 20:17. See also Luke 11:51, where Jesus' reference to Abel and Zechariah implies his knowledge of the Scriptures in the Hebrew order and not the LXX order.

5. Additionally, the rhetorical force of Jesus' question "Have you never read?" does not necessarily reside upon the assumption that Jesus had read the texts, but rather that his interlocutors had read them. *Pace* Dunn, *Jesus*, 314; Evans, "Jewish Scripture," 50.

6. So far as I am aware, the detailing of the contours of this debate that follows is an original contribution.

7. Matt 4:23; 9:35; 12:9; 13:54; Mark 1:21, 39; 3:1; 6:2; Luke 4:15, 16, 33, 44; 6:6; 13:10; John 6:59; 18:20.

individuals and everyone else, particularly manual laborers, manifested physically. On one side of the synagogue service were scribal-literate authorities who would read and interpret the text; on the other side of the service were those who broke from their weekly labor in order to listen to those authorities read and interpret the text. *By claiming that Jesus taught in synagogues rather than received teaching, these traditions place him on a side of the synagogue service that was, in the available sources, exclusively reserved for teachers with scribal literacy.*[8]

The Synoptic debate over Jesus as a synagogue teacher, however, does not technically concern the side of the synagogue service where Jesus *stood*. All agree that he occupied the position of a synagogue teacher rather than the position of an audience member. Rather, the debate concerns the side of the synagogue service where Jesus *belonged*. Here, the Synoptics disagree as to whether Jesus occupied the position of synagogue pedagogue legitimately or presumptuously. Sometimes this disagreement occurs at the level of the narrative, as different synagogue audiences within the same Gospel carry different convictions about the appropriateness of Jesus standing on the scribal-literate side of the synagogue service. At other times, the disagreement occurs at the level of the authors, as one Gospel author disagrees with another over whether Jesus fell into the scribal-literate class. The core texts of this debate narrate Jesus' return to his hometown synagogue: Mark 6:1–6; Matt 13:54–58; and Luke 4:16–30.[9] I begin, however, with the claim in Mark 1:22//Matt 7:29 that Jesus was "not like the scribes," as this statement relates to the broader Markan portrayal of Jesus as a synagogue teacher. Since a full treatment of the Synoptic Problem (as well as a full tradition-history of the Nazareth pericope) is beyond the scope of this book, I note that I assume Matthean and Lukan dependence upon Mark.[10]

1.1. *"Not Like the Scribes" (Mark 1:22//Matthew 7:29)*
The earliest tradition related to Jesus' scribal-literate status occurs in the first chapter of Mark's Gospel. According to Mark 1:21–22, "They [Jesus

8. Note that this claim does not preclude the idea that a scribal-illiterate individual could have presided over a synagogue service. In light of limited evidence, one must acknowledge this possibility. Also in light of the available evidence, however, such a scenario would have been atypical.

9. Only Luke 4:16 names the town as Nazareth. Mark 6:1 and Matt 13:54 both state that Jesus went to "his hometown" (πατρίδα αὐτοῦ).

10. A secondary argument of this chapter (concerning Matthew's and Luke's respective modifications of Mark 6:1–6) depends upon the assumption of Markan Priority; the primary argument of the chapter (that the two different streams of Jesus-memory co-existed) does not.

and the disciples] went to Capernaum; and when the sabbath came, he entered the synagogue and taught (ἐδίδασκεν). They were astounded (ἐξεπλήσσοντο) at his teaching, for he taught them as one having authority (ἐξουσίαν), and not as the scribes (γραμματεῖς)."[11] Matthew 7:29 follows the last sentence of Mark 1:22, which contrasts Jesus with scribes, nearly verbatim, adding only αὐτῶν after γραμματεῖς.[12] Whereas Mark contrasts Jesus' teaching with the scribes in reference to the Capernaum synagogue incident, however, Matthew makes the statement of contrast after narrating the Sermon on the Mount (Matt 5:1–7:27). Those astonished in Matthew, then, are not a synagogue audience, but "the crowds" who listened to Jesus speak on the mountain (5:1; 7:28). Like Mark, however, Matthew uses ἐκπλήσσω in order to describe their reaction and implies a positive response.

Three elements of the Markan narration of Jesus' trip to the Capernaum synagogue are important for the present discussion. The first important element is the claim that Jesus taught in the synagogue (1:21). Jesus is not the reader, but presumably fills the position of the expounder of the holy text.[13] Mark similarly places Jesus in a pedagogical role in the Galilean synagogues in the subsequent context, although preaching instead of teaching (1:39). Jesus' occupation of this position aligns him with scribal-literate teachers, in contrast to the manual-laborer audience, and has already been discussed.

The second important element is Mark's (and Matthew's) narration of the audience's response (Mark 1:22a//Matt 7:28b). The Synoptic portrayals of Jesus as a synagogue teacher become very complex in their narrations of the audiences' responses. As we will see, they both do and

---

11.   Mark 1:22 and Matt 7:29 technically place Jesus outside *grapho-literate* scribal culture by contrasting him with scribes rather than other interpretive authorities who may have only been able to read (Pharisees, Sadducees, etc.). Since the authors of the Synoptic Gospels consistently align and overlap Pharisees and scribes (e.g. Mark 12:38–39//Luke 4:31 claim that scribes enjoy seats of prominence while the Matthean parallel claims it is scribes *and Pharisees* [Matt 23:2], or Mark 2:16's scribes *of the* Pharisees), however, I assume here that the scribes represent scribal culture more generally. C W 33 1241 et al. add Pharisees to the group with whom Jesus is contrasted.

12.   Likely harmonizing with Mark, C L 565 700 et al. omit αὐτῶν at Matt 7:29.

13.   See Philo, *Prob.* 12.81–82, who distinguishes between the reader and interpreter in the Essene Sabbath service. Elsewhere, he describes a synagogue service where the same individual performs both tasks (*Hypoth.* 7.12–13). William Lane, *The Gospel according to Mark* (NICNT 2; Grand Rapids: Eerdmans, 1974), 200, in reference to Mark 6:3: "On the sabbath day Jesus attended the synagogue and was given the opportunity to *expound* the reading from the Torah and the Haftarah" (emphasis added).

do not agree as to *how* and *why* Jesus' audiences responded to his teaching in the manners they did. Despite this complexity, one area of agreement—between the Synoptics collectively and between different synagogue accounts within the same Gospel—is that Jesus' synagogue audiences *initially* responded with astonishment. Mark 1:22 is a prime example. Mark uses ἐκπλήσσω (see also Matt 7:28; 13:54; Luke 2:48) to describe the audience's reaction in 1:22 and θαμβέω in 1:27. Both these verbs are passive with an active sense and imply being overwhelmed.[14] Other texts will use θαυμάζω (Luke 4:22; John 7:15) similarly in reference to Jesus' teaching activity.[15] This verb can have a stronger connotation of impressing in a positive manner while maintaining a meaning of "wonder." It can also have a negative meaning, however, such as when Jesus is "amazed" at the disbelief of his hometown in Mark 6:6. Another verb appearing in these contexts, ἐξίστημι (Luke 2:47), implies being "in a state in which things seem to make little or no sense."[16]

To be sure, the authors use these verbs in order to describe the impact of Jesus' ἐξουσία, as does Mark in Mark 1:22 and elsewhere. But they indicate that this impact sometimes consisted of Jesus' contemporaries not quite knowing what to think of this power/authority. These verbs thus create an opportunity for the narrative to clarify whether the audiences' reactions were ultimately positive or negative, and both reactions occur.[17] In the case of the Capernaum synagogue in Mark 1:22, 27 (or the audience of the Sermon on the Mount in Matt 7:28), the ultimate reaction is positive. The initial response of astonishment turns into admiration, with Jesus' fame spreading from the Capernaum synagogue throughout Galilee (1:28).

The third important element of Mark 1:22//Matt 7:29 is the narrators' explicit assessment of Jesus vis-à-vis scribal-literate teachers. Although Mark's narration of Jesus' teaching in the Capernaum synagogue claims that Jesus occupied a pedagogical position associated with scribal literacy (and ultimately met with fanfare), his own appraisal as narrator contrasts

---

14. "ἐκπλήσσω," BDAG 308: "to cause to be filled with amazement to the point of being overwhelmed, *amaze, astound, overwhelm*"; "θαμβέω," BDAG 442: "be astounded, amazed."

15. "θαυμάζω," BDAG 444–45: "1. to be extraordinarily impressed or disturbed by someth., …*wonder, marvel, be astonished*… 2. wonder, be amazed."

16. "ἐξίστημι," BDAG 350: "1. …to cause to be in a state in which things seem to make little or no sense, *confuse, amaze, astound*… 2. …be out of one's normal state of mind…*lose one's mind, be out of one's senses…be amazed, be astonished.*"

17. Cf. Robert H. Stein, *Mark* (BECNT; Grand Rapids: Baker Academic, 2008), 85: "In the vast majority of instances [in Mark], this astonishment is a positive response."

Jesus' teaching with scribal-literate teachers. Jesus is "not like the scribes" because he teaches "as one having authority" (ὡς ἐξουσίαν ἔχων; Mark 1:22). Mark speaks this opinion directly to the reader rather than placing it on the lips of a character (although he portrays it as representative of the characters' convictions), as does Matthew as well.

Mark may here indicate that, whereas scribes supported their arguments by appealing to prior Jewish traditions, Jesus made no such appeals to external authority.[18] Alternatively, since Mark portrays Jesus' ἐξουσία as an intertwining of teaching, exorcism, and healing, he may indicate that scribes taught without engaging in exorcistic or therapeutic activity.[19]

Those scholars who conceptualize the distinction between Jesus and scribes solely in terms of Jewish texts and traditions, or healings and exorcisms, however, miss the additional significance of the culture in which Jesus lived. In a world where very few received a scribal-literate education, Mark explains the synagogue audience's reaction to Jesus' occupation of a synagogue position typically associated with scribal literacy by contrasting Jesus with those who held scribal literacy. *The crowd's initial astonishment and Mark's own assessment of Jesus' pedagogy both assume, therefore, that Jesus fell outside scribal-literate culture.*[20] This simple point would not bear repeating if it was not so often overlooked by those who focus upon possible stylistic differences between Jesus and the scribes and ignore the possible differences in social class reflected in Mark 1:22//Matt 7:29, with concomitant implications for his scribal-literate status.[21]

18. See R. T. France, *The Gospel of Mark* (NIGTC; Grand Rapids: Eerdmans, 2002), 102: "The general statement that his ἐξουσία differentiated his teaching from that of the γραμματεῖς suggests that he is already expressing some of the radical ideas, boldly contradicting accepted halakhic teaching, which will appear later in relation to, e.g., the sabbath (2:23–3:6), the purity laws (7:1–23), or divorce (10:2–12)." Vincent Taylor, *The Gospel according to St. Mark* (London: Macmillan, 1963), 172, claims Jesus here speaks with "a profound sense of divine inspiration" whereas the scribes' "teaching lacked the note of spontaneity, being based upon tradition."

19. Stein, *Mark*, 87: "For Mark, however, the authority of Jesus's teaching was intimately associated with the coming of the kingdom of God *and his authority to exorcise demons*" (emphasis added).

20. Contra David Daube, *The New Testament and Rabbinic Judaism* (London: Athlone, 1956), 206, who curiously claims the scribes are "not the learned Rabbis but, on the contrary, ordinary teachers without the right to proclaim decisions," and thus that the crowd's surprise indicates that Jesus taught "like one ordained...as if possessing Rabbinic authority."

21. In addition to those mentioned in n. 18, above, consider Strauss, *Life*, 201, who claims unconvincingly that Matt 7:29's description of Jesus as "not like the

Mark 1:21–28 thus involves a certain incongruity. By actively teaching rather than passively listening, Jesus acts in the Capernaum synagogue the way scribal-literate individuals typically acted in synagogues. He does so despite the fact that, according to Mark, his pedagogy was demarcated from scribal-literate teachers. The appearance of this incongruity prepares Mark's and Matthew's readers for Jesus' return to his hometown synagogue. It should come as no surprise that Jesus is rejected as a synagogue teacher on account of his (or his father's) identity as a craftsman (Mark 6:3//Matt 13:55), since a craftsman's social status and proper location in a synagogue service would also have been "not like the scribes."

1.2. *Jesus the* τέκτων *(Mark 6:3; cf. Matthew 13:55)*

In contrast to the Capernaum synagogue incident, when Jesus returns to his hometown synagogue in Mark 6:1–6, many of those among the audience "took offense" (6:3) at his attempt to teach them. Their words in Mark 6:3 specify that the offensive nature of Jesus' actions stemmed particularly from his identity as a τέκτων.

1.2.1. *What is a* τέκτων? English Bibles most often translate τέκτων as "carpenter." This is an accurate translation that reflects early Christian understandings of Jesus as a woodworker.[22] More broadly, a τέκτων could be a "joiner," "builder," or "smith"; that is, generally a manual laborer who works in some fashion with wood, stone, or metal.[23] Translations such as "artisan," "workman," or "craftsman" reflect the wider flexibility of the term. Most important for present purposes, a τέκτων was a manual laborer.

Contrary to some scholars, the claim that Jesus was a τέκτων does not automatically indicate that he was an illiterate peasant.[24] With regard to

---

scribes" actually contrasts him with "doctors of the law" rather than scribes proper and is thus irrelevant for whether Jesus received a scribal education.

22.   Justin Martyr, *Dial.* 88; cf. *Inf. Gos. Thom.* 13:1–3; Origen, *Cels.* 6.34. On the accuracy of "carpenter," see, inter alia, Richard A. Batey, "Is Not This the Carpenter?," *NTS* 30 (1984): 257 n. 2; Chester Charlton McCown, "Ὁ ΤΕΚΤΩΝ," in *Studies in Early Christianity* (ed. Shirley Jackson Case; New York: The Century Co., 1928), 176, 189.

23.   See "τέκτων, ονος, ὁ," BDAG 995; "τέκτων, ονος, ὁ," LSJ 1769; Batey, "Is Not This the Carpenter?," 257 n. 2; Hildebrand Höpfl, "Nonne hic est fabri filius?," *Bib* 4 (1923): 44–47; McCown, "Ὁ ΤΕΚΤΩΝ," 175–89; Lane, *Gospel according to Mark*, 202 n. 9; J. I. Packer, "Carpenter, Builder, Workman, Craftsman, Trade," *NIDNT* 1:279. *TDNT* and *TLNT* do not have entries for τέκτων.

24.   See Chapter 1, specifically in reference to the arguments of Crossan. Paul refers to Jesus as poor in 2 Cor 8:9, but in contrast to his heavenly status and without reference to his identity as a τέκτων.

literate status, Chapter 3 showed that some craftsmen held a functional level of literacy associated with the occupation. With regard to socio-economic standing, if someone was known via his occupation as a work-man—and thus *had* an occupation as a workman—he likely was not among the poorest of the poor.[25] Examples of both these realities appear in Jewish tradition. Exodus 35:30–35 LXX lauds the "master-crafts-manship" (ἀρχιτεκτονίας; 35:32, 35) of Bezalel and Oholiab as work imbued with God's spirit (35:30). Later in the narrative, Exod 39:30 MT will claim these master craftsmen wrote the short phrase "Holy to the LORD" (קדש ליהוה) on the holy diadem, thus manifesting craftsman's literacy.[26] In 2 Kgs 24:12 (24:14 LXX), "all craftsmen" (πᾶν τέκτονα) are included in the prominent Jewish leaders whom Nebuchadnezzar takes into exile, while "the poor of the land" (οἱ πτωχοὶ τῆς γῆς) remain.

Undoubtedly, the distance between the social categories of "craftsman" and "poor" fluctuated in different periods of Jewish history and even from individual to individual.[27] Sirach (second century B.C.E.), however, expresses essentially the same opinion as these other LXX texts—far from being destitute and poor, a τέκτων was an honorable social position in Second Temple Judaism. Sirach 38:27 praises "every artisan and master artisan" (πᾶς τέκτων καὶ ἀρχιτέκτων), claiming that they and all others who "rely on their hands…maintain the fabric of the world" (38:31, 34). So appreciated are skilled manual laborers that "wherever they live, they will not go hungry" (38:32). That there was, at some point in time, a destitute illiterate starving craftsman somewhere in Second Temple Judaism is an extremely safe assumption. But the available evidence suggests that, generally speaking, as a social category in Second Temple society, τέκτονες could be literate to a degree associated with their craft and were not the poorest of Palestinians.

Importantly, however, as Chapter 3 discussed, Sir 38 extols the τέκτων (and other manual laborers) ultimately in order to contrast him with the γραμματεύς. As honorable and important as the craftsman is, he cannot compare to the scribe. Indeed, for Sirach, like Mark, the τέκτων is quite explicitly "not like the scribes." Sirach begins the passage that praises manual laborers by claiming, "The wisdom of the scribe (γραμματέως)

25. Also Luz, "Founding," 240 n. 28. Cf. Schröter, "Jesus of Galilee," 47: "Galilean fishermen, the closest followers of Jesus, were certainly not part of the well-to-do sector of the population, but neither did they belong to the lower end of the social spectrum."

26. LXX omits Exod 39:30 MT; see Exod 39:1–23 LXX (= 38:24–39:1 MT).

27. It did not, however, fluctuate enough to justify the speculation of George Wesley Buchanan, "Jesus and the Upper Class," *NovT* 7 (1964): 207, that "Jesus had once been a businessman but later joined a sect and became a scholar."

depends on the opportunity of leisure; only the one who has little business can become wise" (38:24). Thus, he asks, "How can one become wise who handles the plow?" (38:25), and asserts, "So it is with every artisan (τέκτων) and master artisan who labors by night as well as by day" (38:27). Sirach transitions to praising the scribe by once again emphatically contrasting manual laborers with scribal literates: "Their concern is for the exercise of their trade. How different the one who devotes himself to the study of the law of the Most High!" (Sir 38:34–39:1).

Sirach 38's distinction between the scribe who studies the law and manual laborers who must instead work, including the τέκτων, exhibits the exact same class division between scribal-literate readers/teachers of the law and manual laborers that appears in Second Temple (and rabbinic) descriptions of synagogue audiences.[28] This division is at the crux of Mark 6:3.

1.2.2. *Mark 6:3*. According to Mark 6:1–6, Jesus' attempt to teach in a synagogue met stern resistance in his hometown. Like in Capernaum, once "he began to teach" (ἤρξατο διδάσκειν), the majority of those in the audience "were astounded" (ἐξεπλήσσοντο). Unlike in Capernaum, however, "they took offense" at Jesus for having placed himself upon the wrong side of the synagogue service, as evidenced by their identification of the aspects of his identity that disqualify him from taking such a position: "Is this not the τέκτων, the son of Mary and brother of James and Joses and Judas and Simon, and are not his sisters here with us?" (Mark 6:3).[29] They claim that Jesus' wisdom "has been given to him"

28. Josephus, *Ag. Ap.* 2.17 §175; Philo, *Hypoth.* 7.12–13; *y. Sukkah* 55a–b (5:1); *t. Sukkah* 4:6; cf. Josephus, *Ant.* 16.2.4 §43; Philo, *Prob.* 12.81–82. See further Chapter 3.

29. ℵ A B C D L W Δ Θ *f¹* et al. attest ὁ τέκτων ("the craftsman") at Mark 6:3. Several manuscripts attest the variant τοῦ τέκτονος υἱος ("the son of the craftsman"), including 𝔓⁴⁵ ᵛⁱᵈ *f¹³* and 33ᵛⁱᵈ. (For a helpful discussion of the witnesses, which also include varying references to Mary, see C. E. B. Cranfield, *The Gospel according to St. Mark* [CGTC; Cambridge: Cambridge University Press, 1959], 194–95.) The strength of the manuscript witnesses supports the former reading, which led the committee of the UBS 4th rev. ed. to give it an "A" rating (Bruce M. Metzger, *A Textual Commentary on the Greek New Testament* [2d ed.; Stuttgart: Deutsche Bibelgesellschaft, 2000], 75–76). In addition, what follows will argue that Mark 6:3's reception-history supports the former as the original reading and that the variants are assimilations to Matt 13:55, which had already altered Mark 6:3. Contra Taylor, *Gospel according to St. Mark*, 300, who posits "that Mark wrote ὁ τοῦ τέκτονος υἱός and that an early scribe replaced this reading by ὁ τέκων and added ὁ υἱὸς τῆς Μαρίας," Matthew, and the minority witnesses at Mark 6:3, had more reason to modify Jesus' identity from

(6:2)—that is, not earned via scribal education—because they know he and his family are not part of the educated class.[30] The hometown synagogue crowd thus has the exact same opinion as Sirach concerning the identity of textual authorities—they are not τέκτονες. They are astounded because it is *this* man (6:2)—the τέκτων—who is attempting to teach them.[31] As France notes, "To the people of Nazareth, Jesus is the local boy, and they know no reason why he should have turned out to be any different from the rest of his family."[32] Similarly, Lane styles their complaint: "Is he not a common worker with his hands even as the rest of us are?"[33]

In response to their rejection, Jesus says, "Prophets are not without honor, except in their hometown, and among their own kin, and in their own house" (6:4). Their negative reception of Jesus as a synagogue teacher results in limited miraculous activity on his part (6:5), as failure to accept the pedagogical manifestation of Jesus' ἐξουσία limits the therapeutic manifestation of it. Thus, although Mark describes the initial astonishment of both the Capernaum synagogue and the hometown synagogue with ἐκπλήσσω, the former blossoms into Jesus' fame while the latter deteriorates into hostility.

Mark himself does not identify Jesus as a τέκτων directly, since he places this claim on the lips of Jesus' hometown. Nevertheless, this identification is not one with which Mark appears to disagree. There is no statement of their lack of understanding, as in Mark 6:52 (cf. 8:17, 21). Further, their claim that Jesus is a craftsman coheres with Mark's earlier claim that he did not teach like scribes (1:22) and the common catalyst in both instances is Jesus' teaching in a synagogue.

"a craftsman" to "the son of the craftsman" than the majority of scribes had to strengthen the association of Jesus with craftsman status by making him "the craftsman" rather than the son of one. See further below.

30. Similarly, the chief priests and elders in Matt 21:23 ask, "Who *gave* you this authority?" (emphasis added).

31. Also noting the derogatory attitude reflected in the usage of οὗτος is France, *Gospel of Mark*, 242; Ezra P. Gould, *A Critical and Exegetical Commentary on the Gospel according to St. Mark* (ICC; Edinburgh: T. & T. Clark, 1897), 103; Rudolf Pesch, *Das Markusevangelium. Teil 1, Einleitung und Kommentar zu Kap. 1, 1–8, 26* (HTKNT 2; Freiburg: Herder, 1980), 317.

32. France, *Gospel of Mark*, 242. Also, Gerd Theissen, "Jesus as an Itinerant Teacher: Reflections from Social History on Jesus' Roles," in Charlesworth and Pokorný, eds., *Jesus Research*, 107: "It was not every carpenter who appeared in public as a teacher."

33. Lane, *Gospel according to Mark*, 202.

Combined with the incident in the Capernaum synagogue in Mark 1:22, then, Mark claims that Jesus met mixed results in different locales. He occupied the position of a scribal-literate teacher in a synagogue service with success on multiple occasions. On the basis of those occasions, Jesus' reputation spread throughout the region of Galilee. Once Jesus attempted to occupy this position in the synagogue of those who knew him best, however, he was rejected as a craftsman. Whereas the Capernaum synagogue was astounded because Jesus *taught* unlike the scribes, the hometown synagogue was astounded because Jesus *was* unlike the scribes as a τέκτων and, therefore, should not be teaching. Significantly, once the hometown crowd accosts him on the basis of his status as a craftsman, the Markan Jesus never again sets foot in a synagogue.

1.2.3. *Matthew 13:55.* Matthew 13:54–58 largely follows Mark 6:1–6 in narrating Jesus' trip to his hometown synagogue.[34] He repeats that Jesus "began to teach," although using the inceptive imperfect ἐδίδασκεν (13:54) rather than following Mark's usage of ἄρχω with the infinitive διδάσκειν (Mark 6:2). He also follows Mark in placing the incident in the synagogue and uses ἐκπλήσσω in order to describe the audience's initial astonishment. This astonishment will, as in Mark, ultimately lead to rejection and Jesus' statement that a prophet is not dishonored except in his hometown (13:57–58). Also as in Mark, the Matthean Jesus will not again enter a synagogue after the rejection in his hometown.

Matthew, however, makes one alteration that is particularly important for the present study. Rather than asking "Is this not the carpenter?" as does the synagogue audience of Mark 6:3, the audience of Matt 13:55 asks, "Is this not *the son of* the carpenter (ὁ τοῦ τέκτονος υἱός)?" Already by the early fifth century, Augustine had noted this discrepancy and claimed, "There is nothing to marvel at in this, since He might quite fairly have been designated by both these names. For, in taking Him to be the son of a carpenter, they naturally also took Him to be a carpenter."[35]

Not everyone has been as convinced as Augustine that Matthew's alteration is of no consequence, however, especially since his observation only pushes the question further—if both are equally valid, why change it? As a result, scholars have offered several theories. After stating, "The reasons for the change are not entirely clear," Luz offers two possibilities:

34. W. D. Davies and Dale C. Allison, Jr., *A Critical and Exegetical Commentary on the Gospel of Matthew* (3 vols.; ICC; Edinburgh: T. & T. Clark, 1988–97), 2:452: "There is no reason to think that Mt 13:53–8 is anything other than a revised and abbreviated version of Mk 6:1–6a."
35. Augustine, *Cons.* 2.42.90 (*NPNF*[1]).

It may be that Matthew in Jewish style simply mentions the father's profession. However, it may also be that mentioning Jesus' profession was disturbing, probably not so much because one was ashamed to have a construction worker as a savior as because the tradition nowhere else knows anything about Jesus working at a profession but has him traveling the country as an itinerant preacher.[36]

Another possibility is that dogmatic concerns over the virgin birth and/or Jesus' illegitimacy prompted the alteration, which mitigates Mark's identification of Jesus as "the τέκτων, the son of Mary" by adding a reference to Jesus' father.[37] Schnackenburg offers yet another explanation, claiming, "Matthew's alteration of the Markan version of the question, 'Is this not the carpenter?' to 'Is this not the carpenter's *son?*' can be explained by the fact that Jesus' townsfolk are ignorant of the mystery of his origin."[38] A final possibility is that, contra Luz, Jesus' status as a τέκτων did prove disturbing for some Christians.[39] This might not

36. Ulrich Luz, *Matthew 8–20* (trans. James E. Crouch; Hermeneia; Minneapolis: Fortress, 2001), 302. Similarly, Douglas E. Oakman, *Jesus and the Economic Questions of His Day* (SBEC 8; Lewiston: Edwin Mellen, 1986), 176, claims Jesus' "working class origins" may have been disturbing for Matthew.

37. In 1968, Frans van Segbroeck, "Jésus rejeté par sa patrie (Mt 13,54–58)," *Bib* 48 (1968): 182, claimed this line of reasoning is why "la plupart des exégètes moderns se sont pronounces en faveur de l'originalité de la leçon ὁ τέκτων." See further Cranfield, *Gospel according to St. Mark*, 194–95; Davies and Allison, *Matthew*, 2:456–7; Ethelbert Stauffer, "Jeschu ben Mirjam: Kontroversgeschichtliche Anmerkungen zu Mk 6:3," in *Neotestamentica et Semitica: Studies in Honour of Matthew Black* (ed. E. Earle Ellis and Max Wilcox; Edinburgh: T. & T. Clark, 1969), 121–22, 128; cf. H. E. W. Turner, "The Virgin Birth," *ExT* 68 (1956): 12. Cf. also H. Schürmann, "Zur Traditionsgeschichte der Nazareth-Perikope Lk 4,16–30," in *Mélanges Bibliques en hommage au R. P. Béda Rigaux* (ed. Albert Descamps and André de Halleux; Gembloux: Duculot), 197, who suggests Mark 6:3's "ganz ungewöhnliche Bestimmung Jesu nach der Mutter" indicates that Mark 6:3 is later than Luke 4:22 and possibly even John 6:42. (Joseph A. Fitzmyer, *The Gospel according to Luke I–IX* [AB 28; New York: Doubleday, 1970], 527, criticizes Schürmann's overall tradition-history and correctly notes, "It is better to regard the Lucan story as a reworking of the Marcan source…") Joachim Gnilka, *Das Evangelium nach Markus (1,1–8,26)* (EKKNT 2/1; Zurich: Benziger, 1978), 219, also refers to the matronymic identification of Jesus as "ganz ungewöhnlich." Tempering such statements, Lars Hartmann, "Mk 6,3a im Lichter einiger griechischer Texte," *ZNW* 95 (2004): 276–79, cites several examples showing that matronyms were not entirely unheard of in roughly contemporaneous Greek texts.

38. Rudolf Schnackenburg, *The Gospel of Matthew* (trans. Robert R. Barr; Grand Rapids: Eerdmans, 2002), 138–39 (emphasis original).

39. So, inter alia, Cohick, *Women*, 154 (although she also considers that the Matthean reading in 𝔓[45] [see below n. 48] could be original); Haines-Eitzen,

have disturbed their conception of him as savior, as Luz mentions, but rather their conception of him as teacher. Celsus's second-century chiding of Christians includes the charge that "their διδάσκαλος...was a τέκτων," which he connects to their veneration of a wood cross.[40] He then mocks Christians further, asking, "Would not an old woman who sings a story to lull a little child to sleep have been ashamed to whisper tales such as these?"[41] Under this explanation, it may be no coincidence that Matthew, who alone includes Jesus' claim to be Christians' "only διδάσκαλος" (Matt 23:8, 10), distances Jesus from direct identification as a τέκτων.[42]

While acknowledging that "no single explanation commands acceptance,"[43] and also not denying the possible role that concerns over Mark's identification of Jesus as "the son of Mary" may have played, the broader reception-history of Mark 6:3 makes the final possibility the most plausible explanation for Matthew's alteration. The major objection to this explanation has been that Jews did not despise manual labor and so Matthew would not have viewed the identification of Jesus as a craftsman as a slur.[44] One major problem for this objection is that it goes against the grain of the Markan and Matthean narratives, which portray the audience making the accusation as part of their rejection of Jesus. An additional problem is that those scholars who make this objection cite

---

Guardians, 117–18; Wayne C. Kannaday, *Apologetic Discourse and the Scribal Tradition: Evidence of the Influence of Apologetic Interests on the Text of the Canonical Gospels* (SBLTCS 5; Atlanta: Society of Biblical Literature, 2000), 117–9; Ralph Martin, *Mark: Evangelist and Theologian* (Grand Rapids: Zondervan, 1972), 122–23. Lane, *Gospel according to Mark*, 202–3, posits concerns over τέκτων and the virgin birth. Cohick, *Women*, 154, notes, however, that if Matthew altered Mark, the slur which he addressed primarily was not the reference to Jesus as Mary's son but the reference to him as a carpenter.

40. Origen, *Cels.* 6.34 (PG 11.1348).

41. Origen, *Cels.* 6.34 (Chadwick).

42. On the importance of Matt 23:8 to Matthew, see Byrskog, *Jesus*, 399: "Jesus' statement 'for one is your teacher'...in 23:8 carries a significance which goes far beyond its immediate context. The notion is an important feature in Matthew's whole narrative and an index to realities—conceptions and practices—in his community." More broadly on the theme in early Christianity, see also Friedrich Normann, *Christos Didaskalos: Die Vorstellung von Christus als Lehrer in der christlichen Literatur des ersten und zweiten Jahrhunderts* (Münster: Aschendorffsche, 1967); Riesner, *Jesus*.

43. Peter M. Head, *Christology and the Synoptic Problem: An Argument for Markan Priority* (SNTSMS 94; Cambridge: Cambridge University Press, 1997), 71.

44. Davies and Allison, *Matthew*, 2:457; Head, *Christology*, 70; Maccoby, *Jesus the Pharisee*, 181.

(mostly rabbinic) examples of scribal-literate teachers who engage in manual labor; that is, individuals *within* the scribal-literate class who combine Torah study with manual labor.[45] More pertinent for Mark 6:3 and Matt 13:55, however, is the previously discussed witness of Sir 38–39, which places those who study Torah and τέκτονες and other manual laborers in different classes—one of whom *can* study the law, the other of whom *cannot* (explicitly in Sir 38:24)—all the while expressing respect for manual labor.[46] For, the charge of the synagogue in Mark 6:3 is not that Jesus is a member of the scribal class who does some carpentry in addition to his Torah study, but rather that, as a carpenter, he is a member of the artisan class and therefore has no business teaching.

In this light, it is significant that Mark 6:3's reception-history indicates that Christians at different periods found the designation τέκτων problematic and sought to disassociate Jesus from it.[47] For example, 𝔓[45] and other manuscripts assimilate Mark 6:3 to the Matthean reading "son of the carpenter," thus distancing Jesus from direct identification as a τέκτων in the same manner as Matt 13:55.[48] No known manuscripts assimilate Matthew to the Markan reading, however, suggesting that the appearance of the Matthean reading at Mark 6:3 in 𝔓[45] is not simply harmonization. The Palestinian Syriac tradition (from ca. sixth century) goes further by omitting the reference to Jesus as a τέκτων at Mark 6:3 altogether.[49]

Celsus's well-known reception of Mark 6:3, which was just mentioned, indicates the social conditions that likely prompted anxiety over identification of Jesus as a τέκτων. In the late second century, Celsus mocks Christians for always speaking of "the tree of life and of resurrection of the flesh by the tree," claiming they do so because "their master (διδάσκαλος) was nailed to a cross and was a carpenter (τέκτων) by trade," a reference to Mark 6:3.[50] Origen's third-century[51] response to Celsus is

---

45. See sources in n. 44, above. On manual labor and study, see *m. 'Abot* 2:2.

46. *Pace* Horsley, *Scribes*, 55, 57, who claims Sirach "looks down on" manual laborers.

47. Cf. Head, *Christology*, who finds the argument that Matthew wanted to remove the charge of τέκτων from Jesus unpersuasive on account of Jewish appreciation for manual labor (70), but acknowledges that this argument "has the advantage of coherence with scribal alterations of Mark's text away from the identification of Jesus as a carpenter."

48. 𝔓[45 vid] *f*[13] 33[vid] et al. 𝔓[45] reads τεκτου]ος ο υ[ιος (ibid.).

49. Metzger, *A Textual Commentary*, 75–76.

50. Origen, *Cels.* 6.34 (Chadwick); cf. 6.36. For the Greek text, see PG 11.1348.

51. On the date of *Contra Celsum*, see Henry Chadwick, "Introduction," in *Origen: Contra Celsum* (Cambridge: Cambridge University Press, 1965), xiv–xv.

intriguing: "Furthermore, he [Celsus] did not observe that Jesus himself (αὐτὸς ὁ Ἰησοῦς) is not described as a carpenter (τέκτων) anywhere in the gospels accepted in the churches."[52] Origen's response is intriguing because Mark 6:3 explicitly *does* refer to Jesus as a τέκτων. One possible explanation for Origen's oversight is that his copy(ies) of Mark were already harmonized with Matt 13:55.[53] Alternatively, "possibly he had forgotten the passage in Mark."[54] A third possibility is that Origen was being less than honest, desiring to deny craftsman status to Jesus.[55] Although possible, and fitting with the present argument that it is the best explanation for Matthew's reception of Mark 6:3, this last suggestion is less likely in Origen's particular case. He earlier acknowledges that Jesus' upbringing was "entirely contrary" to "an upbringing at the hands of wealthy people who are able to spend money on the education of their son" and that Jesus "had no general education" and "received no serious instruction from men."[56]

Significant for present purposes, however, Origen here reflects (and affirms) the stream of Christian tradition that places Jesus outside the educated class, agreeing with Celsus on this matter while disagreeing

52.   Origen, *Cels.* 6.36 (Chadwick); PG 11.1352. Kannaday, *Apologetic*, 118, claims, "The care with which he qualified his statement implies that Origen knew of gospels or readings that did in fact describe Jesus as a carpenter." Kannaday suggests that these could have been "apocryphal gospels not read liturgically by the wider church" or "specific manuscripts or textual traditions." To my knowledge, there is no *Gospel* tradition other than Mark 6:3 that identifies Jesus directly as a craftsman. Although Kannaday's suggestion is possible, Origen's comment does not necessarily require that Origen had in mind such traditions. His statement could be a pre-emptive attack on the possible existence of such traditions; that is, even if such traditions exist (as claims Celsus), it would not matter because they are not, for Origen, in the appropriate Gospels.

53.   Batey, "Is Not This the Carpenter?," 256 n. 1; Chadwick, ed. and trans., *Origen*, 352 n. 5; Cranfield, *Gospel according to St. Mark*, 195; Bart D. Ehrman, *Misquoting Jesus: The Story Behind Who Changed the Bible and Why* (New York: HarperCollins, 2005), 203; Bart D. Ehrman, "The Text of the Gospels at the End of the Second Century," in *Codex Bezae: Studies from the Lunel Colloquium, June 1994* (ed. D. C. Parker and C.-B. Amphoux; NTTS 22; Leiden: Brill, 1996), 118; Gnilka, *Evangelium nach Markus (1,1–8,26)*, 231; Metzger, *A Textual Commentary*, 75 n. 1; Riesner, *Jesus*, 218.

54.   Ehrman, "Text," 118. Similarly, Cranfield, *Gospel according to St. Mark*, 195; Ehrman, *Misquoting*, 203; Metzger, *A Textual Commentary*, 75 n. 1. Haines-Eitzen, *Guardians*, 118, finds the suggestion that Origen did not know Mark 6:3 or forgot it to be "unlikely."

55.   Ehrman, *Misquoting*, 203; Ehrman, "Text," 118; Haines-Eitzen, *Guardians*, 118; cf. Kannaday, *Apologetic*, 118–19.

56.   Origen, *Cels.* 1.29 (Chadwick).

with him on its relevance. Admittedly, Origen's acknowledgment of Jesus' background makes his denial that Jesus was a carpenter (*if* not attributable to harmonization or a faulty memory) more perplexing. Regardless of Origen's intentions with such a denial, however, Celsus's accusation indicates that Jesus' identity as a carpenter *was* a problematic source of ridicule that at least warranted a response from Origen. Furthermore, Origen's response indicates that one line of defense against such an accusation was to disassociate Jesus from such an identity.[57] If his response reflects knowledge of the Matthean reading of Mark 6:3, it only indicates further that such an alteration could function apologetically by allowing a Christian to deny that Jesus himself was a τέκτων (regardless of Origen's reason for doing so).

Certainly, not all Christians found Jesus' identity as a τέκτων to be a problem. Several early Christians refer to his identity as such positively or, at least, without comment.[58] The aforementioned receptions of Mark 6:3, however, demonstrate that other Christians in various locales and chronological periods did find it to be a problem, including Matthew, whose alteration to Mark 6:3 finds its best explanation on this premise. Although Matthew's narration of the account preserves the synagogue audience's rejection of Jesus as a scribal-literate teacher, it also distances Jesus from the reason for the rejection in Mark's account—direct identification as a τέκτων. One does not, however, have to look to Mark 6:3's reception-history beyond the first century for clear confirmation that some Christians rejected the Markan idea that Jesus was a τέκτων who did not belong in the pedagogical position of a scribal-literate person. One needs only to look at Luke's reception of Mark 6:3.[59]

1.3. *Jesus in the Temple (Luke 2:41–50)*
Before discussing Luke's re-narration of Mark 6:1–6, however, we should note his placement of Jesus in the scribal-literate category earlier in Luke 2:41–50. This text narrates the twelve-year-old Jesus' activities in the

---

57. Celsus does not appear to be the only critic who seized on Jesus' craftsman status (see Tertullian, *Adv. Jud.* 10) or Christianity's uneducated status. The latter, in fact, was a sustained *topos* in pagan assessments of Christianity. See the summary in Keith, *Pericope*, 224–27.

58. Justin Martyr, *Dial.* 88; Ephraim Syrus, *Hymns on the Nativity* 6; Augustine, *Cons.* 2.42.90. Cf. *Inf. Gos. Thom.* 13:1–4; *Ps.-Mt.* 37. See also *Prot. Jas.* 9.1; *History of Joseph the Carpenter* 2, 15; Origen, *Cels.* 1.28, which refer to Joseph as a carpenter.

59. More generally, Augustine, *Cons.* 2.42.90, claims: "Now Mark, indeed, gives this passage in terms almost precisely identical with those which meet us in Matthew.... Luke, on the other hand, sets forth the same incident on a wider scale, and records a variety of other matters which took place in that connection" (*NPNF*[1]).

temple shortly after Passover and is the first Christian portrayal of Jesus as a member of scribal-literate culture. Luke does not attribute to Jesus scribal-literate skills in this pericope (as he will in Luke 4), but nevertheless rhetorically aligns Jesus with the scribal-literate class (the "teachers" [διδάσκαλοι] discussing the law in the temple[60]) in several manners. First, as demonstrated in the previous chapter, "ordinary" Jewish boys did not typically enjoy the company of rabbis. Luke begins this story by placing Jesus in an atypical position associated with the minority few who received scribal-literate education. Second, Luke describes Jesus not as a pupil of the teachers, but as an equal participant in the discussion. As Bovon observes, "Er sitzt nicht wie ein Jünger zu den Füßen dieser Lehrer.… Seine Position ist eher die des Lehrers."[61] Clearly, the teachers were amazed (2:47) at Jesus based on their assumptions that he was not their equal in light of his age, class, or both.[62] Nevertheless, these are assumptions that Jesus contradicts, with Luke describing Jesus as "in the midst of the teachers" (ἐν μέσῳ τῶν διδασκάλων), listening, questioning, answering, and demonstrating understanding (2:46–47).[63] To the

60. Fitzmyer, *Gospel according to Luke I–IX*, 442: "The Jewish *didaskaloi* in the Temple must be understood as the scribes or lawyers of Jesus' day."

61. François Bovon, *Das Evangelium nach Lukas (Lk 1,1–9,50)* (EKKNT 3/1; Zürich: Benziger, 1989), 157. Similarly, Joel B. Green, *The Gospel of Luke* (NICNT; Grand Rapids: Eerdmans, 1997), 155 n. 10: "Nothing in this text serves to portray Jesus as a *pupil*" (emphasis original). *Pace* those who claim Jesus appears as a pupil in the text (Fitzmyer, *Gospel of Luke I–IX*, 442; Norval Geldenhuys, *The Gospel of Luke* [NICNT; Grand Rapids: Eerdmans, 1951], 127; I. Howard Marshall, *The Gospel of Luke: A Commentary on the Greek Text* [NIGTC; Grand Rapids: Eerdmans, 1978], 127–28).

62. Luke is likely employing a *topos* here of a youth impressing elders in his understanding of the law (see also Josephus, *Vita* 9). It is not clear whether Luke wants readers to think the teachers are amazed at Jesus because they assume he is too young or because they assume he is not from the scribal class. (Cf. my earlier comments, unwittingly to both effects, in Keith, "Claim," 57–58; Keith, *Pericope*, 233–34.) In favor of the former interpretation is that Luke explicitly mentions Jesus' age. In favor of the latter interpretation is that Luke portrays Jesus as part of a family for whom such environments are not the norm; that is, they return after Passover, rather than remain in the temple to discuss the law. These are not mutually exclusive options, however. Luke possibly wants readers to think the teachers are surprised because twelve-year-olds do not normally participate in their discussions of the law, at least not to the degree that Jesus does, and certainly not twelve-year-old pilgrims from Nazareth.

63. In order to qualify Riesner, *Jesus*, 236, then, who says, "Lk 2,46f zeigt Jesus als jüdisches Kind, das durch Fragen, Zuhören und Antworten lernte," the text does not show that Jesus learned *through* the questioning, listening, and answering, but rather

teachers' surprise, and his parents' (2:48), Jesus appears to *belong* in the temple discussing the law with the scribal-literate authorities.

A third manner in which Luke rhetorically aligns Jesus with the scribal-literate teachers is his narration of the teachers' and Jesus' parents' respective reactions of surprise at his presence in the temple. According to Luke 2:47, as just noted, the teachers were amazed (ἐξίσταντο) at Jesus' understanding (συνέσει). According to Luke 2:48, Jesus' parents' also were "astonished" or "overwhelmed" (ἐξεπλάγησαν), with Luke here using ἐκπλήσσω in a manner similar to Mark 1:22 and 6:2. Whereas the teachers were amazed because they were those who heard (οἱ ἀκούντες) Jesus and recognized his understanding (2:47), however, Mary and Joseph are amazed upon seeing (ἰδόντες) him and lack understanding (2:48, 50). Luke uses contrasting characters' responses to Jesus in order to present the reader with two interpretive options: (1) Jesus is surprising because he belongs in the temple (the teachers' surprise); or (2) Jesus is surprising because he does not belong in the temple (Joseph's and Mary's surprise).[64] By stating that Jesus' parents "did not understand" (οὐ συνῆκαν) the explanation of his presence in the temple (2:50), Luke claims implicitly that the teachers' response is the correct reaction of surprise.[65] For Luke, Jesus' family did not understand, but Jesus did belong in the temple among the scribal-literate teachers. Thus, although these διδάσκαλοι encountering the child Jesus are surprised, Lukan characters encountering the adult Jesus do not hesitate to address him as a διδάσκαλος himself,[66] including scribal-literate teachers such as Pharisees, lawyers, Sadducees, and scribes.[67] Interestingly, then, whereas Mark and Matthew align themselves as narrators with characters in their Gospels who place Jesus outside scribal-literate culture, before readers even reach the Nazareth pericope Luke has already aligned himself with characters who place Jesus within scribal-literate culture.

---

that his questioning, listening, and answering implied that he had *already* learned, which is the source of surprise for the teachers.

64. Luke similarly uses characters' contrasting responses to Jesus in order to guide the reader's interpretation with the two criminals crucified with Jesus, one of whom chastises Jesus and the other of whom pronounces his innocence (Luke 23:39–43).

65. Luke's further statement that Mary "treasured all these things in her heart" (2:51) implies that, at some non-narrated or post-narrative point, Mary came to an understanding she did not have when Jesus was twelve.

66. Luke 8:49; 9:38; 12:13; 18:18; 20:21; cf. 21:7.

67. Pharisees—7:40; 19:39; lawyers—10:25; 11:45; Sadducees—20:28; scribes—20:39. Luke also applies Διδάσκαλε to John the Baptist (3:12), who is, in Luke's Gospel, the son of a literate priest (1:8–23, 63), although it is not entirely clear how literate Luke assumes Zechariah to be (see discussion of Luke 1:63 in Chapter 3).

1.4. *The Nazareth Synagogue (Luke 4:16–30)*

Luke 4:16–30 narrates the same account of Jesus' visit to the synagogue in his hometown as Mark 6:1–6 and Matt 13:54–58, although Luke explicitly names the town as Nazareth (4:16).[68] As in the prior accounts, Jesus is able to "amaze" his audience with his pedagogy. Luke uses θαυμάζω to describe this effect (4:22; cf. John 7:15), rather than ἐξίστημι, which he used in 2:47, or ἐκπλήσσω, which he used in 2:48 and Mark and Matthew use in their accounts of the Nazareth synagogue (Mark 6:2//Matt 13:54). As in Mark and Matthew, the crowd's initial amazement ends ultimately in rejection (Luke 4:28–29) and Jesus states that a prophet is not honored in his hometown (4:24). Furthermore, by claiming that Jesus taught in a synagogue rather than listened, Luke too claims Jesus occupied a synagogue position that was normally reserved for scribal-literate authorities. Here, however, the main similarities end.

In contrast to the narratives of Mark and Matthew, where Jesus places himself in the position of a scribal-literate teacher despite the fact that he is a τέκτων or the son of one, the Lukan Jesus stands on the scribal-literate side of a synagogue because he *is* a scribal-literate teacher.[69] At least five differences between Luke and Mark demonstrate that Luke's changes are neither "extremely slight"[70] nor the result of "minimal editorial work,"[71] but rather quite purposeful and result in moving Jesus

---

68. On my assumption of Markan Priority, see above n. 10. Marshall, *Gospel of Luke*, 179, notes the majority opinion: "For many scholars the present narrative is due to Lucan redaction of Mk. 6:1–6." Lane, *Gospel according to Mark*, 201 n. 2, represents the alternative view, claiming that they "describe two distinct visits to Nazareth."

69. Those overlooking the significance of Luke's claim that Jesus could read and handle manuscripts in terms of his placement of Jesus in the scribal-literate class include Darrell L. Bock, *Luke Vol. 1: 1:1–9:50* (BECNT; Grand Rapids: Baker, 1994); Bovon, *Evangelium nach Lukas*; Craig A. Evans, *Luke* (NIBCNT 3; Peabody: Hendrickson, 1990); Geldenhuys, *Gospel of Luke*; Fitzmyer, *Gospel of Luke I–IX*; Green, *Gospel of Luke*; Luke Timothy Johnson, *The Gospel of Luke* (SP 3; Collegeville: Liturgical, 1991); Marshall, *Gospel of Luke*; John Nolland, *Luke 1–9:20* (WBC 35a; Nashville: Thomas Nelson, 1989).

70. Lane, *Gospel according to Mark*, 201 n. 2. Similarly, citing the alteration of Jesus to υἱὸς τοῦ τέκτονος, Luz, *Matthew 8–20*, 301, says, "In comparison with Mark 6:1–6 the narrative is somewhat tightened and in its image of Christ slightly 'retouched,' but not essentially changed."

71. David B. Peabody with Lamar Cope and Allan J. McNicol, eds., *One Gospel from Two: Mark's Use of Matthew and Luke* (Harrisburg: Trinity, 2002), present a recent defense of the Griesbach/Two Gospel Hypothesis and view the alterations to Matthew's and Luke's Nazareth pericopae by Mark (under that theory) as "minimal editorial work" (150). Regardless of one's solution to the Synoptic Problem, the

from the manual-labor class to the scribal-literate class, thus moving him from a position of properly belonging with the craftsmen in a synagogue to a position of properly belonging with the scribal-literate teachers.

The first, and perhaps most readily obvious, difference is that the accusation that Jesus or his father is a τέκτων disappears in Luke's account. Luke's audience identifies Jesus simply as "Joseph's son" (Luke 4:22).[72]

Second, in addition to the difference between how the characters *within* the narratives identify Jesus, Luke's perspective as narrator differs from Mark's. Like Mark 1:22, Luke 4:32 associates Jesus' teaching abilities with his ἐξουσία. Luke does not, however, repeat Mark's explanation that this ἐξουσία made Jesus "not like the scribes." Thus, Luke's narrative of Jesus' activity in synagogues drops from Mark's accounts the crowds' identification of Jesus as a τέκτων and the narrator's statement that he was unlike the scribes, rhetorical moves that corroborate one another.

Third, Luke attributes directly to Jesus scribal-literate skills that status as a τέκτων would preclude. He claims that Jesus stood up "in order to read" (ἀναγνῶναι) in the synagogue and was handed a scroll (βιβλίον) of the prophet Isaiah. Upon receiving it, he "unrolled (ἀναπτύξας)[73] the scroll" (4:17), "found the place where it was written," and "rolled up (πτύξας) the scroll" (4:20) before handing it back and beginning to preach (with Luke narrating the content of the reading between Jesus' rolling and unrolling of the scroll). Despite the assumptions of most commentators, Luke does not actually claim that Jesus read from the scroll; only that he stood in order to do so.[74] Nevertheless, Luke's attri-

---

primary argument at present is that the differences between the crowds' reactions to Jesus in Matthew, Mark, and Luke are the result of more than "minimal editorial work."

72. John 6:42 contains a similar identification of Jesus ("Is not this Jesus, the son of Joseph, whose father and mother we know?"). See below, p. 147.

73. NA[27] prefers ἀναπτύξας, whose witnesses are ℵ D et al., over ἀνοίξας, whose witnesses include A and B, and which NA[25] preferred. Metzger et al. give the former reading a "B" rating, explaining that, although scribes "may have introduced ἀναπτύξας as a pedantic correlative to πτύξας in ver. 20, it is more probable that, being accustomed to books in codex (or leaf) form, they introduced the frequently used verb ἀνοίγειν, 'to open,' as an explanatory substitution for ἀναπτύσσειν (which occurs only here in the New Testament)" (Metzger, *A Textual Commentary*, 114). Roger Bagnall, "Jesus Reads a Book," *JTS* 51, no. 2 (2000): 577–88, however, argues that the referents of ἀναπτύσσω and ἀνοίγω are the exact opposite as those suggested by Metzger et al. Peter van Minnen, "Luke 4:17–20 and the Handling of Ancient Books," *JTS* 52, no. 2 (2001): 690, responds, arguing that, regardless of the reading chosen, codices are not in view.

74. Hugh S. Pyper, "Jesus Reads the Scriptures," in *Those Outside: Noncanonical Readings of the Canonical Gospels* (ed. George Aichele and Richard Walsh; London:

bution of scribal-literate skills to Jesus is clear. He insinuates that Jesus is capable of reading since he claims Jesus stood in order to do so. More important, though, Luke portrays Jesus as familiar with manuscripts. Jesus unrolls the text, locates a particular reading—that is, identifies the beginning and ending in an un- or lightly demarcated script—and rolls the text back up. As Chapter 3 observed, the ability to read publicly, identifying words quickly in script, was not a skill that most Palestinian Jews of the first century C.E. possessed. Even some of the highly textual Qumranites did not possess these skills, as 4Q266 indicates.

Fourth, whereas Mark's and Matthew's Jesus never again enters a synagogue after his rejection, Luke's Jesus is teaching again in a synagogue immediately in the next pericope (Luke 4:31, 33). In fact, his appearance in the Nazareth synagogue was per his custom (κατὰ τὸ εἰωθὸς αὐτῷ; 4:16), whereas the Markan Jesus' custom (ὡς εἰώθει) is to teach crowds as they gather around him (Mark 10:1). Luke's Jesus is, therefore, not a synagogue teacher who is unlike the scribes and whose hometown exposes him as an imposter to the position. Rather, he belongs in the position of a teacher in synagogues on the Sabbath and regularly occupies that position.[75]

Fifth, consistent with the aforementioned changes, Luke also alters the reasons for Jesus' rejection in his narration of the Nazareth synagogue event. Since Jesus is not a τέκτων or the son of one in Luke 4, but rather a legitimate scribal-literate synagogue teacher, the audience ultimately rejects Jesus for reasons unrelated to a class distinction between Jesus and synagogue teachers. In fact, in contrast to Mark's and Matthew's accounts, Luke claims that the initial response to Jesus' teaching, which prompts their patronymic identification of him, is positive: "All spoke well of him and were amazed at the gracious words that came from his mouth. They said, 'Is not this Joseph's son?'" (4:22). Correspondingly, their initial astonishment is due to the sheer power of the spirit evident in Jesus teaching (4:14–15, 18), not *that* he teaches, as in Mark and Matthew. Their eventual rejection, therefore, has a different catalyst in Luke's Gospel than in Mark's or Matthew's—Jesus' seeming pre-emptive attack that, despite their initial positive reception of him, anticipates rejection. After their "gracious words" (4:22), Jesus alters the tone of the situation by stating that he will not perform miracles because "no prophet is accepted in the prophet's hometown" (4:23), adding insult to

T&T Clark, 2005), 6. An exception is Bovon, *Evangelium nach Lukas*, 211: "Kunst-voll, spricht Lukas nicht aus, daß Jesus vorliest, sondern impliziert diesen Tat-bestand…"

   75. Luke 4:15, 16–30, 31–37, 44; 6:6; 13:10.

injury by citing Gentiles who received Elijah's miracles (4:25–27).[76] "When they heard this, all in the synagogue were filled with rage" (4:28).

In summary, Luke agrees with Mark and Matthew that: Jesus occupied the position of a scribal-literate teacher; the event took place in his hometown synagogue; the audience's initial response was astonishment/amazement; this event ultimately led to their rejection of Jesus; and this event led to his statement that a prophet is not honored in his hometown. Luke disagrees, however, over: whether Jesus was a manual laborer or scribal-literate teacher (Luke claims the latter); whether Jesus occupied that pedagogical position surreptitiously (Luke claims he does not, as a handler of manuscripts and reader); whether the initial response of astonishment/amazement was positive (Luke claims it was); whether the ultimate reason for their rejection was Jesus' class or his statements (Luke claims Jesus' statements prompted it); and whether Jesus returned to a synagogue (Luke claims he did, and immediately). These differences between Mark 6:1–6 and Luke 4:16–30 share a common thread that eliminates the identification of Jesus as a member of the manual-labor class and describes him as a member of the scribal-educated class. Already in the first century, Luke was going further than receptions of Mark 6:3 in the first century (Matt 13:55), third century ($\mathfrak{P}^{45}$, Origen), or even sixth century (Palestinian Syriac) in denying the applicability of τέκτων to Jesus.

1.5. *Summary of the Synoptic Debate over Jesus as a Synagogue Teacher*

Chapter 1 argued that scholarly conceptions of Jesus as a teacher play a determinative role in larger reconstructions of the historical Jesus. The above discussion, however, reveals that whether Jesus was a teacher with scribal literacy was already a heated topic of discussion *in the first century*. Further corroborating the previous chapter's description of scribal culture in the Second Temple period, this debate over Jesus demonstrates the divide between scribal literacy and craftsman's literacy, and thus scribal-literate teachers and craftsmen. The Synoptic authors (and characters) disagree as to which one of those two statuses properly applies to Jesus, but their very disagreement serves to confirm that the accusation of "craftsman" is simultaneously a denial of scribal literacy; such that if one wishes to affirm scribal literacy, the accusation of craftsman must be removed.

---

76.   Thus, Jesus' lack of performance of miracles is due to anticipated rejection in Luke, whereas he cannot perform miracles in Mark 6:6//Matt 13:55 because of their immediate rejection. On the Elijianic typology in this passage, see John C. Poirier, "Jesus as an Elijianic Figure in Luke 4:16–30," *CBQ* 71 (2009): 349–63; Rodríguez, *Structuring*, 162–73.

The Synoptic debate also reveals an early Christian social memory that is corporately confused or, better, in a state of disagreement on the matter of Jesus' scribal-literate status. This state of confusion/disagreement persisted into the sixth century when the Palestinian Syriac scribes contributed to it by eliminating the reference to Jesus as τέκτων in Mark 6:3. No doubt aiding the persistence of this debate was the rise of the fourfold canon ca. 150 C.E.,[77] which ensured that the Church's authoritative corpus preserved the tension between these two streams of Jesus-memory.

The temptation of Jesus scholars may be to pronounce, a priori or through argumentation, one of these conflicting streams of Jesus-memory as authentic and the other as inauthentic. Indeed, Chapter 1 showed that this has been the typical approach. Between Luke's thorough recasting of Jesus' class status and the fact that there is no manuscript evidence for the precise text that Luke claims Jesus read (which is a combination of quotations from Isa 61:1–2 and 58:6),[78] in addition to widespread convictions of Markan Priority, it is no surprise that Luke often loses the historicity battle on these terms.[79] As argued in Chapter 2, however, such judgments fail to note the limited contribution to discussions of historicity that redaction criticism can make. To note that Luke has a theological agenda that overtakes Mark's interpretation is not to demonstrate that Luke is therefore ahistorical, as if Mark is a base line for historicity who is not dependent upon, and molding to his own purposes, prior interpretations. Rodríguez thus appropriately asks, "If Luke 4:14–30 is redaction, whence comes Luke's redactional impulse?"[80] Answering this question will be the task of Chapter 5. For present purposes, it suffices to note that, already in the first century, Christians conceptualized Jesus as both a scribal-illiterate and scribal-literate teacher.

77. Graham N. Stanton, *Jesus and Gospel* (Cambridge: Cambridge University Press, 2004), 85.

78. See Evans, *Luke*, 73–74; Rodríguez, *Structuring*, 160. John C. Poirier, "The Roll, the Codex, the Wax Tablet, and the Synoptic Problem," unpublished paper, n. 15, suggests Luke's Isaianic citation comes from a testimony book.

79. Boomershine, "Jesus," 21–22; Crossan, *Birth*, 235. Consider also Richard A. Horsley, "The Origins of the Hebrew Scriptures in Imperial Relations," in *Orality, Literacy, and Colonialism in Antiquity* (ed. Jonathan A. Draper; SemeiaSt 47; Atlanta: Society of Biblical Literature, 2004), 107, who, based on low literacy rates in antiquity, confesses surprise at scholars who "still take at face value Luke's portrayal (4:16–20) of Jesus in the Nazareth synagogue reading from the scroll of the prophet Isaiah."

80. Rodríguez, *Structuring*, 141. Rodríguez asks this question in reference to Luke's account of the Nazareth synagogue as a whole, not in reference specifically to his portrayal of a scribal-literate Jesus, to which it is nonetheless equally applicable.

2. *Jesus' Scribal-Literate Status in the Gospel of John*

The Gospel of John provides further evidence that Jesus' scribal-literate status was a first-century topic of discussion. Indeed, as mentioned previously,[81] the Bread of Life discourse contains an identification of Jesus as "Joseph's son" (6:42) by the Capernaum synagogue audience (6:59) that looks suspiciously like Luke's modification of Mark 6:3 at Luke 4:22.[82] By setting this event in a synagogue, John agrees with the Synoptic authors that Jesus sometimes occupied a synagogue pedagogical position associated with scribal literacy. The controversy that prompts the patronymic identification of him in John, however, is not *that* he teaches in a synagogue, as in Mark and Matthew (this is actually the only occasion in John's narrative that Jesus teaches in a synagogue [cf. 18:20]) but rather the content of his teaching, particularly his claim to have come from heaven (6:42).

Instead, the impetus for questioning Jesus' scribal-literate status in John's Gospel is his teaching in the temple during the Feast of Tabernacles. The debate over Jesus' scribal literacy rises to the surface of the narrative directly in John 7:15 and continues to play a role in characters' assessment of Jesus in 7:45–52. I here also suggest that the insertion of the *Pericope Adulterae* immediately after John 7:52 is best understood as an attempt to contribute to this debate, and thus is part of John 7's reception-history. This section draws upon previous research, where I have argued at length for the key role of scribal literacy/authority in these texts.[83]

---

81. See n. 72, above.

82. If John assumes his readers' knowledge of Mark (as argues Richard Bauckham, "John for Readers of Mark," in Bauckham, ed., *Gospels for All Christians*, 147–71), it is interesting that John 6:42 mirrors Luke 4:22's "Joseph's son" rather than Mark 6:3's "craftsman" or even Matt 13:55's "son of the craftsman," and that John places this event in the Capernaum synagogue (cf. Mark 1:21–28) rather than the Nazareth synagogue, as do each of the Synoptic Gospels. Edwyn Clement Hoskyns, *The Fourth Gospel* (ed. Frances Noel Davey; 2d rev. ed.; London: Faber & Faber, 1947), 296, posits John's dependence upon Luke: "The paternity of Jesus is as well known to the Jews in the synagogue at Capernaum as it is to the crowd in the synagogue at Nazareth (Luke iv. 22, cf. Mark vi. 3; Matt. xiii. 55)." On the *status quaestionis* of the relationship between John and the Synoptics, see Mark Matson, "Current Approaches to the Priority of John," *SCJ* 7, no. 1 (2004): 73–100; and, earlier, D. Moody Smith, *John among the Gospels: The Relationship in Twentieth-Century Research* (Minneapolis: Fortress, 1992).

83. Keith, "Claim," 50–54; Keith, "Performance," 50–52; Keith, *Pericope*, 141–202, and throughout.

2.1. *Did Jesus Know Letters? (John 7:15)*
According to John 7:14, in the middle of the Feast of Tabernacles, "Jesus went up into the temple and began to teach (ἐδίδασκεν)." Like the Markan/Matthean account(s) of Jesus in the synagogue, the very act of beginning to teach warrants a response, as John too uses the inceptive imperfect ἐδίδασκεν (cf. Matt 13:54). Also similar, Jesus' audience, which here consists of "the Jews," was amazed, with John employing θαυμάζω in John 7:15 (cf. Luke 4:22).

More important for present purposes is the Jews' verbal response to Jesus' teaching activity in John 7:15: "How does this man have such learning, when he has never been taught?" The phrase in this verse that the NRSV translates as "have such learning" is literally "know letters" (γράμματα οἶδεν). John 7:15's unique status as the only location in all Jesus tradition where characters within a narrative explicitly discuss Jesus' literacy is remarkably overlooked.[84] This is not to suggest that scholars ignore the passage altogether, however. The Jews' questioning of Jesus' literacy has been a steady source of confusion. As Chapter 1 presented, scholars have disagreed over whether the passage indicates a literate or illiterate Jesus, whether it refers to reading or writing skills, and whether this indication (whatever it may be) is an accurate reflection of the historical Jesus.[85] It is thus necessary to clarify the precise claim of John 7:15.

As to the phrase itself, the previous chapter demonstrated that, in Jewish tradition, γράμματα οἶδεν can refer to reading or writing abilities and various levels of each, such as the ability to read the law reflected in *T. Levi* 13:2 or the signature literacy that Babatha lacks in *P. Yadin* 15.35–36; 16.35; 22.34. The context of John 7:15 removes any lingering ambiguity with the phrase, however. The narrative amply affirms the majority opinion that the γράμματα under question are those of the Mosaic Law; for Jesus goes on to discuss Moses and the law in the immediate subsequent context (7:19–24).[86] Insofar as Jewish literate education at the time of Jesus seems to have consisted of reading ability, not writing,[87] one can assume that the Jews' question concerns Jesus' ability to read Torah.

---

84. An exception is Kelber, *Oral*, 18.
85. See also the brief history of research in Keith, "Claim," 48–54.
86. Hoskyns, *Fourth Gospel*, 314: "If these words stood by themselves, they would mean simply that Jesus was illiterate, unable to read and write, since the Greek adjective *without letters* meant precisely this… But in its context, and especially in reference to v. 46, *letters* means the writings of Moses" (emphases original).
87. See Chapter 3.

More important, however, is that questioning Jesus' ability to read Torah is to question Jesus' *scribal* literacy.[88]

It is more important for interpreters to focus upon the fact that the Jews question Jesus' scribal literacy in general, rather than getting tangled up on whether it refers to reading or writing, because John narrates neither reading skills for Jesus (as does Luke 4:16–17, 20) nor writing skills (as does the *Pericope Adulterae* at John 8:6, 8; see below).[89] In other words, despite the fact that the Jews explicitly question Jesus' scribal-literate education, the impetus for their question is not Jesus' (lack of) demonstration of those skills. Rather, the catalyst for their query about Jesus' scribal literacy is, according to John, Jesus' teaching (7:14, 16). John 7:14–15 thus joins Mark 6:3//Matt 13:55 in claiming that Jesus' audiences drew lines of connection between his pedagogical activity and his scribal-literate status. Mark and Matthew both engage in such assessment as narrators as well, telling their readers that Jesus' teaching was "not like the scribes" (Mark 1:22//Matt 7:29).

Unlike Mark 1:22//Matt 7:29 and Mark 6:3//Matt 13:55, however, which *contrast* Jesus' teaching with scribal-literate authorities (again, Jesus is "not like the scribes," a τέκτων or his son), the Jews' response in John 7:15 both *compares* and *contrasts* Jesus to scribal-literate authorities. Each of the respective clauses of the Jews' response, "How does this man know letters, since he has never been taught?," carries an important assumption. The main clause ("How does this man know letters?....") assumes, based on Jesus' teaching activity, that he "knows letters," that he is a scribal-literate teacher who can access Torah for himself. The dependent clause ("...since he has never been taught") assumes, based, in context, on his status as a Galilean (see below), that he is not a scribal-literate teacher because he has not been the recipient of a scribal education.[90] The Johannine Jesus is a walking paradox for the Jews: *he teaches*

---

88. Consider Bultmann's interpretation of their reaction: "How can Jesus appeal to the Scriptures! He has not made a proper study of them! He does not belong to the guild of Scribes" (Rudolf Bultmann, *The Gospel of John: A Commentary* [trans. G. R. Beasley-Murray, R. W. N. Hoare, and J. K. Riches; Philadelphia: Westminster, 1971], 273). Similarly, Jürgen Becker, *Das Evangelium nach Johannes, Kapitel 1–10* (ÖTBK 4/1; Würzberg: Echter, 1979), 258.

89. *Pace* Thomas J. Kraus, "John 7:15B: 'Knowing Letters' and (Il)literacy," in *Ad fontes*, 175, who claims Jesus "reads fluently" in John 7:15.

90. Arguments that John 7:15 indicates that Jesus could be literate but had not received a "higher education" (see Chapter 1) fall on the concessive participial phrase μὴ μεμαθηκώς. The only literacy in view in John 7:15 is the type that makes one an authoritative interpreter of the Mosaic Law, and this is a literacy that the Jews' μὴ μεμαθηκώς denies to Jesus. As Jerome H. Neyrey, "The Trials (Forensic) and

as a scribal-literate person even though they know he is not. (This interpretation of the Jews' response makes clear why scholars have argued that
John 7:15 indicates a literate Jesus and that it indicates an illiterate Jesus.
Their response contains within it evidence to support both interpretations to an extent.)

John 7:15 adds a further layer to the confused corporate early Christian
memory concerning Jesus' scribal-literate status by simultaneously
including both sides of the debate. The response of the Jews in John 7:15
is similar to Luke 4:16–30 insofar as it claims Jesus teaches as a scribal-
literate person teaches and similar to the synagogue crowd's assessment
in Mark 6:3 (cf. Matt 13:55) insofar as it assumes Jesus is not a member of
the scribal-educated class. It is dissimilar, however, to the narrators'
statements in Mark 1:22//Matt 7:29, which claim that Jesus does not
teach like scribal-literate teachers.

The ultimate claim of John 7:15, however, depends upon the narrator's
perspective, not the characters'. Unlike Mark and Matthew, whose claims
that Jesus was not like the scribes support their characters' placement of
him in the craftsman class, and unlike Luke as well, who explicitly attributes to Jesus scribal literacy, John offers no authoritative commentary on
whether the assumptions of the Jews in their statement are correct. His
authoritative statement on Jesus' scribal-literate status is neither that he
held it nor that he did not, but rather that *Jesus was the type of teacher
who was able to confuse his audience concerning his scribal-literate status.*[91]

2.2. Galileans Who Know Not the Law (John 7:45–52)[92]

The issue of scribal literacy appears again in 7:45–52, giving further
explanation for the Jews' assumption in John 7:15 that Jesus was not the
recipient of a scribal-literate education. The Pharisees send "temple
police" to arrest Jesus in 7:32 due to the public unrest his teaching is
causing. They return empty-handed in 7:45, however, and must answer
for their lack of action. When they attest to Jesus' teaching prowess in
7:46, their superiors offer a quick rebuke, in which they distinguish
between the uneducated gullible crowd and the educated teachers of the
law: "Surely you have not been deceived too, have you? Has any one of

---

Tribulations (Honor Challenges) of Jesus: John 7 in Social Science Perspective," *BTB*
26 (1996): 111, states: "This charge reasons that Jesus cannot know the Law and so
teach correctly, for he has no formal education" (emphasis removed).

91. So far as I am aware, I was the first to suggest this interpretation of John 7:15
in Keith, "Claim," 50–54.

92. The following two paragraphs are drawn from ibid., 53–54, with slight
modifications (© 2010 Cambridge University Press; used with permission).

the authorities or of the Pharisees believed in him? But this crowd, *which does not know the law*—they are accursed" (John 7:47–49; emphasis added). That is, the crowd can be understood, or perhaps pitied, for having been duped by Jesus and questioning if he might be the Messiah (7:40–43). They may even have a limited knowledge of the Scriptures, as 7:42 suggests. But compared to the "chief priests and Pharisees" in 7:45, they cannot be said to "know the law" (7:49) at all. The Jewish leadership, however, knows the law, and thus knows better.

Further confirming this dividing line and explaining the assumptions of the Jews of John 7:15 about Jesus is the immediate chastisement of Nicodemus. Ironically questioning his comrades' knowledge of Torah, he implies the illegality of their pre-emptive (negative) judgment of Jesus' messianic/prophetic status: "Our law does not judge people without first giving them a hearing to find out what they are doing, does it?" (7:51). They reply, "Surely you are not also from Galilee, are you? *Search* and you will see that no prophet is to arise from Galilee" (7:52; emphasis added).[93] The Pharisees' command, "search," is key to understanding their complaint. Based on his ability to search the holy text, an ability apparently not shared by the accursed crowd of Galileans, Nicodemus should know that Jesus could not be a/the prophet.[94] The common thread between the Jewish leadership's chastisement of the temple police and their chastisement of Nicodemus is their insistence that those who know Torah, who can search it for themselves—that is, the Jewish leadership— should carry the official opinion with regards to Jesus' identity. Stated otherwise, authoritative opinion and pronouncement are the prerogatives of those who fall on the scribal-literate side of the dividing line. The temple police of 7:45 are chastised for suggesting that Jesus—a Galilean— fell too close to the Jewish leadership's side of that line. Jesus' teaching earlier produced the same confusion for the Jews of 7:15 who, as a result, ask how he "knows letters." Frustrating the attempts of the Jewish leadership to discount Jesus entirely in John 7, then, according to the Johannine narrator, is that Jesus carries himself as one of their own, despite their conviction that he—again, a Galilean—is like the crowd who "does not know the law."[95]

93. On the possibility of the Jews' statement here being an example of Johannine irony, since Jonah was from Galilee, see Keener, *Gospel of John*, 1:734–35.

94. NA[27] follows the majority of witnesses with the indefinite reading προφήτης; 𝔓[66] offers the definite reading ὁ προφήτης.

95. Similarly, Hoskyns, *Fourth Gospel*, 314: "To the Jewish authorities Jesus is one of the ignorant crowd which is accursed and *knoweth not the law* (vii. 49), and His claim to interpret it in public is a blasphemous impertinence" (emphasis original).

2.3. *Jesus Began to Write (John 8:6, 8 in the* Pericope Adulterae*)*[96]
Like the events in John 7 and John's Gospel as a whole, the *Pericope Adulterae* turns on the issues of the Mosaic Law, who has proper authority concerning it, and Jesus' identity.[97] The scribes and the Pharisees attempt to trap Jesus by having him pronounce on the prescribed Mosaic punishment of a woman who committed a Decalogue-prohibited sin (adultery) in John 8:4–5. Within this context, the *Pericope Adulterae* contains, in John 8:6, 8, the claim that Jesus was grapho-literate, able to write. In response to the scribes and Pharisees' questions, Jesus twice bent down and "began to write," with the narrator describing the actions with καταγράφω in 8:6 and γράφω in 8:8.[98] In Jesus' and the early Church's context(s), this is a substantial claim. Even among the minority literate, fewer could write than could read.

Scholars have been reticent to see John 8:6, 8 as a claim for Jesus' literacy, however,[99] so much so that John 8:6, 8 plays virtually no role in the history of research on Jesus' literacy (see Chapter 1). Scholars' hesitance has primarily centered on the meaning of καταγράφω, which is a *hapax legomenon* in the New Testament and had not received a full lexical study until my 2009 monograph. In that study, I demonstrate that, although the ancient record includes usages of the verb that do not reference alphabetic writing,[100] synchronic usages of the verb in Hellenistic texts, Oxyrhynchus papyri, and the LXX overwhelmingly indicate that its

96. I propose a third-century insertion date for the *Pericope Adulterae* in Keith, *Pericope*, 249–56.

97. On the theme of Moses in the Gospel of John, see T. Francis Glasson, *Moses in the Fourth Gospel* (SBT 40; London: SCM, 1963); Stan Harstine, *Moses as a Character in the Fourth Gospel: A Study of Ancient Reading Techniques* (JSNTSup 229; Sheffield: Sheffield Academic, 2002); Wayne A. Meeks, *The Prophet-King: Moses Traditions and the Johannine Christology* (NovTSup 14; Leiden: Brill, 1967).

98. On the variants in, for example, D (καταγράφω in 8:6 and 8:8) or *f*[13] (most MSS with γράφω in 8:6, 8), see Keith, *Pericope*, 168–69, where I agree with NA[27] and Hermann Freiherr von Soden, *Die Schriften des Neuen Testaments in ihrer ältesten erreichbaren Textgestalt auf Grund ihrer Textgeschichte* (2 vols.; Göttingen: Vandenhoeck & Ruprecht, 1911–19), 1:1:523, 2:427, in preferring the majority reading.

99. Bernard, *Gospel according to St. John*, 2:719; Boomershine, "Jesus," 22; Dunn, *Jesus*, 314 n. 284; Evans, "Context," 16; Foster, "Educating," 19–21; Derek Krueger, *Writing and Holiness: The Practice of Authorship in the Early Christian East* (Philadelphia: University of Pennsylvania Press, 2005), 7; Meier, *Marginal Jew*, 1:268; Millard, *Reading*, 178; Lionel R. M. Strachan, trans., *Light from the Ancient East* by Adolf Deissmann (rev. ed.; London: Hodder & Stoughton, 1927), 245 n. 3; Lee Martin McDonald and James A. Sanders, "Introduction," in *The Canon Debate* (ed. Lee Martin McDonald and James A. Sanders; Peabody: Hendrickson, 2002), 9 n. 20.

100. For example, Josephus, *J. W.* 5.214; Pausanias, *Descr.* 1.28.2; or Herodotus, *Hist.* 3.108.4, who uses it in reference to what a lion cub does to its mother's uterus!

primary referent was alphabetized writing.[101] In light of the Mosaic themes in the *Pericope Adulterae*, the LXX is the most important background for καταγράφω. Of its twelve occurrences there,[102] eight make explicit the alphabetized nature of the writing, with three stating that it occurs in a book (Exod 17:14; 1 Chr 9:1; 2 Chr 20:34) and two reproducing the written document in the body of the text (1 Esd 2:12; 1 Macc 14:26). Three more employ the verb to reference writing metaphorically or to reference the symbolic significance of "that which is written" (Num 11:26; Job 13:26; Sir 48:10[103]). The only clearly non-literary LXX usage is the appearance of καταγράφω as a variant at Ezek 8:10 in a ninth-/tenth-century witness to Symmachus's second-century C.E. revision of the LXX.[104] In addition, when καταγράφω and γράφω occur together (Exod 32:15; 2 Chr 20:34; 1 Macc 14:18/14:26), they have no clearly differentiated meanings. The synonymous meanings are indicated by the fact that they often represent the same action (2 Chr 20:34[105]) or translate the same Hebrew word, כתב ("to write"; Exodus 32:15; 1 Macc 14:18/14:26), and a manuscript tradition that interchanges the two verbs.[106] Against this background, and additionally since γράφω means alphabetized writing in all 190 of its occurrences in the New Testament outside John 8:8,[107] the most natural meaning for καταγράφω in John 8:6 is the same as γράφω in 8:8—both are claims that Jesus wrote.

I further propose that this unique claim in canonical and noncanonical Gospel tradition guided the insertion of the *Pericope Adulterae* into

---

101.   Keith, *Pericope*, 27–49.

102.   Exod 17:14; 32:15; Num 11:26; 1 Chr 9:1; 2 Chr 20:34; 1 Esd 2:12; Job 13:26; Sir 48:10; Hos 8:12; 1 Macc 9:22; 14:26 (ET 14:27). The twelfth occurrence of καταγράφω in the LXX is as a variant in Ezek 8:10 in a ninth-/tenth-century witness of Symmachus' second-century C.E. LXX (MS 86 [Vatican 549, Codex Barberinus]).

103.   *Pace* Foster, "Educating," 21, who claims Sir 48:10 "gives little indication to decide whether καταγράφω refers, in this context, to writing using some form of alphabet, *or* is just a loose metaphor for an event that cannot be changed" (emphasis mine). The italicized "or" reveals a false choice by Foster (either a reference to writing *or* a metaphor) that misunderstands the nature of metaphors, and thus that Sir 48:10 is a both/and—a metaphor *of* writing, not a metaphor *instead of* writing or vice versa. See further Keith, *Pericope*, 45.

104.   MS 86 (Vatican 549, Codex Barberinus); noted by Joseph Ziegler, ed., *Ezechiel* (LXXG 16.1; Göttingen: Vandenhoeck & Ruprecht, 1952), 119; HRCS, 730.

105.   In 2 Chr 20:34 LXX, καταγράφω and γράφω appear synonymously, but translate different Hebrew words (עלה and כתב, respectively).

106.   For example, at Exod 32:15, B (fourth century C.E.) attests καταγράφω, then γράφω, while A and F (both fifth century C.E.) attest γράφω at both locations. Similarly, MS 126 (1475 C.E.) exchanges γράφω for καταγράφω at Exod 17:14.

107.   Keith, *Pericope*, 49–52.

John's Gospel at John 7:53–8:11, and thus that the insertion of the passage is part of the reception-history of John 7:15–52. The interpolator uses this image of a grapho-literate Jesus in order to respond to the Jews who question Jesus' scribal literacy in John 7:15 and the Jewish leaders who question whether Galileans who cannot "search" the law can truly "know" the law in 7:45–52.[108] If this interpretation is plausible, then it is no surprise that the scribes, the very practitioners of grapho-literacy in Second Temple Judaism, appear alongside the Pharisees in the same pericope that portrays Jesus' own grapho-literacy (and appear nowhere else in John's Gospel).[109]

There is, however, an additional layer to the narrator's usage of καταγράφω in 8:6 and γράφω in 8:8. Although the verbs occur together in other LXX passages, the only passage in which they occur in the same syntactical order, with the compound verb first and the simple verb second, is Exod 32:15.[110] Translated literally, Exod 32:15 reads:

> And turning back, Moses went down from the mountain, and the two tablets of testimony were in his hands, stone tablets having been written (καταγεγραμμέναι) on both of their sides, from here and from here they had been written (γεγραμμέναι).[111]

108.   That the interpolator was responding to the entire complex of events from 7:15 to 7:52 is my own claim. After arriving at this conclusion, however, I discovered that Edgar J. Goodspeed had already suggested the interpolator was responding to 7:15 in particular in his *A History of Early Christian Literature* (Chicago: University of Chicago Press, 1942), 70, and *Problems of New Testament Translation* (Chicago: University of Chicago Press, 1945), 108.

109.   This interpretation thus assumes that the scribes in John 8:5 represent more than scribal-educated Torah interpreters generally (as suggested for their appearance in Mark 1:22//Matt 7:29 in n. 11, above) and instead represent the *most* educated of scribal-literate Torah authorities.

110.   I came to the conclusion that John 8:6, 8 is an allusion to Exod 32:15 independently of Josep Rius-Camps, "Origen Lucano de la Perícopa de la Mujer Adúltera (Jn 7,53–8,11)," *Filología Neotestamentaria* 6 (1993): 171–2, who suggests this connection as well. In this article, Rius-Camps argues that the *Pericope Adulterae* was originally in Luke. Later, in Josep Rius-Camps, "The Pericope of the Adulteress Reconsidered: The Nomadic Misfortunes of a Bold Pericope," *NTS* 53, no. 3 (2007): 379–405, he amends this argument to suggest that the story was instead originally in Mark. Neither of these arguments is persuasive since there is no evidence that early Christians encountered the *Pericope Adulterae* in a canonical Gospel in any location other than John 7:53–8:11 until the ninth/tenth century C.E. See Chris Keith, "The Initial Location of the *Pericope Adulterae* in Fourfold Tradition," *NovT* 51 (2009): 209–31.

111.   The two Greek participles translate the same underlying Hebrew participle, כְּתֻבִים.

This passage refers to God's authorship of the Decalogue and expresses that authorship as a differentiation between God as the *author* of the law and Moses as the *deliverer* of the law. Just prior, Exod 31:18 LXX had claimed the first stone tablets were "written with the finger (τῷ δακτύλῳ) of God." Exodus 32:16 goes on to identify God's role as author of the first tablets with similarly explicit language: "And the tablets were the work of God, and the writing is the writing of God." Although the Torah else-where claims the law came to the Israelites "by the hand of Moses" (ἐν χειρὶ Μωυσῆ),[112] Exod 31:18 and 32:15–16 quite explicitly reject that notion for the original tablets.[113] According to these texts, Moses did not write the Decalogue, God himself did.

Therefore, when the narrator describes Jesus' response to the challenge of the scribes and Pharisees for Jesus to oppose Moses (note the emphatic σύ in 8:5), he does so with vocabulary and syntax that he borrows from a LXX passage that describes God, not Moses, as the author of the law and thus its ultimate authority. For the narrator, Jesus' lack of condemnation of the woman caught committing a Decalogue sin in the *Pericope Adulterae* derives from the same scribal authority that originally authored the Decalogue. The lexical connections between John 8:6, 8 and the Decalogue narrative add further weight to suggestions by previous scholars of a Mosaic background based on the fact that Jesus uses his finger in 8:6 (τῷ δακτύλῳ), as does God in his authorship of the Deca-logue in Exod 31:18//Deut 9:10.[114]

As part of the reception-history of John 7:15–52 specifically and the Gospel of John generally, the insertion of the *Pericope Adulterae* at John 7:53–8:11 indicates that the interpolator too read John 7:15–52 as a narrative in which Jesus' scribal-literate status is under question. He entered that debate by inserting a pericope that claims not only that Jesus was as scribal-literate as the most educated of his interlocutors, but was indeed the scribal-literate Torah authority *par excellence*, whose scribal authority in matters of the Mosaic Law exceeds that of Moses himself.[115]

2.4. *Summary of Jesus' Scribal-Literate Status in the Gospel of John*
Whereas the Synoptic Gospels reveal a debate over Jesus' scribal-literate status between sources, the Gospel of John places such debate within his

112.   Lev 26:46; Num 4:37, 41, 45, 49; 9:23; 10:13; 15:23; 36:13; cf. Bar 2:28.
113.   Exod 34:27–28 claims Moses served as God's amanuensis for the writing on the second set of tablets.
114.   This interpretation of John 8:6, 8 goes back at least to Ambrose, *Epistle* 68. For a full listing of its supporters, see Keith, *Pericope*, 12–13.
115.   Similarly, John 6:32 distinguishes between God's role and Moses' role in the giving of the manna, paralleling Jesus with God over Moses.

life. According to John 7:15, Jesus was capable of inspiring assumptions
that he was not educated (like the rest of Galileans), but was also capable
of forcing his contemporaries to reassess those assumptions by teaching
as if he had been educated. The subsequent narrative context, and particularly John 7:45–52, provides background to these assumptions by portraying Pharisees who explicitly cite the ability to search the law (7:52) as
a difference between themselves and the gullible crowd that does not
know the law (7:45). Later, a scribe or scribal school entered into the
Johannine debate by inserting the *Pericope Adulterae* immediately after
the Pharisees' chiding of Nicodemus to "search" the law. With John 8:6,
8, the interpolator claims that Jesus is not only scribal-literate, but
grapho-literate; and not only grapho-literate, but divinely so.

3. *The Predominance of the Scribal-Literate Jesus*

Eventually, the stream of Jesus-memory in which Jesus appears as a
legitimate scribal-literate teacher predominated over the stream in which
he is denied scribal literacy. The craftsman Jesus did not, of course, dis-
appear. If nothing else, manuscripts of Mark's Gospel preserved the
charge of the synagogue audience in Mark 6:3, to which scribes continued
to respond by altering the text, as manuscripts from the third to sixth
centuries indicate. In addition, Celsus appropriates this portrayal of Jesus
in the late second century, as does Origen in his subsequent response.
The image of Jesus as a scribal-literate teacher, however, became more
prominent, spreading into (what would become) orthodox, apocryphal,
and heretical Christian tradition. The following sources place Jesus into
the scribal-literate category by portraying him as a writer/dictator of
epistles, an author of gospel tradition, or other scribal-literate terms. The
present claim is not that these sources (attempt to) represent the historical Jesus in the same manner as first-century Gospels, but that they
reveal the eventual trajectory of a corporate Jesus-memory that emerged
initially in the first century.

3.1. *The Epistolary Jesus*

Portrayals of an "epistolary Jesus" who authors letters (whether through
dictation or his own handwriting) abound in early Christianity. Such
images place Jesus in the educated elite by portraying him as someone who can write himself or is important enough to have someone else
write for him.[116] In the late first century, the Apocalypse portrays the

---

116.   As noted in the previous chapter, the ability (financially, educationally, etc.)
to dictate to a scribe was most typically associated with the educated elite.

resurrected Jesus as dictating the seven letters to the seven churches (Rev 1–3) to John, who serves as amanuensis.[117] The incipit of the *Gospel of Thomas* (late first or second century)[118] similarly portrays Jesus dictating its contents to Thomas the amanuensis: "These are the secret sayings which the living Jesus spoke and which Didymos Judas Thomas wrote down."[119]

The Abgar Legend, in which Jesus sends a letter to King Abgar of Edessa, appears in Eusebius's *Ecclesiastical History* (ca. 325 C.E.) and is the center of the early fifth-century Syriac *Doctrina Addai*.[120] Eusebius's Greek claims the letter is "by Jesus through the courier (lit. 'fast-runner')

---

117.   I discuss this example in Keith, *Pericope*, 236, and note on p. 241 that J. K. Elliott, *The Apocryphal Jesus: Legends of the Early Church* (Oxford: Oxford University Press, 1996), 64, overlooks it (and the *Narrative of Joseph of Arimathea*) when he claims that the Abgar Legend "represents the only example of a text written in Jesus' name." Subsequently, in a review of my study, Elliott claims, "Keith…tells us that Jesus wrote the letters to the seven churches in Revelation, although he cannot provide us with the chapter and verse for this" (J. K. Elliott, review of Chris Keith, *The* Pericope Adulterae, *the Gospel of John, and the Literacy of Jesus, JTS* 61, no. 1 [2010]: 294). In response, I can only note that I do not provide chapter and verse for that claim because I nowhere make the claim that "Jesus wrote the letters." In fact, I claim the exact opposite: "This section of the text presents Jesus as the source of the seven letters to the seven churches in the opening of the Apocalypse, *but nowhere claims that Jesus writes the letters himself. Jesus instead authors the letters to the churches through the amanuensis John*" (Keith, *Pericope*, 236; emphasis added).

118.   On the date of the *Gospel of Thomas*, see Uwe-Karsten Plisch, *The Gospel of Thomas: Original Text with Commentary* (trans. Gesine Schenke Robinson; Stuttgart: Deutsche Bibelgesellschaft, 2008), 15–16.

119.   *Gos. Thom.* incipit (Lambdin). Cf. also *Ap. Jas.* 1:1–19.

120.   Eusebius, *Hist. eccl.* 1.13.10. For text and English translation of the *Doctrina Addai*, see George Howard, trans., *The Teaching of Addai* (SBLTT 16/ECLS 4; Chico: Scholars, 1981). (W. Cureton, *Ancient Syriac Documents* [Eugene: Wipf & Stock, 1864], 6–23, provided an earlier English translation.) Howard, "Introduction," in *Teaching*, vii, claims *Doctrina Addai* is "usually dated c. AD 400"; similarly, Cureton, *Ancient*, 147. See also H. J. W. Drijvers, "The Abgar Legend," in *New Testament Apocrypha* (ed. Wilhelm Schneemelcher; trans. R. McL. Wilson; 2 vols.; rev. ed.; Louisville: Westminster John Knox, 1991), 1:493. Kevin P. Sullivan and T. G. Wilfong, "The Reply of Jesus to King Abgar: A Coptic New Testament Apocryphon Reconsidered (P. Mich. Inv. 6213)," *BASP* 42 (2005): 109–10, claim one cannot date the Abgar Legend itself with any more precision than "between 100–300 C.E." For the most recent full treatment of the Abgar Legend, including the *Doctrina Addai*, see Martin Illert, *Die Abgarlegende: Das Christusbild von Edessa* (Fontes Christiani 45; Turnhout: Brepols, 2007). *Decretum Gelasianum* 8.5.1–2 identifies *Epistula Iesu ad Abgarum* and *Epistula Abgari ad Iesum* as *apocrypha* (for the text, see Ernst von Dobschütz, *Das Decretum Gelasianum* [TUGAL 3.3.4/38.4; Leipzig: J. C. Hinrichs, 1912], 13).

Ananias" (ΥΠΟ ΙΗΣΟΥ ΔΙΑ ΑΝΑΝΙΟΥ ΤΑΧΥΔΡΟΜΟΥ), with a variant
in several manuscripts identifying this Ananias as a letter-carrier (γραμ-
ματοκομιστός).[121] Similarly, Rufinus's translation of the *Ecclesiastical
History* in 402 C.E. claims Jesus sent the letter "through the courier
Ananias" (*per Ananiam cursorem*).[122] The Latin *Itinerarium of Egeria*,
based on a pilgrimage to Jerusalem ca. 384 C.E. that includes a stop in
Edessa, claims likewise that Jesus "sent [the letter] to King Abgar through
the courier Ananias" (*ad Aggarum regem per Ananiam cursorem misit*).[123]
According to these traditions, then, Jesus wrote the letter himself and
Ananias, the courier, only delivered it.[124] The Coptic version of the
legend, whose composition Drioton dates to between 359–362 C.E.,[125]
makes Jesus' role as author explicit. Jesus states, "It is I, Jesus, who have
written this letter with my hand."[126]

    In stark contrast, the Syriac versions of the Abgar Legend portray Jesus
avoiding writing himself by dictating to Ananias/Hanan, who is thus an
amanuensis. For example, Cureton translates a Syriac copy of Eusebius's
Ecclesiastical History from the British Museum with the following
introduction to Jesus' letter: "Copy of those things which were written
from Jesus by the hand of Hananias, the Tabularius, to Abgar, the Chief
of the country."[127] Hanan also appears in the *Doctrina Addai* as Jesus'

---

121.   Eusebius, *Hist. eccl.* 1.13.5. The variant appears at 1.13.9 in Codex Lauren-
tianus 70, 20; Codex Mosquensis 50; Codex Parisinus 1431; Codex Parisinus 1433.

122.   Rufinus's Latin appears alongside Eusebius's Greek in Friedhelm Winkelmann, ed., *Eusebius Werke* (3 vols.; GCS n.s. 6.1–6.3; Berlin: Akademie, 1999), 1:88–
89.

123.   *Itinerarium of Egeria* 17.1. For the Latin text alongside a German
translation, see Illert, *Abgarlegende*, 120–21; for the date, see p. 24.

124.   The parallel description of Abgar's initial letter to Jesus confirms this
interpretation, since the epistle is described as "written by Abgar the Toparch"
(ΓΡΑΦΕΙΣΗΣ ΥΠΟ ΑΒΓΑΡΟΥ ΤΟΠΑΡΧΟΥ) and sent to Jesus "through Ananias the
fast-runner" (ΔΙ' ΑΝΑΝΙΟΥ ΤΑΧΥΔΡΟΜΟΥ) (Eusebius, *Hist. eccl.* 1.13.5–6).

125.   Et. Drioton, "Un Apocryphe anti-arien: la version copte de la Correspondance d'Abgar, roi de'Edesse, avec Notre-Seigneuŕ," *Revue de l'Orient chrétien* 20
(1915): 368.

126.   Translation is that of Sullivan and Wilfong, "Reply," 113–14, who note on
p. 114 that most of the Coptic tradition stresses further that Jesus wrote in his "own"
hand. See also the translation of Drioton, "Apocryphe," 321, who provides the
known Coptic texts in 1920 on pp. 310–25.

127.   *Cod. Add.* 14,639, folio 15b (Cureton, *Ancient*, 3, 140). Drijvers, "Abgar
Legend," 1:495, posits: "The original form of the legend knew two letters. The trans-
formation of a letter of Jesus into an oral but written answer can be explained on
dogmatic grounds: Christ wrote nothing." Although this is possible, it may also be
that the Syriac tradition seeks to elevate Jesus' status by portraying him as the type of
person who has functionaries write for him.

amanuensis and Abgar's archivist.[128] Although these versions of the legend disagree as to whether Jesus wrote the letter himself or employed an amanuensis, and thus as to whether Ananias/Hanan is a courier or archivist, they agree in portraying Jesus as a scribal-literate individual who could write a letter or have someone write for him.

Eusebius and the Coptic version of the Abgar Legend were not the only early Christians to claim literary activity for Jesus himself. The third-/fourth-century *Narrative of Joseph of Arimathea*[129] similarly contains an epistolary Jesus and is one of only two places outside the Gospels that directly applies γράφω to him.[130] In addition, it is the only early Christian text, of which I am aware, that portrays Jesus writing *and* reading. *Narrative of Joseph* 3.4 claims that Jesus "wrote" (γράψας) a letter to the cherubim guarding paradise as he hung from the cross.[131] Although the discussion of verbs for reading and writing in the LXX in Chapter 3 shows that they can mean that someone else did the writing, the text mentions no amanuensis—despite the fact that Jesus is hanging from the cross. After sending his letter, Jesus receives a post-mortem response from the cherubim, which he then read (ἀνέγνω).[132] According to Augustine in the early fifth century, the Manichaeans also preserved an image of an epistolarly Jesus, claiming to possess an *Epistle of Christ*.[133]

3.2. *Jesus as Author of Gospel Tradition*

Other early Christian portrayals of a scribal-literate Jesus attribute to him authorship of gospel tradition. These texts find their immediate background in the polemics of early Christian debates over authoritative Gospel texts. For example, Adamantius's *Dialogue on the True Faith in*

---

128.   *Doctrina Addai* 9–10, 43, respectively (following versification in Howard, *Teaching*). Further, Howard, "Introduction," vii: "In the Teaching of Addai there is no mention of Jesus writing a letter. Addai says simply that Jesus sent a reply by Hanan, Abgar's archivist."

129.   The editors of the *Ante-Nicene Fathers* place the *Narrative of Joseph of Arimathea* in their collection of third- and fourth-century New Testament apocrypha. For the English text, see *ANF* 8.468–71. For the Greek text, see Constantinus Tischendorf, ed., *Evangelia apocrypha: adhibitis plurimis codicibus graecis et latinis maximam partem nunc primum consultis atque ineditorum copia insignibus* (rev. ed.; Leipzig: Hermann Mendelssohn, 1876), 459–70.

130.   The other is Adamantius, *Dialogue* 2.13; cf. however, *Barn.* 12:9 (both are discussed below).

131.   *Narrative of Joseph* 3.4.

132.   *Narrative of Joseph* 4.3. This text joins Luke 4:16 in applying ἀναγινώσκω to Jesus.

133.   Augustine, *Faust.* 28.4; cf. also *Cons.* 1.7.11.

God, a fourth-century anti-Marcionite text,[134] attributes to Marcionites the claim that Jesus wrote the gospel.[135] This text is the second piece of Christian literature outside John 8:8 that applies γράφω to Jesus. Adamantius places on the lips of Marcus, a Marcionite, the claim that Peter did not write the gospel, but Christ did (οὐ Πέτρος ἔγραψεν ἀλλ᾽ ὁ Χριστὸς τὸ εὐαγγέλιον).[136] Similarly, the fourth-century Syriac *Demonstrations* of Aphrahat the Persian Sage contain the claim that Jesus authored gospel tradition.[137] Jerome's fifth-century statement that Jesus *nullum volumen doctrinæ suæ proprium dereliquet* ("left his teaching in no book of his own") despite the claims of apocryphal tradition reveals further claims for Jesus as author of gospel tradition.[138]

3.3. *Other Early Christian Images of a Scribal-Literate Jesus*

Several other early Christian sources also portray Jesus as a scribal-literate individual. Worth brief mention in this context is the *Epistle of Barnabas* (dated between 70 and 132/135 C.E.).[139] Barnabas does not portray Jesus *using* scribal-literate skills. In a symbolic word play on Ἰησοῦ, however, he applies γράφω to Jesus when claiming that Moses gave his instructions to write (γράψον) in a book (12:9) to Jesus, Son of God, not Joshua, son of Nun.[140] *Barnabas* 12:9 is not a direct application of γράφω to Jesus in the same sense as John 8:8, *Narrative of Joseph* 13:4, or *Dialogue* 2.13, as it is more of a symbolic transposition of that claim

---

134. Adamantius, *Dialogue on the True Faith in God* (trans. Robert A. Pretty; Gnostica 1; Leuven: Peeters, 1997). Pretty dates the *Dialogue* to between 290 and 300 C.E. (16–17). Kenji Tsutsui, *Die Auseinandersetzung mit den Markioniten im Adamantios-Dialog: Ein Kommentar zu den Büchern I–II* (PTS 55; Berlin: de Gruyter, 2004), 108, dates the text between ca. 350 and 360/378 C.E.

135. Adamantius, *Dialogue* 1.8; 2.13; cf. 2.14.

136. Adamantius, *Dialogue* 2.13. For the Greek text, see Tsutsui, *Auseinandersetzung*, 331.

137. For example, Aphrahat, *Demonstrations* 21.1: "It happened one day, that a man, who is called wise amongst the Jews, questioned me, saying:—Jesus, Who is called your Teacher, wrote for you, that *If there shall be in you faith like one grain of mustard...*" (NPNF[2]). John Gwynn, "Introductory Dissertation: Ephraim the Syrian and Aphrahat the Persian Sage," NPNF[2] 12.153, dates Aphrahat's *Demonstrations* to 337–345 C.E.

138. Jerome, *Comm. Ezech.* 44.29 (PL 25.443). His full statement reads: *Unde et Salvator nullum volumen doctrinæ suæ proprium dereliquit, quod in plerisque apocryphorum deliramenta confingunt.*

139. For the date, see Holmes, *Apostolic Fathers*, 272; James Carleton Paget, "The *Epistle of Barnabas*," in *The Writings of the Apostolic Fathers* (ed. Paul Foster; London: T&T Clark, 2007), 73–75.

140. *Barn.* 12:8–10; cf. Exod 17:14.

for Joshua to Jesus. It is, however, another early Christian text that applies γράφω to him.

In the late second century, the *Infancy Gospel of Thomas* portrays a five- to twelve-year-old Jesus who transcends literate education.[141] The narrative is set chronologically before Jesus' trip to Jerusalem at twelve years of age in Luke 2, which serves as the ending of *Infancy Gospel of Thomas*.[142] To an extent, then, the *Infancy Gospel of Thomas* is part of the reception-history of Luke's scribal-literate Jesus.

A central conflict in the narrative is Joseph's attempts to secure a literate education for Jesus. In light of Jesus' "aptitude, and his great intelligence for his age, [Joseph] resolved that Jesus should not remain illiterate."[143] On three occasions teachers attempt to teach Jesus the alphabet.[144] The first two teachers write out the alphabet for Jesus and attempt to instruct him,[145] with the second even stating, "First I'll teach him Greek, then Hebrew."[146] In response to both attempts, Jesus taunts the teachers by underscoring their lack of true knowledge. To the first, he says, "Since you don't know the real nature of the letter alpha, how are you going to teach the letter beta? You imposter, if you know, teach me first the letter alpha and then I'll trust you with the letter beta."[147] Similarly, to the second teacher Jesus says, "If you're really a teacher, and if you know the letters well, tell me the meaning of the letter alpha, and I'll tell you the meaning of beta."[148] Jesus' responses, known as the Alpha-Beta logion, appear elsewhere in early Christianity. In the second century, Irenaeus knows a version of it and attributes it to apocryphal tradition.[149] It appears also in the seventh-century *Gospel of Pseudo-Matthew*, an adaptation of *Infancy Gospel of Thomas* that has the teacher

---

141.   For the most recent English translation of the *Infancy Gospel of Thomas*, see Hock, trans., "Infancy Gospel of Thomas," in *The Complete Gospels* (ed. Robert J. Miller; Santa Rosa: Polebridge, 1994), 371–79. I follow Hock's versification. On the date of the *Infancy Gospel of Thomas*, see Oscar Cullmann, "Infancy Gospels," in Schneemelcher, ed., *New Testament Apocrypha*, 1:442; Foster, "Educating," 22 n. 84; Ronald F. Hock, "Infancy Gospel of Thomas: Introduction," in *Complete Gospels*, 369–70.

142.   *Inf. Gos. Thom.* 19:1–13.

143.   *Inf. Gos. Thom.* 14:1 (Hock).

144.   *Inf. Gos. Thom.* 6:1–8:3; 14:1–5; 15:1–7.

145.   *Inf. Gos. Thom.* 6:15; 14:2.

146.   *Inf. Gos. Thom.* 14:2 (Hock).

147.   *Inf. Gos. Thom.* 6:19–20 (Hock).

148.   *Inf. Gos. Thom.* 14:3 (Hock).

149.   Irenaeus, *Haer.* 1.20.1.

attempt to teach Jesus Hebrew first and Greek second.[150] In response to the Alpha-Beta logion in *Infancy Gospel of Thomas*, the second teacher strikes Jesus upon the head and, as a result, ends up unconscious, face-down on the ground.[151] Jesus brings the second teacher back to consciousness only on account of the third teacher's proper response to him. The third teacher simply acknowledges Jesus' lack of a need for literate education after hearing Jesus teach the law without reading from it.[152] In response, Jesus "immediately smiled" and healed the first teacher.[153]

The *Infancy Gospel of Thomas* presents an interesting case for the present study. As a late second-century reception of the two streams of Jesus-memory presented above, it intertwines them rather than fully accepting or rejecting one over the other. Jesus is an illiterate[154] son of a carpenter[155] who nevertheless appears in a context of literate education (even a schoolroom),[156] waxes eloquent on the alphabet, including reciting "the letters from alpha to omega very quickly,"[157] and generally upstages his literate teachers.[158] In setting the stage for Jesus' appearance in the temple at twelve, the *Infancy Gospel of Thomas* portrays the child Jesus as a teacher already who needs not literate education in order to shame the learned, demonstrating *en route* both rote-memory and philosophical knowledge of the alphabet.[159] In claiming he taught from the law, however, the author goes out of the way to specify that Jesus took

---

150.   *Ps.-Mt.* 31, 38, respectively. Jan Gijsel, *Libri de Nativitate Mariae: Pseudo-Matthei Evangelium Textus et Commentarius* (CCSA 9; Turnhout: Brepols, 1997), 62, cautiously places *Gospel of Pseudo-Matthew*'s composition between 600 and 625 C.E. Cullmann, "Infancy Gospels," 1:458, dates *Gospel of Pseudo-Matthew* to the eighth or ninth century.

151.   *Inf. Gos. Thom.* 14:5.

152.   *Inf. Gos. Thom.* 15:3.

153.   *Inf. Gos. Thom.* 15:7 (Hock).

154.   *Inf. Gos. Thom.* 14:1.

155.   *Inf. Gos. Thom.* 13:1.

156.   *Inf. Gos. Thom.* 15:3.

157.   *Inf. Gos. Thom.* 6:18 (Hock).

158.   The Gnostic *Gospel of Truth*, roughly contemporaneous with the *Infancy Gospel of Thomas*, similarly places Jesus in a school context: "He went into the midst of the schools (and) he spoke the word as a teacher. There came the wise men—in their own estimation—putting him to the test. But he confounded them because they were foolish" (*Gos. Truth* 19:19–25; Macrae). Hock, "Infancy Gospel of Thomas: Introduction," in *Complete Gospels*, 370, mentions this text as a possible allusion to *Infancy Gospel of Thomas*. George W. MacRae, "Introduction," in *The Nag Hammadi Library in English* (ed. Marvin W. Meyer; Leiden: Brill, 1977), 37, dates the *Gospel of Truth* to 150–200 C.E.

159.   *Inf. Gos. Thom.* 6:18, 21–23.

a book but "did not read the letters."[160] The Jesus of the *Infancy Gospel of Thomas* thus mixes both streams of Jesus-memory that emerged in the first-century Synoptic Gospels, as Jesus demonstrates all the tangible effects of a literate education despite never submitting to one.

A final source of early Christian portrayals of a scribal-literate Jesus is fourth-century iconographical representations of Jesus teaching with a scroll in his hand. These images appear on sarcophagi in the Vatican Museum (for example, and inter alia, sarcophagus inv. no. 191 and sarcophagus inv. no. 193).[161] Natanson shows similar images of Jesus in carvings of Gospel scenes dated from the fourth to the sixth centuries, including one example where Jesus holds a codex instead of a scroll.[162] Along with the aforementioned literary witnesses, these images of Jesus demonstrate that, in various corners of Christendom, the image of the scribal-literate Jesus predominated over the scribal-illiterate Jesus in the second to sixth centuries.

4. *Summary and Conclusion*

This chapter has demonstrated the co-existence in early Christianity of two streams of Jesus-memory concerning his scribal-literate status. In one stream, whose earliest definite instantiations are Mark 1:22//Matt 7:29 and Mark 6:3//Matt 13:55, early Christians remembered Jesus as an outsider to scribal-literate culture and explicitly as a craftsman or the son of a craftsman. In another stream, whose earliest definite instantiation is Luke 4:16–30, early Christians remember Jesus as a scribal-literate teacher who possesses scribal-literate skills. The relationship between these texts reveals appropriations of these two streams of Jesus-memory in a state of disagreement.

Slightly later than these texts but also in the first century, the Gospel of John attests both streams of Jesus-memory by claiming that Jesus provided sufficient fodder for his enemies to maintain conflicting assumptions/conclusions about his scribal-literate status. As narrator,

---

160.   *Inf. Gos. Thom.* 15:3 (Hock).

161.   Images of these two sarcophagi appear in Keith, *Pericope*, 245–46, with discussion. See a third example in Harris, *Ancient*, figure 8, and more in Robin M. Jensen, "The Economy of the Trinity at the Creation of Adam and Eve," *JECS* 7, no. 4 (1999): 527–46. Graydon F. Snyder, *Ante Pacem: Archaeological Evidence of Church Life Before Constantine* (Mercer: Mercer University Press, 1985), 61, mentions two other sarcophagi but does not seem certain that the teacher is Jesus.

162.   Joseph A. Natanson, *Early Christian Ivories* (London: Alec Tiranti, 1953), figures 2, 10, 12, 28, 50 (codex).

John does not provide an authoritative opinion, but rather claims simply that Jesus' teaching sparked the debate. Among later appropriations of the two streams of Jesus-memory, the late second-century *Infancy Gospel of Thomas* is particularly notable. Whereas the Gospel of John appropriates both streams by narrating confusion among Jesus' audience, the *Infancy Gospel of Thomas* claims, as matters of fact, that Jesus was an unlettered son of a carpenter *and* knew the alphabet and could out-teach his scribal-educated teachers.

Later sources from within and without early Christianity attest the continuance of both streams of Jesus-memory, although the scribal-literate image of Jesus became more commonplace. Collectively, therefore, and from the first century, the early Church remembered Jesus, sometimes vigorously, as someone who did not have scribal literacy, someone who did, and someone who was able to blur the lines between scribal literacy and scribal illiteracy. The final chapter proposes a historical Jesus who was capable of setting these streams of Jesus-memory into motion.

Chapter 5

Jesus and Scribal Literacy

> *Every impact has to be tested as to its*
> *adequacy to the original impulse from*
> *which it derives its authority.*[1]
>
> *We must explain, as much as possible,*
> *the creative impulse in each*
> *individual case.*[2]
>
> *So it is with every* τέκτων. (Sir 38:27)

This chapter will bring the previous chapters to a culmination and argue that the most plausible explanation for why early Christians remembered Jesus as a scribal-illiterate teacher, a scribal-literate teacher, and as someone who confused his audiences on the issue, is that Jesus' own life and ministry produced conflicting convictions about his scribal-literate status. This overall argument consists of two more specific arguments concerning Jesus, which will provide the structure for what follows. First, I will argue that Jesus was not a scribal-literate teacher. Second, I will argue that he managed (whether intentionally or not) to convince many of his contemporaries that he was.

1. *Prior Suggestions on the Transition to a Scribal-Literate Jesus*

Before proceeding, however, it may help to clarify the precise contours of my proposal by distinguishing it from a seeming alternative suggestion. Like my argument in this chapter, this suggestion is concerned not

---

1.   Petr Pokorný, "Demoniac and Drunkard: John the Baptist and Jesus according to Q 7:33–34," in Charlesworth and Pokorný, eds., *Jesus Research*, 172. Consider also Le Donne, *Historiographical*, 13: "The multiple (and sometimes contradictory) interpretations of Jesus found in the Gospels allow the historian to chart trajectories of memory refraction that have been propelled forward by the initial perceptions of Jesus by his contemporaries."
2.   Becker, *Jesus*, 15.

just with Jesus' scribal-literate status, but also with explaining the relationship between the various images of him in the Gospels. According to
this solution, the alterations to the portrayals of Jesus in the canonical
Gospels mirror the development of Christianity into an increasingly
scribal religion. That is, Christians originally remembered Jesus as a
teacher who did not hold scribal literacy (e.g. Mark 6:3) because he
was, in fact, a teacher who did not hold scribal literacy. As Christianity
became more textually aware and ventured into literate culture, however,
its images of Jesus morphed in order to reflect its new identity, with
Christians eventually remembering Jesus as a scribal-literate teacher (e.g.
Luke 4:16–20 or later sarcophagi images where he holds a scroll). Kelber
and Crossan are representatives of this theory.

1.1. *Werner Kelber*
Kelber claims, "All four canonical gospels…supply us with the general
picture of Jesus as speaker of authoritative and often disturbing words,
and not as a reader, writer, or head of a school tradition."[3] Kelber concedes, however, that two canonical texts, John 8:6, 8 and John 7:15,
attribute to Jesus literate skills.[4] He dismisses the former as a "parody of
formal, literary writing," but says the latter portrays Jesus as "a man of
literacy and probably scriptural knowledge (*grammata oiden*), but
without formal rabbinic training (*mē memathēkōs*)."[5] Kelber explains
how an "early synoptic orality" Jesus became a "man of literacy" by
identifying Matthew as the culprit: "The specifically scribal, Rabbinic
model of Jesus the authoritative interpreter of the Torah was clearly
shaped by the theological interests of Matthew."[6] "The gospels will have
retained a genuine aspect of the oral performer," therefore, not when
they show a literate Jesus, but only "insofar as he is featured as a pro-
phetic speaker and eschatological teacher."[7] For Kelber, Jesus himself was
not a man of letters; he only became so at the hands of Matthew, whose
theological interests enabled the later image of him in John 7:15.

1.2. *John Dominic Crossan*
Another version of this proposal is that of Crossan. For Crossan, "Jesus
was illiterate until the opposite is proven."[8] Crossan acknowledges that

---

3.   Kelber, *Oral*, 18.
4.   Ibid.
5.   Ibid.
6.   Ibid.
7.   Ibid.
8.   Crossan, *Birth*, 235. See also Crossan, *Jesus*, 25; Crossan, *Essential*, 21.

Luke portrays Jesus as a reader in Luke 4:16–20, but claims that this image mainly reflects Luke's presumption about Jesus: "And it [Jesus' literacy] is not proven but simply presumed by Luke."[9] Far more historically reliable for Crossan, insofar as it reflects Jesus' peasant status, is Mark 6:3's identification of Jesus as a τέκτων.[10] Like Kelber, Crossan proposes a trend in early Christianity that moves from an illiterate historical Jesus to a religion with written texts. The wake of this shift enabled a steadily more scribal memory of Jesus, to the point that Luke could presume that Jesus could read: "Jesus' kingdom-of-God movement began as a movement of peasant resistance but broke out from localism and regionalism under scribal leadership."[11] Therefore, for Crossan, the shifting of Jesus' class that occurs between Mark's and Luke's accounts of the Nazareth pericope simply mirrors a larger shifting of class occurring in Christianity as a whole.

1.3. *Points of Agreement*
Earlier chapters addressed some details of these proposals critically, such as the lack of distinction between illiteracy in general and scribal illiteracy in particular and, related, the hasty assumptions that a manual laborer (τέκτων) would be a peasant and/or completely illiterate. Without engaging these details further, however, I note two points of concurrence.

1.3.1. *Jesus Was Not a Scribal-Literate Teacher.* First, Jesus most likely was not a scribal-literate teacher. With regard to my own proposal, this position resides neither upon a judgment that Luke's portrayal of a scribal-literate Jesus is a polemical reaction to Mark 6:3 (a judgment with which I agreed in Chapter 4) nor upon a judgment that Mark is—*on those grounds*—more historically reliable (a judgment with which I would not agree).[12] To repeat, demonstrating that Luke has theological or cultural motivation to alter the Jesus-memory he inherited does not demonstrate that the inherited Jesus-memory (that is, Mark) is theologically (more) neutral. The main difference between Luke's reception of Mark 6:1–6 and Mark's reception of prior Jesus-memory concerning Jesus' trip to the Nazareth synagogue, from the standpoint of scholarly assessment, is that

---

9. Crossan, *Birth*, 235. See also Crossan, *Jesus*, 26.

10. Crossan, *Jesus*, 23–26. For criticism of this interpretation of τέκτων, see Chapter 4.

11. Crossan, *Birth*, 235. See also Oakman, *Jesus and the Peasants*, 308.

12. As will be clear, I agree that Mark is more historically reliable in his portrayal of Jesus as outside the scribal class, but not simply because his portrayal is earlier than Luke's.

we have a past interpretation with which to compare Luke's Jesus-memory and see how he has altered it. We can make no such comparison between Mark 6:1–6 and prior tradition.

My judgment that Jesus did not hold scribal literacy stems primarily from adherence to the Jesus-memory approach to positing the historical Jesus.[13] The difference between the role of socio-historical context in this approach and those studies that Chapter 1 rehearsed is slight but nonetheless crucial. For most of those prior studies, the historical background is *determinative* for the scholar's conception of Jesus; that is, many of those scholars assert that Jesus was educated because most boys were educated or that he was illiterate because most people were illiterate. The problem with such an approach, regardless of which side of the argument one takes, is that history is littered with exceptions to generalities. As this study as a whole has made clear, I affirm that the vast majority of Jews at the time of Jesus were illiterate. Nevertheless, I also affirm that this observation—in and of itself—tells us little about the particular case of Jesus of Nazareth.

The problem with applying historical generalities to singular cases does not, however, mean that socio-historical contexts are irrelevant to the task of critical reconstruction of history. It simply indicates the problem with assuming that those contexts are determinative. By shifting focus onto the sources, which deal with individuals but spring from concrete historical circumstances, one can bring the general contexts of the ancient world to bear upon a particular case. More specifically, the historical task starts with the claims in the sources; the socio-historical context then provides the primary background for the scholar's conclusions concerning which claims have the greatest likelihood of historical accuracy, and for what reasons. In this sense, the socio-historical context is indispensable to historical Jesus studies not because it is *determinative* for the scholar's proposal, but rather because it is *informative* for the scholar's understanding of the sources, which form the foundation of his or her proposal.[14]

In terms of the present topic, then, a Second Temple Palestinian context favors the theory that Jesus was a scribal-illiterate teacher not simply because most people were scribal illiterates, but because the sources have conflicting claims and the socio-historical context suggests

13. See Chapter 2.
14. Schröter, "Jesus of Galilee," 40: "It must remain one of the tasks of historical Jesus Research to paint as accurate a picture as possible of the world in which Jesus lived and worked.... The setting in which Jesus lived and worked is...not a secondary 'framework' that can be ignored, but part of the 'historicizing tendency' of the first stories told by Jesus."

that one of those claims (scribal illiteracy) has a far greater likelihood than the other (scribal literacy). The lack of any convincing evidence for a popular-level educational system in Palestine (and the rest of the ancient world) and concomitant severely limited literacy rates place the burden of proof upon scholars who would argue that, unlike around 90 percent of Galileans, Jesus did receive a scribal-literate education. Also against this background, the notion that Jesus was a manual laborer, a τέκτων, as was his father Joseph, is inherently likely.

I note further that the claim that Jesus did not hold scribal literacy does not negate the possibility that he held some level of literacy, such as signature literacy or craftsman's literacy. The sources never address this matter, but it is possible that a τέκτων possessed some degree of literate skills associated with his labor. Whatever degree of craftsman's literacy Jesus may have held, however, the world of the τέκτων was nevertheless far removed from the world of the scribal-literate Torah student.

1.3.2. *The Directional Development of Early Christian Jesus-Memories.*
In addition to Jesus' socio-historical context, the second reason he most likely was not a scribal-literate teacher is that this proposed historical reality best explains the existence and development of the diverse Jesus-memories of his scribal-literate status. Related to this reason is the second issue upon which I agree with Kelber and Crossan: Jesus-memories in the early Church developed in a more explicitly scribal direction. Indeed, in the previous chapter and earlier work, I have detailed the "increasingly overt portrayals of a literate Jesus" and shown that, although the transition was not wholly uniform, the scribal-literate Jesus eventually carried the day in the early Church.[15]

The development of the tradition away from a scribal-illiterate Jesus and toward a scribal-literate Jesus is significant because, in the final analysis, there are of course only two real possibilities: either Jesus was a scribal-literate teacher or he was not. The question one must ask, then, in light of the varying Jesus-memories in the early sources, is whether it is more likely that (1) Jesus was a scribal-illiterate teacher whom the Church had reason or desire to remember as a scribal-literate teacher or (2) Jesus was a scribal-literate teacher whom the Church had reason or desire to remember as a scribal-illiterate teacher.[16]

15. Keith, *Pericope*, 227–49, 251 (quotation from section title on p. 251).
16. The argument that follows concerns the likely embarrassment of early Christians, a concept that finds a home in the criterion of embarrassment. It may appear, then, that I here go against the Jesus-memory approach to the historical Jesus, which I advocated in Chapter 2 as an explicit rejection of criteria of authenticity. My argument in Chapter 2, however, is not against the usefulness of social factors such

I have already argued that Jesus' own context favors the notion of a scribal-illiterate Jesus. Additionally, the wider socio-historical context of the early Church in the first to third centuries and beyond strongly favors the transition of the tradition in the first option over the second. For, in the words of Holmes, "As Christianity emerged from the shadow of the synagogue it became increasingly visible to the rest of Greco-Roman society, which in general was not impressed with what it saw."[17] Lucian (second century C.E.), Galen (second century C.E.), and Minucius Felix (late second or third century C.E.) all draw attention, sometimes mockingly, to Christians' uneducated simplemindedness.[18] In addition, Celsus's second-century pointed criticisms of Jesus' status as a τέκτων and lack of education,[19] his apostles' lack of education,[20] and Christian adherents' lack of education and illiteracy[21]—*criticisms that Origen concedes*—reveal just the type of pressures in the present of the tradition-handlers that could inspire their re-categorization of Jesus' social class and concomitant scribal-literate abilities in their commemorations of his past. The previous chapter has already argued that Mark 6:3's reception-history (including Matt 13:55 and Luke 4:16–20) is a particular example that indicates as much. It is readily understandable, then, that some early Christians would alter the image of a scribal-illiterate Jesus into a scribal-literate Jesus.

Less understandable is the alternative—that early Christians had reason or desire to alter the image of a scribal-literate Jesus into a scribal-illiterate Jesus. At first, this may seem an attractive hypothesis. D. Strauss, in fact, proposes a possible Christological motivation along these lines:

as embarrassment in understanding the interpretations of Jesus that exist in the early sources. Rather, it is against the idea that scholars can bypass those interpretations and access authentic Jesus tradition, whether by means of embarrassment, dissimilarity, or other methods.

17. Holmes, *Apostolic*, 10.

18. Lucian, *Peregr.* 11; Richard Walzer, *Galen on Jews and Christians* (OCPM; London: Oxford University Press, 1949), 15; Minucius Felix, *Oct.* 5.2–4, respectively. For fuller discussion, see Stephen Benko, "Pagan Criticisms of Christianity During the First Two Centuries AD," *ANRW* 23.2.1055–118; Allen Hilton, "The Dumb Speak: Early Christian Illiteracy and Pagan Criticism" (Ph.D. diss., Yale University, 1997).

19. Origen, *Cels.* 1.28; 6.34. Origen understands Celsus's criticisms of the manual-labor stock of Jesus and his family to imply Jesus' lack of education in *Cels.* 1.29.

20. Origen, *Cels.* 1.62.

21. Origen, *Cels.* 1.27; 6.13–14. See also Justin Martyr, *1 Apol.* 60, who states, "[There are] those among us who do not even know the letters of the alphabet, who are uncultured and rude in speech" (Falls, FC).

> The consideration that it must have been the interest of the Christian legend to represent Jesus as independent of human teachers, may induce a doubt with respect to these statements in the New Testament [that distance Jesus from rabbinical education, such as John 7:15], and a conjecture that Jesus may not have been so entirely a stranger to the learned culture of his nation.[22]

The theory that early Christians had Christological interest in downplaying Jesus' learnedness in order to emphasize that his wisdom is divine is sensible because early Christians were, from early on, clearly quite concerned with showing Jesus as (a source of) divine wisdom (e.g. 1 Cor 1:24; Eph 1:8).

The problem for this theory, however, is that such an impulse is not clearly discernible in the traditions that concern Jesus' scribal-literate status. Such Christological polemic is observable under only three circumstances in the earliest traditions. The first circumstance is if Jesus tradition that distances Jesus from scribal education (such as Mark 1:22// Matt 7:29 and Mark 6:3//Matt 13:55) is, as D. Strauss suggests concerning John 7:15, actually a cover-up for an educated Jesus.[23] The second circumstance is Mark 6:3—if Mark is dependent upon Matthew and Luke— since Mark identifies Jesus directly as a τέκτων rather than as one's son (Matt 13:55) or as a scribal-literate teacher (Luke 4:22). The third possibility is John 7:16, which shows Jesus responding to the Jews' questioning of his scribal-literate status in 7:15 with an affirmation of the divine origin of his teaching.

Each of these options presents difficulties. The first possibility is not an argument or demonstration but rather an a priori hypothesis that cannot move beyond the suggestive stage. D. Strauss does not demonstrate that texts that distance Jesus from scribal education and pedagogy are, in fact, downplaying an otherwise learned historical Jesus in order to emphasize the divine source of his knowledge. He merely suggests the possibility, and hesitantly at that. He follows his suggestion by stating that the lack of firm evidence means that "we can arrive at no decision on this point."[24] Strauss is right to be hesitant. We simply do not know the traditions upon which Mark, for example, is dependent, and these traditions would offer the best fodder for informed guesses on why he presents Jesus as "not like the scribes" and a τέκτων. Certainly, one can affirm that Mark's

22. Strauss, *Life*, 202.
23. As the previous chapter argues, D. Strauss's emphasis on the contrast between Jesus and scribal-educated authorities in John 7:15 is insufficient since John 7:15 also compares Jesus with scribal-educated authorities.
24. Strauss, *Life*, 202.

present theological agenda impacted his portrayal of Jesus' life. It is, however, difficult to know precisely how Mark's present theological agenda impacted his narration of this particular aspect of Jesus' life without comparing and contrasting it to the tradition he appropriated. Without a base line of comparison, discussion of the impact of Mark's theological agenda upon his portrayal of Jesus can quickly devolve into a chicken-and-egg scenario. Did Mark inherit a scribal-literate Jesus but portray him as a scribal-illiterate teacher because his theological agenda is to distance Jesus from scribal authority? (That is, Mark's agenda overrides the tradition.) Or did Mark inherit a scribal-illiterate Jesus and portray him as such because he believed Jesus was a scribal-illiterate teacher? (That is, Mark's agenda grows from the tradition.) There is no convincing manner in which scholars can adjudicate between these, or other, possibilities. The sole thing scholars can observe is that Mark and his characters do distance Jesus from scribal-literate authority.

Of course, regarding the second circumstance of possibly detectable Christological downplaying of Jesus' access to scribal education, those who affirm Markan dependence upon Matthew and Luke will argue that scholars *do* have the tradition Mark inherited. From this perspective, one could argue that Mark's identification of Jesus directly as a τέκτων heightens his distance from scribal education compared to the Matthean and Lukan accounts of the Nazareth pericope. In so doing, then, Mark emphasizes the divine source of Jesus' wisdom and provides an example of early Christian tradition moving from a scribal-literate Jesus (Luke) to a scribal-illiterate Jesus (Mark), and from a τέκτων's son (Matthew) to a τέκτων (Mark).

In addition to requiring an affirmation of the minority Griesbach hypothesis, however, this theory explains only a single piece of evidence, namely Mark 6:3's reception of Matt 13:55 and Luke 4:16–20. It does not explain Luke's reception of Matthew, which goes in (under this proposal) the opposite direction by making Jesus a scribal-literate teacher instead of the son of a τέκτων. It also does not explain the Markan and Matthean manuscript traditions, where scribes harmonized Mark 6:3 with Matt 13:55 but did not harmonize Matt 13:55 with Mark 6:3. Thus, even under this minority solution to the Synoptic Problem, one still has early Christian traditions reflecting a move away from a scribal-illiterate τέκτων Jesus and only one tradition (Mark 6:3) reflecting a move toward this image.

The third possibility, John 7:16, may at first glance provide the best fodder for the theory that early Christians intentionally downplayed Jesus' scribal literacy for Christological purposes. For here Jesus responds to the Jews' questioning of his scribal-literate status by claiming that his teaching is that of the Father. The association between Jesus' scribal-literate status and the divine origin of his teaching is thus explicit. John 7:15–16 also, however, calls into question the hypothesis that an author's conviction that Jesus was the source of divine wisdom *necessarily* led him to portray Jesus as independent of human knowledge/education. Although the association between the ideas is explicit, the Johannine narrator technically portrays the divine origins of Jesus' pedagogy as the catalyst for debate over Jesus' scribal-literate status, not as evidence for the resolution of the debate. That is, and taking the broader Johannine narrative into consideration, despite asserting that Jesus is the divine λόγος (1:1)[25] and having Jesus claim that his teaching is that God himself in 7:16 and elsewhere (6:45; 8:28), John does not feel compelled to settle his characters' debates over Jesus' and Galileans' scribal-literate status in John 7:15–52. As argued earlier, his claim is simply that Jesus inspired such debates.

From another perspective, one may be tempted to see the portrayal of Jesus as a scribal-illiterate teacher in Mark 6:3//Matt 13:55 against the background of other religious traditions that polemically assert that their founding figure was illiterate in order to stress the divine origin of the sacred text he authored or translated. Some Mormons forward such a claim for Joseph Smith's translation of the Book of Mormon.[26] Similarly, some Muslims forward such a claim for Muhammad's authorship of the Quran.[27] Once again, although this comparison may make sense on one level, that particular impulse does not appear in earliest Christianity. In contrast to these religions, the earliest Christians of the first to third centuries attributed no written works to Jesus. This claim found a home only among later Christians in the fourth and fifth centuries, who met quickly with vehement criticism. Those making the claims, along with their texts, were labeled heretical and apocryphal by those who represented orthodox Christianity.[28] Even those later "heretical" Christians

---

25. For a succinct statement on the Wisdom Christology in the Johannine Prologue, see D. Moody Smith, *The Theology of the Gospel of John* (NTTh; Cambridge: Cambridge University Press, 1995), 17–19, 101.

26. "Origin of the Book of Mormon," in the front matter of the Book of Mormon (London: West European Mission, 1959), n.p., begins by asserting that Joseph Smith translated the book "by the gift and power of God," which some Mormon apologists claim must be the case because Smith received only a rudimentary education.

27. On the centrality of Muhammad's illiteracy to Islam, see Thomas W. Lippman, *Understanding Islam: An Introduction to the Muslim World* (2d rev. ed.; New York: Meridian, 1995), 37.

28. Augustine, *Faust.* 28.4; *Cons.* 1.7.11; Jerome, *Comm. Ezech.* 44.29; *Decretum Gelasianum* 8.5.1–2.

did not, to our knowledge, assert Jesus' illiteracy as part of their claim for the sacred nature of their texts. Unlike other religious traditions, then, early Christians do not appear to have been interested in asserting Jesus' scribal illiteracy as a means of affirming the divine nature of his teachings or the texts that transmitted them.

In summary, a clear desire to promote Jesus as a scribal-literate teacher is observable in several early Christian traditions, as is a socio-historical context where Christians stood to gain from doing so. In contrast, a clear desire to promote a scribal-illiterate Jesus is not readily observable, even if such a desire would (from one perspective) make Christological sense. In light of this evidence, it is more likely that Christians came to remember a historically scribal-illiterate Jesus as a scribal-literate individual than vice versa. Therefore, I agree with the general conclusions of Kelber and Crossan that (1) Jesus was a scribal-illiterate teacher and (2) later Christian portrayals of a scribal-literate Jesus are departures from the most likely historical reality. This proposal best explains the sources we have.

1.4. *Points of Disagreement—Why and When*
In what remains of this chapter and book, however, I seek to build on Kelber's and Crossan's proposals by re-directing scholarly focus in light of important points of disagreement.[29] My overall disagreement with the Kelber/Crossan solution concerns not *whether* early Christian Jesus-memory developed away from a scribal-illiterate Jesus and toward a scribal-literate Jesus, but *why* and *when*.

Kelber attributes the scribal-literate Jesus to the interpretive pro-clivities of Matthew while Crossan attributes it to the presumption of Luke. The problem is not that positing that a handler of the Jesus tradition remembered Jesus in his own scribal-literate image is illegiti-mate. Indeed, this undoubtedly happened with all the handlers of Jesus-memory to one degree or another. Thus, one should acknowledge that the Kelber/Crossan solution is possible and capable of explaining the evidence.

Rather, the problem is that this solution leaves the historical task incomplete. By locating the redactional impulse solely in the present theological interests of the early Church, Kelber and Crossan fail to account for the role of the past in the production/enabling of those pre-sent categories. Their suggestions are thus symptomatic of the presentist

---

29. As the following discussion will reveal, my own proposal is not actually contrary to their proposals, but rather a criticism that they unnecessarily truncate the historical task.

form-critical legacy in Jesus scholarship that is also evident in the structural framework of the criteria of authenticity. As a result, they present the scribal-literate Jesus as something of a Matthean or Lukan *creatio ex nihilo*.[30] Thus, despite my agreement with Kelber and Crossan that the portrayals of Jesus as a scribal-literate teacher are a movement away from historical reality, I here disagree with them on the stage of that development at which the scribal-literate Jesus emerged. It is not impossible that Luke, for example, is responsible for the scribal-literate image of Jesus; it is simply much more likely that Jesus himself is responsible.

2. *Scribal Literacy and the Perception(s) of Jesus*

The remainder of this chapter will argue that many individuals in Jesus' audiences likely concluded that he was a scribal-literate teacher despite the fact that he was not. Therefore, the conflicting or confused state of early Christian Jesus-memory concerning his scribal-literate status is traceable to the life and ministry of Jesus and not initially, or solely, a product of the theological concerns of early Christians such as Luke. I here offer what Schröter rightly describes as the proper goal of historical Jesus studies: a hypothesis "about how things could have been" that accounts for the extant sources and Jesus' historical context, and necessarily draws upon "historical imagination."[31]

30. Rodríguez, *Structuring*, 141, is once again apropos: "If Luke 4.14–30 is redaction, whence comes Luke's redactional impulse?"

31. Schröter, "Jesus of Galilee," 38 (emphasis removed). More fully: "The sources have a corrective function or…a 'right of veto.' They prohibit certain interpretations and can protect us from making mistakes, but they do not tell us what a story sketched out on a critical basis should look like. To achieve this we also need the power of 'historical imagination.'" See also Allison, *Constructing*, 22: "We should proceed by abduction—that is, by inference to the best explanation, always looking for a Jesus who makes the most sense of the available facts and what we otherwise know of Judaism and nascent Christianity." Earlier, Allison states, "Espying a pattern is not enough; we need to account for it sensibly" (p. 21). See also Le Donne, *Historiographical*, 7; "Theological Distortion," 165.

It is necessary, however, to distinguish between my approach, which coheres with that of Schröter and Allison, and Le Donne's approach. I agree with Le Donne that "it is the effects of the past that are available for analysis and not the past itself" (*Historiographical*, 76). Whereas Le Donne then proceeds on the same page to qualify Schröter by claiming that scholars cannot speak intelligently about an actual past that existed apart from its perception ("But once qualified it is no longer helpful to draw a distinction between the real Jesus and the remembered Jesus"), I affirm with Schröter that scholars can at least offer theories "about how things could have been." No doubt, Le Donne would consider my appropriation of social memory

Along these lines, significant for present purposes is Chapter 3's sixth important factor for interpreting claims about literacy—the perception of literacy. In addition to—but sometimes distinct from—the actual possession of literate skills, the perceptions and judgments of others determined whether one was considered literate, what type of literacy one was considered to have, and the social significance of that form of literacy. Village scribes, for example, could defend each other as members of the literate class while truly elite members of the upper class could chastise the limited abilities and education of those village scribes.[32] In similar fashion, Libanius could scold provincial governors who were able to write shorthand—undoubtedly a rare skill in terms of the general population and the product of an education—as having no knowledge.[33] The assessor's own class and education affected his or her qualitative assessment of another's literate skills and/or status. Further, most Judeans would have viewed all judges, teachers, scribes, priests, Pharisees, and Sadducees as authoritative representatives of Torah even if some in their midst were, in reality, not scribal-educated or only at the beginning pedagogical stages.[34] In other words, the assessment that someone belonged to the scribal-literate class depended upon the perception of a social package, a perception to which a host of factors contributed. Demonstration of scribal-literate abilities was only one of these factors, and a factor that did not always need to be present for a conclusion on the individual to be reached.

In this context, the most fundamental reason that Jesus was likely perceived as both a scribal-illiterate teacher and a scribal-literate teacher is that his audiences regularly consisted of different classes. I suggest that individual audience members would have interpreted and remembered Jesus' pedagogical activity, particularly his interpretive battles with known scribal-literate authorities, from perspectives that inherently reflected their own class and scribal-literate status (as well as other factors) and come to differing conclusions. For the sake of clarity, I state explicitly that this argument does not require that Jesus *intended* to create multiple

---

theory to these ends to be closer to critical realism than his appropriation of social memory theory (see *Historiographical*, 8–10; cf., however, his affirmation that "one cannot isolate a historical event from its impact and the trajectory of stories set in motion thereby" and the role of "the historical agent which set the episode in motion" [62, 63, respectively]—I would argue that, in these statements, Le Donne preserves a role not just for the earliest perceptions, but for the historical impetuses of those perceptions).

32. Youtie, "βραδέως," 239–40; Josephus, *J. W.* 1.24.3 §479.
33. Libanius, *Or.* 18.158.
34. Schwartz, *Imperialism*, 68; similarly, Carr, *Writing*, 288.

perceptions of his scribal-literate status, although I consider it rather unlikely that he was entirely unaware of the effects of his activities. This argument requires only that Jesus engaged in the types of activities that inevitably resulted in multiple perceptions, regardless of his intentions for doing so.

2.1. *Jesus' Activities Invited Assessment*

In order to arrive at an understanding of how Jesus' audiences likely perceived his scribal-literate status, the first thing to note is that Jesus often engaged in activity that invited assessment of him vis-à-vis known scribal-literate authorities. This point is simple but important. Since scribal literacy was a social construct in terms of its perception and manifestation in cultural contexts, scribal-literate authorities were recognizable as much for their social roles as they were for their possession and utilization of scribal-literate skills; as much for their ability to avoid manual-labor occupations as their study of Torah;[35] as much for their leisure lifestyle that enabled writing a book as the linguistic ability to do so;[36] as much for their proclivity for walking in robes in the market[37] and sitting on Moses' seat in the synagogue[38] as their ability to read Moses aloud. That is, the acquisition and usage of scribal literacy was so intertwined with larger social, political, and economic realities that a whole host of activities, which included (but were not limited to) demonstration of scribal-literate abilities, reflected a lifestyle associated with scribal-literate education and authority.

As Chapters 3 and 4 demonstrated, reading and interpreting Torah in a synagogue were recognizably scribal-literate positions, just as passively hearing and receiving Torah instruction were recognizably manual-laborer positions. Therefore, if Jesus ever stood up to teach in a synagogue service rather than listen, and so occupied the position of a scribal-literate teacher instead of a manual-labor member of the audience, then he placed himself in the social role of a scribal-literate authority. This very action would have invited assessment of his scribal-literate status, especially if other aspects of his life were perceived to be at variance with it. Similarly, if Jesus ever challenged or addressed the teaching of the scribes (Mark 9:11; 12:35; Matt 23:1–12), if he ever debated known scribal-literate authorities (Matt 16:1–4) over the interpretation of Jewish

---

35. Sir 38:24–34.

36. Josephus, *Ag. Ap.* 1.9 §50 (on leisure and writing); *Ant.* 20.12.1 §263–265 (on ability in Greek).

37. Mark 12:38.

38. Matt 23:2.

Scriptures (Mark 12:18–40; John 7:53–8:11) or proper interpretive authority (Matt 20:23–27; Luke 20:2–8; John 5:39–47), if he ever cited Scripture during such a debate (Mark 2:25//Matt 12:3//Luke 6:3; Mark 12:10//Matt 21:42; Mark 12:26//Matt 22:31; Matt 12:5; 19:4–5; Luke 10:26; cf. Mark 12:24; Luke 20:17) or accused his opponents of not knowing Scripture in such a debate (Mark 12:24//Matt 22:29), if he ever offered interpretations of Torah to crowds (Matt 5:17–48), if he ever taught in the shadow of the temple hierarchy (Matt 21:23; Luke 19:47; 21:37–38; John 8:2–3), if he ever did any of these things, then his scribal literacy and authority for such actions would inevitably have come under scrutiny.

I here take it as a safe assumption that Jesus did at least some of these things in his ministry.[39] There is, therefore, no reason to doubt the shared claim of Mark 1:22//Matt 7:29; Mark 6:3//Matt 13:55, and John 7:15 that Jesus' various audiences compared and contrasted him with known scribal-literate Torah authorities. There is likewise no reason to doubt that, as part of that assessment, Jesus' opponents and/or audiences questioned his authority (Mark 11:28//Matt 21:23//Luke 20:2; cf. Mark 6:3//Matt 13:55). These individual episodes do not have to be historical in order for scholars to acknowledge that, if Jesus ever did anything of the sort, it would inevitably have led to assessments of his scribal-literate status.[40]

Stated otherwise, as soon as Jesus presented himself as a teacher, he would have met particular social expectations among his audiences. As Theissen observes,

> Everyone becomes part of a society with predetermined patterns of behavior. Everyone is faced with role expectations that are attached to certain positions and which cannot be avoided. It was the same for Jesus. Being perceived in the role of teacher and prophet, he had to deal with the accompanying role *expectations*.[41]

39. Allison, *Constructing*, 15–16: "Certain themes, motifs, and rhetorical strategies recur again and again throughout the primary sources; and it must be in those themes and motifs and rhetorical strategies—which, taken together, leave some distinct impressions—if it is anywhere, that we will find memory.... The historian should heed before all else the general impressions that our primary sources produce."

40. In a study that is also focused upon Jesus' interpretive battles with scribal-literate authorities, Thatcher, *Jesus*, xxi, makes a similar point: "I am not concerned about particular riddles recorded in the Gospels but about whether he engaged in riddling *at all*. I claim that if Jesus engaged in riddling *at all*, this fact is significant to key aspects of our understanding of his social posture and message" (emphases original).

41. Theissen, "Jesus," 98 (emphasis added).

Similarly, Snyder notes, "Jesus and Christian teachers…would have encountered in their audiences the *expectation* that their teacher was skilled in the literature of his or her tradition."[42] This point brings the current discussion to the various factors that affected whether Jesus' audiences judged him to have met their expectations.

2.2. *Mixed Audiences*

Since Jesus' activities frequently invited assessment of him vis-à-vis scribal-literate authorities, it is significant that his audiences often consisted of both scribal-illiterate individuals/groups and scribal-literate individuals/groups. According to Matthew, Jesus' audience for the healing of the paralytic included the paralytic and his friends (9:2), scribes (9:3), and "the crowds" (9:8). Further, Jesus interacts with Pharisees when they see him eating with tax collectors and sinners (Matt 9:10–11). Likewise, after the Pharisees and scribes questioned Jesus about handwashing (15:1), he turned to "the crowd" in order to teach on true defilement (15:10–11), after which the disciples tell Jesus that the Pharisees were offended because they were listening (15:12). Mark too tells this story, though with the additional detail that the Pharisees and scribes "had come from Jerusalem" (Mark 7:1). Among other similar exchanges, Mark also notes that scribes from Jerusalem joined in the same audience as "the crowd" and Jesus' family in his hometown at the beginning of his ministry (3:19–22), and that Pharisees came to Jesus while he was teaching "the crowds" (10:1–2). Luke claims a Pharisee invited Jesus to his home while listening to Jesus speak (11:37) to "the crowds" (11:29). After Jesus offended both the Pharisees and the lawyers (11:45) at the host's home, Luke claims Jesus' audiences continued to consist of multiple groups and classes: "When he went outside, the scribes and the Pharisees began to be very hostile toward him and to cross-examine him about many things…. Meanwhile, when the crowd gathered by the thousands…he began to speak first to his disciples" (Luke 11:53–12:1). Luke 15:1–2 begins the famous lost parables by noting that Jesus' audience consisted of "all the tax collectors and sinners" as well as "Pharisees and scribes." John 7 presents a chaotic melee where Jesus tells "the Jews" of John 7:15, "None of you keeps the law," but "the crowd" responds that Jesus is demon-possessed (7:20). Further, the Pharisees, who later distinguish between the crowd and themselves based on knowledge of the law (7:48–49), overhear the crowd's reaction to Jesus' teaching and reach a quite different conclusion on whether Jesus might be the Messiah (7:25–32). The showdown over the adulterous woman in

42. Snyder, *Teachers*, 190 (emphasis added).

John 7:53–8:11 occurs between Jesus and "the scribes and the Pharisees" (8:3) yet in front of "all the people" (8:2).

Although one could add many, many more examples to these few texts, they suffice to show a common claim among early narratives about Jesus, which is that his audiences often consisted simultaneously of common people who "did not know the law" (John 7:49) and scribal-literate individuals (Pharisees, Sadducees, scribes, lawyers, chief priests, etc). This broad claim of the Gospels is not one that I am prepared to question, nor are others.[43] If one affirms that Jesus ministered in Galilee and died in Jerusalem, one has already affirmed two historical contexts that guaranteed the presence of these demographics in some of his audiences.

2.3. *Mixed Perceptions*

Since Jesus often engaged in pedagogical activities that raised the issue of his scribal-literate status, and did so before audiences with varying class and scribal-literate backgrounds, I suggest that different members of Jesus' audiences could have perceived and remembered his scribal-literate status in different terms. A completely illiterate farmer in Jerusalem for a festival and a scribe from the temple could have witnessed the exact same interpretive battle between Jesus and Pharisees and walked away with opposite convictions about Jesus. Much like the differing assessments of the village scribe Ischyrion—one of which claimed he was illiterate, the other of which claimed he was literate—the backgrounds of the assessors would have played a programmatic role in the formation of their perceptions.[44] The farmer, unfamiliar with the intricacies of Torah study and scribal education, could have concluded from the fact that Jesus was arguing Torah with Pharisees that Jesus, too, was a scribal-literate individual. In contrast, the temple scribe, familiar with the intricacies of Torah study and scribal education, could have surveyed the same scene and concluded that Jesus was not a scribal-literate authority.[45]

---

43. In offering an explanation for who wrote early Gospel texts since his own proposal associates Jesus so strongly with the illiterate peasant stratum of society, Crossan, *Birth*, 235, claims, "So even if Jesus was a peasant talking to peasants, others besides peasants were listening." Consider also Allison, *Constructing*, 30 n. 122: "But there must have been various sorts of eyewitnesses." Elsewhere, Allison, *Resurrecting*, 54, references "the varied nature of Jesus' audiences," although he is here more interested in the hermeneutical implications of Jesus speaking differently to different audiences than how different audiences could have heard the same message differently.

44. Youtie, "βραδέως," 239–40.

45. An anachronistic but relevant analogy may clarify the point. If I recite the *Shema* in Hebrew from rote memory to my freshmen students, the majority of them

The point of this illustration is that Jesus lived, taught, and debated in a socio-historical context where he did not have to read Torah in public in order for some members of his audience to conclude or assume that he could have. Thus, contradictory Jesus-memories concerning his scribal-literate status were likely already present in his lifetime and among eyewitnesses, who would have further transmitted their individual Jesus-memories, contributing to the corporate shape of early Christian social memory of Jesus. Regardless of Luke's precise reasons for portraying Jesus as a scribal-literate synagogue teacher, he likely was not the first person to have this conviction. A scribal-literate Jesus was not, in the first instance, his sole creation but an interpretive category that was already available. Further, that this interpretive category was already present in early Christianity was likely a contributing factor to why Luke challenged Mark's image of a scribal-illiterate Jesus with success. Many Christians already conceived of Jesus as a scribal-literate teacher, just as many Christians already conceived of Jesus as a scribal-illiterate τέκτων. Luke and Mark were hardly in isolation in early Christianity with regard to this difference of opinion. Looking down the historical line, then, one possible reason why early Christians corporately held the two images of Jesus in tension, a tension that is observable in the Church's corporate acceptance of both images (in the rise and dominance of the fourfold canon) and occasional rejections of one over the other (through alteration to traditions and manuscripts), is that this tension was part of the received tradition from the outset.

2.4. *The Influence of Those Who Knew Better?*
In raising the possible connection between the perceptions of Jesus in his own lifetime and those in the canonical Gospels, I should reiterate that my specific argument is only that the interpretive category of the scribal-literate Jesus was available to Luke and others in the corporate early Jesus-memory as a result of Jesus' own ministry. That is, I suggest that *some* people remembered Jesus as a scribal-literate teacher and continued to pass on such an image of Jesus, not that all Christians were confused on the matter or that the scribal-literate image of Jesus carried equal

will likely conclude that I am an expert in the Hebrew Scriptures with the ability to open any Hebrew text at random and read/translate at will. If, however, I recite the same text before someone who has spent a lifetime studying and memorizing the Hebrew Scriptures, or even just as much as I have, he or she will likely recognize that what I have recited is something that even introductory Hebrew students learn. Thus, the same recitation would indicate to this person nothing about the possibility of more advanced knowledge of the Hebrew Scriptures. The level of familiarity that one brings to the interpreted event affects what conclusion one reaches.

authority in all corners of the early Church.[46] My argument does not require or assume, for example, that Jesus' disciples or family members were confused about his scribal-literate status (although it also does not rule out the possibility of varying opinions even among his followers); nor does it deny that they could have exerted their growing authority in the early Church on the formation of early Christian Jesus-memory.[47] Peter and James the Just, for example, may have known that Jesus was, in fact, not a scribal-literate authority and used their influence in the period between Jesus' life and the formation of the Gospel narratives in order to corral the confusion over the issue. Indeed, two matters are difficult to overlook in this regard. First, despite the differences between the Gospels' portrayals of Jesus' scribal-literate status that the previous chapter presented, there is also considerable similarity, at least between Mark, Matthew, and John. Each of these Gospels agrees that Jesus received criticism from some of his audiences based on an assumed lack of scribal literacy (whether the assumption is that of the narrator, the characters, or both); only Luke claims Jesus' scribal-literate status was never under question. That is, Matthew and John may soften Jesus' association with scribal illiteracy compared to Mark, but only Luke removes it entirely and explicitly asserts scribal literacy for Jesus. Second, in light of Luke's sharp difference with Mark, Matthew, and John—and without wanting to push its significance too far considering the thorny issue of the authorship of the Gospels—it is interesting to note that Luke is the only Gospel author whom early Christian tradition does not anchor to an original disciple of Jesus in one form or another.[48]

Despite these considerations, however, two further points are important with regard to my argument that disagreement or confusion over Jesus' scribal-literate status in the corporate early Christian social memory would have persisted from his own lifetime and enabled or aided Luke's successful portrayal of Jesus as a scribal-literate teacher. First, it is not certain that all early Christians who knew that Jesus did not hold scribal literacy would have been motivated to correct perceptions of him

---

46. I thank Dale Allison for encouraging me to clarify this aspect of my proposal.

47. See Gerhardsson's famous argument for the *collegium* of apostles in Jerusalem in *Memory*, 274–80.

48. The historical reliability of the early Church attributions of Gospel authorship is beyond the scope of this study. The most recent discussions of patristic evidence concerning the authorship of Mark, Matthew, and John is Bauckham, *Jesus*, 202–39, 412–71; on John, see further his *Testimony*, 33–72; repr. from *JTS* 44 (1993): 24–69. For early Christian identifications of Luke as the companion of Paul and Luke's Gospel as Paul's proclamation, see Irenaeus, *Haer.* 3.1.1, 14.1; Tertullian, *Marc.* 4.2, 5; Muratorian Canon 1.

as a scribal-literate teacher. If the authors of Matthew and John are any indication, some authoritative early Christians may have been happy to retain/acknowledge the criticism Jesus received, but lighten it and so move Jesus slightly closer to scribal literacy (Matthew), or simply acknowledge the criticism without offering an authoritative opinion on its accuracy (John). If the socio-historical context traced in the previous chapter is at all indicative of early Christianity, some Christians may have found it beneficial to allow misperceptions of Jesus to continue while others (such as the authors of Mark and Luke) expressed firmer opinions.

Second, even if some of Jesus' earliest followers knew he was not a scribal-literate authority and were concerned to correct misunderstandings of Jesus' scribal-literate status, their influence over the corporate shape of Jesus-memory was limited and local, not universal and total. If it is possible that John the Baptist had adherents who had visited Palestine and carried their memories and knowledge of the baptismal movement to the Diaspora, and thus out of the control of the regional authorities (Acts 19:1–7), it is also possible that Jews who encountered Jesus while in Palestine carried their memories, based on limited exposure, back with them outside the control of Jerusalem and transmitted them. Similarly, Theissen asks, "Would there not also have been stories among the Jesus traditions that had traveled outside the circle of his closest associates?"[49] Further, the debate between Paul and the Jerusalem authorities that appears in Gal 1–2 and Acts 15 similarly indicates that, although the early Church had a central authority in Jerusalem, its authority knew boundaries, as did Paul's. In other words, the social, historical, and ecclesial contexts of the early Church were sufficiently diverse that memories of a scribal-literate Jesus could have persisted in early Christianity even if some authoritative shapers of that memory in certain locales were concerned to correct it.

The present point, however, is not to trace with detail the many and varied developments of Jesus-memory after Jesus' life. My present point is only that it is plausible that the impact of Jesus' own life and ministry created the contradictory and confusing categories concerning his scribal-literate status that Mark, Luke, and other Christians later employed.

2.5. *Other Factors*

Additional factors increase the likelihood that the confusion present in our earliest sources was also present in the life of Jesus. First, previous knowledge of Jesus would have influenced how his audience members

49. Gerd Theissen, *The Gospels in Context: Social and Political History in the Synoptic Tradition* (trans. Linda M. Maloney; Minneapolis: Fortress, 1991), 97.

assessed his pedagogy vis-à-vis scribal-literate authorities. When Jesus stepped into the social position of a scribal-literate authority, a person who had no previous knowledge of him, and had heard no rumors about him, may have given him the benefit of the doubt and accepted that he was a scribal-literate authority (or at least held judgment and waited for him to prove that he is not). Meanwhile, someone who knew he was not a scribal-literate authority may have perceived his occupation of that position suspiciously or with immediate disdain. There is no reason to dismiss the claim of Mark that, at the beginning of his ministry, a synagogue outside Jesus' hometown (Mark 1:28, 39; cf. 3:1) could have been surprised that Jesus was a synagogue teacher but nonetheless allowed him to proceed while those who grew up with him scoffed at the very idea of him as a synagogue teacher (Mark 6:3). Equally, an individual who had heard laudatory claims that Jesus was a powerful pedagogical authority may have viewed a victory of Jesus in an interpretive showdown with scribal-literate authorities as evidence that he is one of them. Meanwhile, an individual who had heard that he was a scribal-illiterate Galilean who had managed to dupe a few unlearned audiences may have viewed such a victory as a fluke occurrence. The lack or presence of previous knowledge of Jesus could have affected how a given audience member perceived his occupation of scribal-literate social roles and his public disputations with known scribal-literate authorities.

Second, the impact of previous knowledge of Jesus on assessments of his scribal-literate status would not have been limited to first-time encounters. Some members of Jesus' audience may have seen him only once, but many undoubtedly saw him numerous times and at least his committed followers heard him over and over. Repeated exposures to Jesus' pedagogy could have reinforced initial assessments or forced reassessment of those initial assumptions (as John 7:15 claims for the Jews who hear Jesus teach), contributing to overall confusion. And, again, an assessor's own standards for what qualifies as indicating scribal-literate status would have impacted this revision process, as would have the next factor.

Third, the previous discussion raises the overlooked but intriguing issue that Jesus' audiences perceived him, at least occasionally, as the victor of interpretive battles with scribal-literate figures.[50] The Synoptic Gospels portray a Jesus who outwits scribal-literate authorities on their own turf and in a public nature. For example, Mark portrays Jesus

---

50. On the significance of Jesus citing Scripture in such battles, see immediately below.

successfully turning the tables on the chief priests, scribes, and elders in Jerusalem. When they challenge his authority, he responds by giving them a riddle concerning John the Baptist that they cannot answer (Mark 11:27–33). As a result of similar encounters, the Synoptics claim that Jesus emerged from the controversies as the winner: "After that no one dared to ask him any question.... And the large crowd was listening to him with delight" (Mark 12:34, 37); "No one was able to give him an answer, nor from that day did anyone dare to ask him any more questions" (Matt 22:46); "When he said this, all his opponents were put to shame; and the entire crowd was rejoicing at all the wonderful things that he was doing" (Luke 13:17); "And they could not reply to this" (Luke 14:6); "For they no longer dared to ask him another question" (Luke 20:40).[51]

Once again, one does not have to affirm the historical accuracy of each of these texts in order to affirm the likelihood of their broad claim— someone somewhere perceived Jesus to have won a public battle of wits with Pharisees, scribes, or other scribal-literate authorities. If this ever occurred, then it requires no great leap of imagination to understand that some members of Jesus' audiences could have moved from the perception that Jesus successfully responded to a challenge from scribal-literate authorities to the conclusion that he himself held such authority and was, thus, himself a scribal-literate individual.

Fourth, and to add further to the previous suggestion, I view it as particularly likely that at least some members of Jesus' audience(s) could have concluded that he was a scribal-literate teacher if he cited Scripture during his pedagogical sessions or his interpretive battles. It is at this point, therefore, that Jesus' references to the Scriptures in such battles become relevant to scholarly discussions of Jesus' scribal-literate status. Although texts such as Mark 12:10 ("Have you not read this scripture?...") do not constitute claims on the parts of the Gospel authors that Jesus was able to read Scripture, they do constitute claims that Jesus was part of cultural events that could have led to the conviction that he was able to read Scripture, particularly if he was viewed as the winner.[52] In

---

51. By way of contrast, neither the narrator's nor the characters' public acknowledgment that Jesus won interpretive battles is a sustained theme in John's Gospel. The late addition to the Gospel of John, the *Pericope Adulterae*, however, does include a similar scene. After the scribes and the Pharisees approach Jesus to test him over the interpretation of the Mosaic Law, they leave defeated: "When they heard it, they went away, one by one, beginning with the elders" (John 8:9).

52. In a similar manner, the Gospel authors' claims that Jesus had followers who referred to him as "rabbi" or "teacher" do not indicate that Jesus was a *scribal-literate*

other words, Jesus did not have to be able to read the Scriptures in order
to know what they said. And if he cited what they said in an authoritative
manner while arguing with known scribal-literate authorities, an
audience member who perceived him as the winner could easily have also
perceived him as a scribal-literate teacher and pointed to his authoritative
citation of Scripture against known authorities as reason for his or her
conclusion.

Other aspects of Jesus' cultural context also likely created the possibility for some of his audiences or audience members to conclude that he
was a scribal-literate teacher despite the fact that he was not.[53] The
preceding discussion, however, demonstrates the complexity of scribal
culture and its social perception at the time of Jesus, and thus describes
some conditions under which someone could have come to that conclusion. Once Jesus placed himself in social locations and situations that
invited the assessment of his scribal-literate status, the assessor's previous
knowledge of Jesus, the negotiation of revision between initial and
repeated impressions, and the perception that Jesus (at least sometimes)
out-witted or out-interpreted known scribal-literate authorities and

---

teacher, even as circumstantial evidence (see Evans, "Context," 17 [on the circumstantial nature of the evidence], 19; Evans, "Jewish Scripture," 48–49; and the
discussion in Chapter 1). They do, however, indicate a historical circumstance that
could have led some observers to that conclusion, and equally led others to reject the
idea, depending on their respective familiarity levels with scribal culture, Jesus, and
his disciples.

53. For example, if Jesus was perceived to have supernatural exorcistic and
therapeutic abilities *and* was perceived to employ these abilities while occupying the
social position of a scribal-literate teacher, some of his audience members could have
concluded that he was a powerful scribal-literate teacher. Note Mark's claim that the
Capernaum synagogue intertwined Jesus' pedagogy and exorcism in just such a
manner. After casting a demon out, they respond: "What is this? A new *teaching*—
with authority! He commands even the unclean spirits, and they obey him" (Mark
1:27; emphasis added). On account of this intertwined pedagogical and exorcistic
activity, Jesus' "fame began to spread throughout the surrounding region of Galilee"
(1:28). (Similarly, Graham H. Twelftree, *Jesus the Miracle Worker: A Historical and
Theological Study* [Downers Grove: IVP, 1999], 95: "Although miracles are
important to Mark, Jesus the miracle worker cannot be separated from Jesus the
teacher.") Mark's claim here is rather precise. He himself does not believe Jesus is a
scribal-literate teacher (1:22) but notes that his reputation sprang from a combination of his presentation of himself as one and his supernatural abilities. I reiterate
that one does not need to affirm the historical accuracy of this text, or the existence
of demons, in order to affirm that the perception that Jesus had such abilities could
have contributed to the perception that he was a scribal-literate teacher under certain
social conditions.

(at least sometimes) cited Scripture during such events, all could have enabled such perceptions. All this happening concurrently among audiences of different classes offers a plausible context from which multiple perceptions of Jesus, and indeed corporate confusion, could have emerged.

3. *Conclusion*

Jesus most likely did not hold scribal literacy. This alone, however, was not enough to keep some of his audiences, or members of his audiences, from concluding that he did.[54] Although he was not a scribal-literate teacher, he was the type of teacher who was able to make people assume or conclude that he was. Therefore, within Jesus' own lifetime there likely were contradictory and confused perceptions of his scribal-literate status.

From one perspective, the proposal that Jesus' audiences reached differing conclusions concerning his scribal authority and, thus, his scribal-literate status, is common sense. Surely no one doubts that different sectors of Jesus' audiences reached different conclusions about him,[55] or even that various members of Jesus' audience within the same class carried different convictions about him.[56] Related to this, several scholars have demonstrated the likelihood that ambiguity marked Jesus' teaching or public appearances.[57] If this is the case, it increases the complexity of the assessment of Jesus' pedagogy and thus increases the possibility for differing conclusions among Jesus' audiences. Furthermore, if one affirms that Jesus lived in a socio-historical context where scribal-literate authority was a primary factor in the distribution of power,[58] and that Jesus ran afoul of those who held such power by

54. See also Fredriksen, *Jesus*, 242–45, who argues that Jesus' life and ministry were sufficient to convince some that he was not a messianic claimant and threat to Rome (242–43) and others that he was (245). Regardless of whether one agrees with Fredriksen that Jesus himself did not claim to be the Messiah (242), her general proposal that Jesus' life would have generated multiple convictions about the matter is convincing and resonates with my proposal concerning his scribal-literate status.

55. Luke 11:53–12:1; 13:17; John 7:47–52.

56. John 7:12, 25–31, 43–44; 9:16; 10:19. I note again Mark's portrayal that some Galilean synagogues accepted Jesus as a synagogue teacher (1:21–28, 39) while his hometown did not (6:1–6).

57. Haacker, "What," 153; Thatcher, *Jesus*, esp. 3–15.

58. With regard to the ancient world in general, see the essays in Bowman and Woolf, eds., *Literacy and Power*. With regard to Jewish and early Christian contexts in particular, see Fox, "Literacy," 126–48; Goodman, "Texts," 99–108. See also Saldarini's description of scribal-literate authorities as educated (127) brokers of

engaging them publicly, then it is sensible that there also were different convictions about Jesus' own relationship to that power. Jesus' scribal-literate status was simply one more thing that his contemporaries disagreed upon, or were confused about, concerning him.

More important, however, is that the thesis that Jesus was not a scribal-literate teacher but was perceived to be one by some people offers a more satisfactory explanation for the various early Christian Jesus-memories that appear in the sources. More precisely, it accounts better for the impact of the past on the differing Jesus-memories we see in first-century (and later) sources than previous proposals. The sources portray a Jesus who was not a scribal-literate teacher, a Jesus who was, and a Jesus who confused individuals on the matter. In a very real sense, each of these claims has a purchase in the historical Jesus, although their claims are not equal. The Markan portrayal of Jesus as a τέκτων who is outside the scribal-literate class but nevertheless occupies social positions associated with scribal literacy, and meets various receptions for doing so, most clearly reflects the actual past. Similarly, the Johannine claim that Jesus was assumed to be uneducated, but was able to force at least some of his audiences to re-assess those assumptions, has a high degree of historical plausibility.[59] Matthew maintains the rejection of Jesus in his hometown, but transitions Jesus away from direct identification with the scribal-illiterate manual-labor class and towards scribal pedagogical authority (Matt 23:1–12). Luke completes the transition towards scribal literacy by presenting Jesus as a fully legitimate scribal-literate synagogue teacher.

Roman authority to "the mass of uneducated villagers" (58) (Anthony J. Saldarini, *Pharisees, Scribes, and Sadducees in Palestinian Society* [BRS; Grand Rapids: Eerdmans, 1988]) and Snyder's more precise description of them as "text-brokers" (Snyder, *Teachers*, 11); see Keith, *Pericope*, 99–102, for a summary.

59. Keith, "Claim," 60–63.

CONCLUDING REMARKS:
THE CONTROVERSY OF JESUS THE TEACHER

The difficulty arose simply because Jesus set himself up
as an interpreter of texts
in the first place.[1]

Doubting that Jesus was literate is not new. Several aspects of my argument that he did not hold scribal literacy in particular, however, are new. I close this study by noting its contributions and offering some brief remarks on the relevance of my conclusions for the interpretation of the controversy narratives.

1. *The Contributions of this Study*

First, although others have addressed the topic of Jesus' literacy in articles and book chapters, this is the first book-length study. Advances in our knowledge of the complexities of ancient scribal and literary culture in the last thirty years in particular enable a more thorough consideration of Jesus' literacy than was previously possible. In the wake of Harris, specialists in Biblical Studies and cognate fields, such as Jaffee, Hezser, Snyder, Carr, Horsley, and van der Toorn have awakened their fields to this important aspect of Palestinian culture in new ways, opening the door for this study's consideration of Jesus' place within it.[2]

Second, this study makes a methodological advancement from previous studies by being the first effort to bring the insights of social memory theory to bear upon the issue of Jesus' scribal-literate status. Adopting the Jesus-memory approach to the historical Jesus, I have argued that any theory about Jesus' scribal-literate status must explain the different portrayals of him that appear in the early sources.

---

1. Snyder, *Teachers*, 215–16.
2. Harris, *Ancient*; Jaffee, *Torah*; Hezser, *Jewish*; Snyder, *Teachers*; Carr, *Writing*; Horsley, *Scribes*; van der Toorn, *Scribal Culture*; respectively.

A third and original contribution of this book concerns its insistence that the issue of Jesus' scribal-literate status is not quite as simple as a bald statement that affirms or denies scribal literacy for Jesus. Although I propose that Jesus likely did not hold scribal literacy, I also propose that if one were able to ask Jesus' contemporaries whether he was a scribal-literate teacher, the answer one received would depend upon which contemporary of Jesus one asked. This third contribution relates directly to the first two, insofar as it stems from a commitment to explain the Jesus-memories in the Gospels and other sources in light of the multifaceted world of first-century Palestinian scribal culture, where different groups and individuals perceived different literate skills differently.

A fourth and, to my knowledge, also original contribution of this study is my argument that the Synoptic Gospels and John show that, already by the first century, there was explicit disagreement and/or confusion in early Christianity over whether Jesus was a scribal-literate teacher. This tension in the corporate early Christian Jesus-memory is particularly clear in the accounts of Jesus' return to his hometown synagogue in Nazareth. Mark represents one end of the spectrum, claiming earlier in his narrative that Jesus was "not like the scribes" (Mark 1:22), that others recognized him as such, and that his hometown rejected him as a synagogue teacher on account of this fact by identifying him as a τέκτων (Mark 6:3). Luke represents the other end of the spectrum, removing the charge that Jesus is a τέκτων and presenting him as a scribal-literate teacher who is capable of reading and interpreting Scripture publicly in a synagogue (Luke 4:16–20). When scholars debate the scribal-literate status of Jesus, they are joining a two-thousand year-old conversation.

2. *The Scribal-Illiterate Jesus and the Controversy Narratives*

To bring the current discussion back to one of the main points of the Introduction and Chapter One, the issue of Jesus' scribal-literate status matters to Jesus scholarship. Whether one considers Jesus a scribal-literate or scribal-illiterate person impacts one's conception of Jesus as a Jewish teacher and, ultimately, how one sees Jesus functioning in the culture of his day. Along these lines, I conclude this study with a few brief remarks on the relevance of my argument for the interpretation of the controversy narratives. For, it is here, in the Gospels' portrayals of Jesus' conflict with the authorities of his day, that the exegetical effects of my argument will perhaps most readily be felt.

First, if Jesus was not a scribal-literate teacher, then the controversy narratives ultimately do not reflect in-house debates between equally qualified/authoritative teachers (contrary to the suggestions of some that

Jesus himself was a Pharisee).[3] Rather, the debates between Jesus and Pharisees, Sadducees, priests, scribes, and others were likely attempts on the part of the scribal-literate authorities to expose Jesus as an imposter to the position of interpretive authority. Not all interactions between Jesus and scribal-literate teachers were antagonistic, but those interactions that were antagonistic were likely designed to demonstrate publicly that Jesus was *not* one of their own. Questions such as "By whose authority are you doing these things, and who gave you this authority?" (Matt 21:23) were rhetorical and intended to shame Jesus. By the same token, questions such as "Have you never read what David did?" (Mark 2:25) on the part of Jesus were likewise rhetorical and intended to shame his scribal-literate opponents.

Second, in light of the previous point, one must note a certain irony in the difference between the intended effects of scribal-literate authorities' public engagements of Jesus and their likely actual effects in the observing audiences. If scribal-literate authorities simply ignored Jesus, they would not have created the social circumstances by which some audience members concluded that he was one of them. By debating Jesus publicly in order to demonstrate that he was not a scribal-literate authority, however, they created situations that led some of the audiences to conclude the precise opposite—that Jesus too was a scribal-literate authority. Ironically, then, the actual effect (or at least one effect) of their admission of Jesus into debate with them stood in diametrical opposition to their intentions for doing so.

Third and finally, this scenario raises the question of why scribal-literate authorities did not simply ignore Jesus altogether. This matter also takes us to the beginnings of Jesus' conflict with the scribal-literate authorities, a conflict that eventually ended with Jesus on a Roman cross. I suggest that my argument concerning Jesus' scribal-literate status—he was not a scribal-literate teacher but managed to convince many that he was—provides an explanation for why the Jewish authorities could not ignore Jesus in the early period of his ministry. Undoubtedly, the content of Jesus' preaching and teaching, as well as his reputation as an exorcist and healer, also led their attention and concern to turn toward Galilee. But a central contributing factor to why they could not ignore Jesus altogether was that some of his audiences were accepting Jesus as a scribal-literate authority in his own right. Jesus was trading on the very social factor that created and enabled their own authoritative status in Second Temple Judaism: their reputations as scribal-literate interpreters of the law. Thus, when Jesus presented dissenting views from scribal

3. Falk, *Jesus the Pharisee*; Maccoby, *Jesus the Pharisee*; Winter, *On the Trial*, 133.

authorities, some members of his audience understood those views as deriving from an authority equal to their own. To qualify the quotation at the beginning of these concluding remarks, then, Jesus became a problem that demanded attention from the Jewish leadership, and continued to be throughout his ministry, not just because he set himself up as a scribal-literate interpreter of texts, but because he did so, in some times and at some places, successfully.

BIBLIOGRAPHY

Critical Biblical Texts

Aland, Barbara, Kurt Aland, Johannes Karavidopoulos, Carlo M. Martini, and Bruce M. Metzger, eds. *Novum Testamentum Graece*. 27th ed. 8th printing. Stuttgart: Deutsche Bibelgesellschaft, 2001.

Elliger, K., and W. Rudolph, eds. *Biblia Hebraica Stuttgartensia*. Revised by A. Schenker. 5th ed. Stuttgart: Deutsche Bibelgesellschaft, 1997.

Ralfs, Alfred, ed. *Septuaginta: Editio altera*. Revised by Robert Hanhart. Stuttgart: Deutsche Bibelgesellschaft, 2006.

Septuaginta: Vetus Testamentum Graecum Auctoritate Academiae Scientiarum Gottingensis editum. 20 vols. Göttingen: Vandenhoeck & Ruprecht, 1931–.

Primary Sources

Adamantius. *Dialogue on the True Faith in God*. Edited by Garry W. Trompf. Translated with Commentary by Robert A. Pretty. Gnostica 1. Leuven: Peeters, 1997.

Angeli, Anna. *Agli amici di scuola (PHerc. 1005)*. LSE 7. Naples: Bibliopolis, 1988.

The Ante-Nicene Fathers. Edited by Alexander Roberts and James Donaldson. 1885–87. 10 vols. Repr., Peabody: Hendrickson, 1994.

The Apostolic Fathers: Greek Texts and English Translations. Edited and revised by Michael W. Holmes. Grand Rapids: Baker Academic, 1999.

The Biblical Antiquities of Philo. Translated by M. R. James. Translations of Early Documents 1. London: SPCK, 1917.

Book of Mormon. London: West European Mission, 1959.

Charles, Robert Henry, ed. *The Ethiopic Version of the Hebrew Book of Jubilees*. Anecdota Oxoniensia. Oxford: Clarendon, 1895.

———. *The Greek Versions of the Testaments of the Twelve Patriarchs*. Oxford: Oxford University Press, 1966.

Charlesworth, James H., ed. *The Old Testament Pseudepigrapha*. 2 vols. Garden City: Doubleday, 1983, 1985.

Curenton, W., ed. and trans. *Ancient Syriac Documents Relative to the Earliest Establishment of Christianity in Edessa and the Neighbouring Countries, from the Year after Our Lord's Ascension to the Beginning of the Fourth Century*. Eugene, Wipf & Stock, 1864.

Denis, Albert-Marie, ed. *Fragmenta Pseudepigraphorum Quae Supersunt Graeca*. PVTG 3. Leiden: Brill, 1970.

Dionysius of Halicarnassus. *The Critical Essays*. Translated by Stephen Usher. 2 vols. LCL. London: William Heinemann, 1974–85.

Dobschütz, Ernst von, ed. *Das Decretum Gelasianum*. Texte und Untersuchungen zur Geschichte der altchristlichen Literatur 3.3.4/38.4. Leipzig: J. C. Hinrichs, 1912.

Eusebius. *The Ecclesiastical History*. Translated by Kirsopp Lake and J. E. L. Oulton. 2 vols. LCL. Cambridge, Mass.: Harvard University Press, 1957–59.

García Martínez, Florentino, and Eibert J. C. Tigchelaar, trans. *The Dead Sea Scrolls: Study Edition*. 2 vols. Grand Rapids: Eerdmans, 1997, 1998.

Hock, Ronald F. "The Infancy Gospel of Thomas." Pages 380–96 in *The Complete Gospels*. Edited by Robert J. Miller. Santa Rosa: Polebridge, 1994.

Howard, George, trans. *The Teaching of Addai*. SBLTT 16/ECLS 4. Chico: Scholars Press, 1981.

Itinerarium of Egeria. Pages 120–31 in *Die Abgarlegende: Das Christusbild von Edessa* by Martin Illert. Fontes Christiani 45. Turnhout: Brepols, 2007.

Jonge, M. de, ed. *The Testaments of the Twelve Patriarchs: A Critical Edition of the Greek Text*. PVTG 1/2. Leiden: Brill, 1978.

Josephus. Translated by H. St. J. Thackeray et al. 12 vols. LCL. Cambridge, Mass.: Harvard University Press, 1926–81.

Justin Martyr. *Writings of Saint Justin Martyr*. Translated by Thomas B. Falls. FC 6. Washington, D.C.: Catholic University of America Press, 1948.

Lactantius. *De mortibus persecutorum*. Translated by J. L. Creed. OECT. Oxford: Clarendon, 1984.

———. *Minor Works*. Translated by Mary Francis McDonald. FC 54. Washington, D.C.: Catholic University of America Press, 1965.

Lewis, Naphtali, Yigael Yadin, and Jonas C. Greenfield, eds. *The Documents from the Bar Kokhba Period in the Cave of Letters: Greek Papyri*. JDS. Jerusalem: Israel Exploration Fund, 1989.

Lucian. *The Works of Lucian*. Translated by A. M. Harmon. 8 vols. LCL. London: William Heinemann, 1977.

Minucius Felix. *The Octavius of Marcus Minucius Felix*. Translated by G. W. Clarke. ACW 39. New York: Newman, 1974.

The Nag Hammadi Library in English. Edited by Marvin W. Meyer. Translated by members of the Coptic Gnostic Library Project of the Institute for Antiquity and Christianity. Leiden: Brill, 1977.

New Testament Apocrypha. Edited by Wilhelm Schneemelcher. Translated by R. McL. Wilson. Rev. ed. 2 vols. Louisville: Westminster John Knox, 1991.

The Nicene and Post-Nicene Fathers, Series 1. Edited by Philip Schaff. 1886–89. 14 vols. Repr., Peabody: Hendrickson, 1994.

The Nicene and Post-Nicene Fathers, Series 2. Edited by Philip Schaff and Henry Wace. 1890–1900. 14 vols. Repr., Peabody: Hendrickson, 1994.

Origen: Contra Celsum. Translated by Henry Chadwick. Cambridge: Cambridge University Press, 1965.

Patrologia graeca. Edited by J.-P. Migne. 162 vols. Paris, 1857–86.

Patrologia latina. Edited by J.-P. Migne. 217 vols. Paris, 1844–64.

Philo. Translated by F. H. Colson and G. H. Whitaker. 10 vols. LCL. Cambridge, Mass.: Harvard University Press, 1929–62.

Plisch, Uwe-Karsten. *The Gospel of Thomas: Original Text with Commentary*. Translated by Gesine Schenke Robinson. Stuttgart: Deutsche Bibelgesellschaft, 2008.

Quintilian. *Institutio Oratoria: Books I–III.* Translated by H. E. Butler. LCL. Cambridge, Mass.: Harvard University Press, 1920.

Seneca. *Epistulae Morales.* Translated by Richard M. Gummere. 3 vols. LCL. London: William Heinemann, 1917–25.

The Talmud of the Land of Israel. Vol. 17, *Sukkah.* Translated by Jacob Neusner. Chicago: University of Chicago Press, 1988.

The Talmud of the Land of Israel. Vol. 19, *Megillah.* Translated by Jacob Neusner. CSHJ. Chicago: University of Chicago Press, 1987.

Tischendorf, Constantinus, ed. *Evangelia apocrypha: adhibitis plurimis codicibus graecis et latinis maximam partem nunc primum consultis atque ineditorum copia insignibus.* Rev. ed. Leipzig: Hermann Mendelssohn, 1876.

The Tosefta: Translated from the Hebrew with a New Introduction. Translated by Jacob Neusner. 2 vols. Peabody: Hendrickson, 2002.

Vermes, Geza, trans. *The Complete Dead Sea Scrolls in English.* New York: Penguin, 1997.

Winkelmann, Friedrich, ed. *Eusebius Werke.* 3 vols. Die griechischen christlichen Schriftsteller der ersten Jahrhunderte new series 6.1–6.3. Berlin: Akademie, 1999.

Wise, Michael, Martin Abegg, Jr., and Edward Cook, trans. *The Dead Sea Scrolls: A New Translation.* San Francisco: HarperCollins, 1996.

Secondary Sources

Ackroyd, P. R., and C. F. Evans, eds. *The Cambridge History of the Bible.* Vol. 1, *From the Beginnings to Jerome.* Cambridge: Cambridge University Press, 1970.

Aguilar, Mario I. "The Archaeology of Memory and the Issue of Colonialism: Mimesis and the Controversial Tribute to Caesar in Mark 12:13–17." *BTB* 35 (2005): 60–66.

———. "Rethinking the Judean Past: Questions of History and a Social Archaeology of Memory in the First Book of the Maccabees." *BTB* 30 (2000): 58–67.

Aitken, Ellen Bradshaw. *Jesus' Death in Early Christian Memory: The Poetics of the Passion.* NTOA/SUNT 53. Göttingen: Vandenhoeck & Ruprecht, 2004.

Alexander, Loveday. "Memory and Tradition in the Hellenistic Schools." Pages 113–53 in Kelber and Byrskog, eds., *Jesus in Memory.*

Allison Jr., Dale C. *Constructing Jesus: Memory, Imagination, and History.* Grand Rapids: Baker Academic, 2010.

———. *The Historical Christ and the Theological Jesus.* Grand Rapids: Eerdmans, 2009.

———. *Jesus of Nazareth: Millenarian Prophet.* Minneapolis: Fortress, 1998.

———. *Resurrecting Jesus: The Earliest Christian Tradition and Its Interpreters.* London: T&T Clark, 2005.

Arnal, William E. *Jesus and the Village Scribes: Galilean Conflicts and the Setting of Q.* Minneapolis: Fortress, 2001.

Assmann, Aleida. "Was sind kulturelle Texte?" Pages 232–44 in Poltermann, ed., *Literaturkanon.*

Assmann, Jan. "Cultural Texts Suspended between Writing and Speech." Pages 101–21 in *Religion and Cultural Memory.* Repr. and trans. from "Kulturelle Texte im Spannungsfeld von Mündlichkeit und Schriftlichkeit. Pages 270–92 in Poltermann, ed., *Literaturkanon.*

———. *Moses the Egyptian: The Memory of Egypt in Western Monotheism.* Cambridge, Mass.: Harvard University Press, 1997.

————. *Religion and Cultural Memory.* Translated by Rodney Livingstone. CMP. Stanford: Stanford University Press, 2006.

Aune, David E. "Literacy." Pages 275–76 in *The Westminster Dictionary of New Testament and Early Christian Literature and Rhetoric.* Louisville: Westminster John Knox, 2003.

Bacher, Wilhelm. "Das altjüdische Schulwesen." *Jahrbuch für jüdische Geschichte und Literatur* 6 (1903): 48–81.

Bagnall, Roger S. "Jesus Reads a Book." *JTS* 51, no. 2 (2000): 577–88.

————. *Reading Papyri, Writing Ancient History.* AAW. New York: Routledge, 1995.

Baines, John. "Literacy (Ancient Near East)." *ABD* 4:333–37.

————. "Literacy and Ancient Egyptian Society." *Man* 18 (1983): 572–99.

Bakhos, Carol. "Orality and Writing." Pages 482–500 in *The Oxford Handbook of Jewish Daily Life in Roman Palestine.* Edited by Catherine Hezser. Oxford: Oxford University Press, 2010.

Bar-Ilan, Meir. "Illiteracy in the Land of Israel in the First Centuries CE." Pages 46–61 in *Essays in the Social Scientific Study of Judaism and Jewish Society,* vol. 2. Edited by Simcha Fishbane, Stuart Schoenfeld, and A. Goldschlaeger. New York: Ktav, 1992.

————. "Writing in Ancient Israel and Early Judaism Part Two: Scribes and Books in the Late Second Commonwealth and Rabbinic Period." Pages 21–38 in Mulder, ed., *Mikra.*

Barclay, William. *The Mind of Jesus.* New York: Harper & Row, 1961.

Barkay, Gabriel. "The Iron Age II–III." Pages 302–73 in Ben-Tor, ed., *Archaeology of Ancient Israel.*

Batey, Richard A. "Is Not This the Carpenter?" *NTS* 30 (1984): 249–58.

Bauckham, Richard. "For Whom Were the Gospels Written?" Pages 9–48 in Bauckham, ed., *Gospels for All Christians.*

————, ed. *The Gospels for All Christians: Rethinking the Gospel Audiences.* Edinburgh: T. & T. Clark, 1998.

————. *Jesus and the Eyewitnesses: The Gospels as Eyewitness Testimony.* Grand Rapids: Eerdmans, 2006.

————. "John for Readers of Mark." Pages 147–71 in Bauckham, ed., *Gospels for All Christians.*

————. *The Testimony of the Beloved Disciple: Narrative, History, and Theology in the Gospel of John.* Grand Rapids: Baker Academic, 2007.

Bauer, D. Walter. *Das Johannesevangelium.* 2d ed. HNT 6. Tübingen: Mohr Siebeck, 1925.

Baumgarten, Albert I. *The Flourishing of Jewish Sects in the Maccabean Era.* JSJSup 55. Atlanta: Society of Biblical Literature, 1997.

Beard, Mary, Alan K. Bowman, Mireille Corbier, Tim Cornell, James L. Franklin, Jr., Ann Hanson, Keith Hopkins, and Nicholas Horsfall. *Literacy in the Roman World.* JRASup 3. Ann Arbor: Journal of Roman Archaeology, 1991.

Becker, Jürgen. *Das Evangelium nach Johannes, Kapitel 1–10.* ÖTBK 4/1. Würzburg: Echter-Verlag, 1979.

————. *Jesus of Nazareth.* Translated by James E. Crouch. Berlin: de Gruyter, 1998.

Beilby, James K., and Paul Rhodes Eddy. "The Quest for the Historical Jesus: An Introduction." Pages 9–54 in *The Historical Jesus: Five Views.* Edited by James K. Beilby and Paul Rhodes Eddy. Downers Grove: IVP Academic, 2009.

Benko, Stephen. "Pagan Criticism of Christianity During the First Two Centuries A.D." *ANRW* 23.2.1055–1118. Part 2, *Principat*, 23.2. Edited by Wolfgang Haase. Berlin: de Gruyter, 1980.

Ben-Tor, Amnon, ed. *The Archaeology of Ancient Israel.* Translated by R. Greenberg. New Haven: Yale University Press, 1992.

Ben-Yehuda, Nachman. *The Masada Myth: Collective Memory and Mythmaking in Israel.* Madison: University of Wisconsin Press, 1995.

Bernard, J. H. *A Critical and Exegetical Commentary on the Gospel of John.* Edited by A. H. McNeile. 2 vols. ICC. Edinburgh: T. & T. Clark, 1928.

Bienkowski, Piotr, Christopher Mee, and Elizabeth Slater, eds. *Writing and Ancient Near Eastern Society: Papers in Honour of Alan R. Millard.* JSOTSup 426. London: T&T Clark, 2005.

Birkeland, Harris. *The Language of Jesus.* SNVA 1954/1. Oslo: Jacob Dybwad, 1954.

Black, Matthew. "Language and Script: The Biblical Languages." Pages 1–11 in Ackroyd and Evans, eds., *Cambridge History of the Bible,* vol. 1.

Blass, F., and A. DeBrunner. *A Greek Grammar of the New Testament and Other Early Christian Literature.* Translated and revised by Robert W. Funk. Chicago: University of Chicago Press, 1961.

Blomberg, Craig L. Review of Craig S. Keener, *The Historical Jesus of the Gospels. Review of Biblical Literature* (2010). No pages. Cited 10 September 2010. Online: http://www.bookreviews.org/pdf/7385_8048.pdf.

Bock, Darrell L. *Luke Vol. 1: 1:1–9:50.* BECNT. Grand Rapids: Baker, 1994.

Bockmuehl, Markus. *Seeing the Word: Refocusing New Testament Study.* STI. Grand Rapids: Baker Academic, 2006.

———. *This Jesus: Martyr, Lord, Messiah.* Downers Grove: IVP, 1994.

Bodnar, John. *Remaking America: Public Memory, Commemoration, and Patriotism in the Twentieth Century.* Princeton: Princeton University Press, 1992.

Bond, Helen K. *Caiaphas: Friend of Rome and Judge of Jesus?* Louisville: Westminster John Knox, 2004.

Boomershine, Thomas E. "Jesus of Nazareth and the Watershed of Ancient Orality and Literacy." Pages 7–35 in Dewey, ed., *Orality.*

Booth, A. D. "The Schooling of Slaves in First-Century Rome." *TAPA* 109 (1979): 11–19.

Boring, M. Eugene. *The Continuing Voice of Jesus: Christian Prophecy and the Gospel Tradition.* Louisville: Westminster John Knox, 1991.

Bovon, François. *Das Evangelium nach Lukas (Lk 1,1–9,50).* EKKNT 3/1. Zurich: Benziger, 1989.

Bowman, Alan K., and Greg Woolf, eds. *Literacy and Power in the Ancient World.* Cambridge: Cambridge University Press, 1994.

Brueggemann, Walter. *Abiding Astonishment: Psalms, Modernity, and History Making.* Louisville: Westminster John Knox, 1991.

———. *David's Truth in Israel's Imagination and Memory.* Philadelphia: Fortress, 1985.

Buchanan, George Wesley. "Jesus and the Upper Class." *NovT* 7 (1964): 195–209.

Bultmann, Rudolf. *The Gospel of John: A Commentary.* Translated by G. R. Beasley-Murray, R. W. N. Hoare, and J. K. Riches. Philadelphia: Westminster, 1971.

———. *The History of the Synoptic Tradition.* Translated by John Marsh. Rev. ed. Peabody: Hendrickson, 1963.

Burge, Gary M. *Jesus, the Middle Eastern Storyteller.* ACAF. Grand Rapids: Zondervan, 2009.

Burge, Gary M., Lynn H. Cohick, and Gene L. Green. *The New Testament in Antiquity: A Survey of the New Testament within Its Cultural Contexts.* Grand Rapids: Zondervan, 2009.

Byrskog, Samuel. "A Century with the *Sitz im Leben*: From Form-Critical Setting to Gospel Community and Beyond." *ZNW* 98 (2007): 1–27.

———. "The Early Church as a Narrative Fellowship: An Exploratory Study of the Performance of the *Chreia.*" *TTKi* 78 (2007): 207–26.

———. "Introduction." Pages 1–20 in Kelber and Byrskog, eds., *Jesus in Memory.*

———. *Jesus the Only Teacher: Didactic Authority and Transmission in Ancient Israel, Ancient Judaism and the Matthean Community.* ConBNT 24. Stockholm: Almqvist & Wiksell, 1994.

———. "A New Quest for the *Sitz im Leben*: Social Memory, the Jesus Tradition and the Gospel of Matthew." *NTS* 52 (2006): 319–36.

———. *Story as History—History as Story: The Gospel Tradition in the Context of Ancient Oral History.* WUNT 123. Tübingen: Mohr Siebeck, 2000.

Cadoux, C. J. *The Life of Jesus.* Gateshead on Tyne: Pelican, 1948.

Calderini, Rita. "Gli ἀγράμματοι nell'Egitto greco-romano." *Aegyptus* 30 (1950): 14–41.

Calvert, D. G. A. "An Examination of the Criteria for Distinguishing the Authentic Words of Jesus." *NTS* 18 (1972): 209–18.

Carr, David M. *Writing on the Tablet of the Heart: Origins of Scripture and Literature.* New York: Oxford University Press, 2005.

Catto, Stephen K. *Reconstructing the First-Century Synagogue: A Critical Analysis of Current Research.* LNTS 363. London: T&T Clark, 2007.

Chadwick, Henry. "Introduction." Pages ix–xxxii in *Origen: Contra Celsum.* Cambridge: Cambridge University Press, 1965.

Charlesworth, James H. "Introduction: Why Evaluate Twenty-Five Years of Jesus Research?" Pages 1–15 in Charlesworth and Pokorný, eds., *Jesus Research.*

Charlesworth, James H., and Petr Pokorný, eds. *Jesus Research: An International Perspective.* Grand Rapids: Eerdmans, 2009.

Chilton, Bruce D. *A Galilean Rabbi and His Bible: Jesus' Use of the Interpreted Scripture of His Time.* GNS 8. Wilmington: Michael Glazier, 1984.

———. *Rabbi Jesus: An Intimate Biography.* New York: Doubleday, 2000.

Chilton, Bruce, and Craig A. Evans, eds. *Authenticating the Words of Jesus and Authenticating the Activities of Jesus.* 2 vols. NTTS 28. Leiden: Brill, 1999.

Cohen, Shaye J. D. *From the Maccabees to the Mishnah.* 2d ed. Louisville: Westminster John Knox, 2006.

Cohick, Lynn H. *Women in the World of the Earliest Christians.* Grand Rapids: Baker Academic, 2009.

Coser, Lewis A. "Introduction." Pages 1–34 in Halbwachs, *On Collective Memory.*

Craffert, Pieter F., and Pieter J. J. Botha. "Why Jesus Could Walk on the Sea but He Could Not Read or Write." *Neot* 39, no. 1 (2005): 5–35.

Cranfield, C. E. B. *The Gospel According to St. Mark.* CGTC. Cambridge: Cambridge University Press, 1959.

Crenshaw, James L. *Education in Ancient Israel: Across the Deadening Silence.* ABRL. New York: Doubleday, 1998.

Cribiore, Raffaella. "The Grammarian's Choice: The Popularity of Euripides' *Phoenissae* in Hellenistic and Roman Education." Pages 241–59 in *Education in Greek and Roman Antiquity.* Edited by Yun Lee Too. Leiden: Brill, 2001.

————. *Gymnastics of the Mind: Greek Education in Hellenistic and Roman Egypt.* Princeton: Princeton University Press, 2001.

————. *Writing, Teachers, and Students in Graeco-Roman Egypt.* ASP 36. Atlanta: Scholars Press, 1996.

Crossan, John Dominic. *The Birth of Christianity: Discovering What Happened in the Years Immediately after the Execution of Jesus.* New York: HarperCollins, 1998.

————. *The Essential Jesus: What Jesus Really Taught.* New York: HarperCollins, 1994.

————. *The Historical Jesus: The Life of a Mediterranean Jewish Peasant.* New York: HarperCollins, 1991.

————. *Jesus: A Revolutionary Biography.* New York: HarperCollins, 1994.

Crossan, John Dominic, Luke Timothy Johnson, and Werner H. Kelber. *The Jesus Controversy: Perspectives in Conflict.* RLS. Harrisburg: Trinity, 1999.

Cullmann, Oscar. "Infancy Gospels." Pages 414–69 in vol. 1 of Schneemelcher, ed., *New Testament Apocrypha.*

Dahl, Nils Alstrup. *Jesus in the Memory of the Early Church.* Minneapolis: Augsburg, 1976.

Daube, David. *The New Testament and Rabbinic Judaism.* London: Athlone, 1956.

Davies, Philip R. *Memories of Ancient Israel: An Introduction to Biblical History—Ancient and Modern.* Louisville: Westminster John Knox, 2008.

Davies, W. D., and Dale C. Allison, Jr. *A Critical and Exegetical Commentary on the Gospel of Matthew.* 3 vols. ICC. Edinburgh: T. & T. Clark, 1988–97.

Deissmann, Adolf. *Light from the Ancient East.* Translated by Lionel R. M. Strachan. Rev. ed. London: Hodder & Stoughton, 1927.

Demsky, Aaron. "Writing in Ancient Israel and Ancient Judaism Part One: The Biblical Period." Pages 2–20 in Mulder, ed., *Mikra.*

Derrenbacker Jr., R. A. *Ancient Compositional Practices and the Synoptic Problem.* BETL 186. Leuven: Peeters, 2005.

Dewey, Joanna. "The Gospel of John in Its Oral-Written Media World." Pages 239–52 in Fortna and Thatcher, eds., *Jesus in Johannine Tradition.*

————, ed. *Orality and Textuality in Early Christian Literature.* SemeiaSt 65. Atlanta: Society of Biblical Literature, 1995.

————. "Textuality in an Oral Culture: A Survey of the Pauline Traditions." Pages 37–65 in Dewey, ed., *Orality.*

Dibelius, Martin. *From Tradition to Gospel.* Translated by Bertram Lee Wolf. SL 124. New York: Charles Scribner's Sons, 1934.

Dodd, C. H. *The Founder of Christianity.* New York: Macmillan, 1970.

Douglas, Mary. "Introduction." Pages 1–19 in Halbwachs, *The Collective Memory.*

Draper, Jonathan A. "Vice Catalogues as Oral-Mnemonic Cues: A Comparative Study of the Two-Ways Tradition in the *Didache* and Parallels from the Perspective of Oral Tradition." Pages 111–33 in Thatcher, ed., *Jesus.*

Drazin, Nathan. *History of Jewish Education from 515 BCE to 220 CE.* Baltimore: The Johns Hopkins Press, 1963.

Drijvers, H. J. W. "The Abgar Legend." Pages 492–99 in vol. 1 of Schneemelcher, ed., *New Testament Apocrypha.*

Drioton, Et. "Un Apocryphe anti-arien: la version copte de la Correspondance d'Abgar, roi d'Édesse, avec Notre-Seignuŕ." *Revue de l'Orient chrétien* 20 (1915): 306–26, 337–73.

Duling, Dennis C. "Social Memory and Biblical Studies: Theory, Method, and Application." *BTB* 36, no. 1 (2006): 2–3.

Dunn, James D. G. "'All that glisters is not gold': In Quest of the Right Key to Unlock the Way to the Historical Jesus." Pages 131–61 in Schröter and Brucker, eds., *Der historische Jesus*.

———. *Jesus Remembered*. CM 1. Grand Rapids: Eerdmans, 2003.

———. *A New Perspective on Jesus: What the Quest for the Historical Jesus Missed*. London: SPCK, 2005.

———. "On History, Memory and Eyewitnesses: In Response to Bengt Holmberg and Samuel Byrskog." *JSNT* 26, no. 4 (2004): 473–87.

———. "Social Memory and the Oral Jesus Tradition." Pages 179–94 in Stuckenbruck, Barton, and Wold, eds., *Memory in the Bible*.

Ebner, Eliezer. *Elementary Education in Ancient Israel During the Tannaitic Period (10–220 C.E.)*. New York: Bloch, 1956.

Eddy, Paul Rhodes, and Gregory A. Boyd. *The Jesus Legend: A Case for the Historical Reliability of the Synoptic Tradition*. Grand Rapids: Baker Academic, 2007.

Edersheim, Alfred. *Sketches of Jewish Social Life*. Updated ed. Peabody: Hendrickson, 1994.

Ehrman, Bart D. *Jesus: Apocalyptic Prophet of the New Millennium*. New York: Oxford University Press, 1999.

———. *Misquoting Jesus: The Story Behind Who Changed the Bible and Why*. New York: HarperCollins, 2005.

———. *The Orthodox Corruption of Scripture: The Effect of Early Christological Controversies on the Text of the New Testament*. New York: Oxford University Press, 1993.

———. "The Text of the Gospels at the End of the Second Century." Pages 95–122 in *Codex Bezae: Studies from the Lunel Colloquium, June 1994*. Edited by D. C. Parker and C.-B. Amphoux. NTTS 22. Leiden: Brill, 1996.

Elliott, J. K. *The Apocryphal Jesus: Legends of the Early Church*. Oxford: Oxford University Press, 1996.

———. Review of *The Pericope Adulterae, the Gospel of John, and the Literacy of Jesus* by Chris Keith. *JTS* 61, no. 1 (2010): 293–6.

Ellis, E. Earle. "The Synoptic Gospels as History." Pages 49–57 in Chilton and Evans, eds., *Authenticating the Activities of Jesus*. Repr. from pages 83–91 in *Crisis in Christology: Essays in Quest of Resolution*. Edited by William R. Farmer. Livonia: Dove, 1995.

Emerton, J. A., ed. *Congress Volume: Jerusalem 1986*. Leiden: Brill, 1988.

Epp, Eldon Jay. "The Codex and Literacy in Early Christianity and at Oxyrhynchus: Issues Raised by Harry Y. Gamble's *Books and Readers in the Early Church*." Pages 521–50 in *Perspectives*. Repr. from *Critical Review of Books in Religion* 11 (1998): 15–37.

———. "The Oxyrhynchus New Testament Papyri: 'Not without honor except in their hometown'?" Pages 743–801 in *Perspectives*. Repr. from *JBL* 123, no. 1 (2004): 5–55.

———. *Perspectives on New Testament Textual Criticism: Collected Essays, 1962–2004*. NovTSup 116. Leiden: Brill, 2005.

Esler, Philip F. "Collective Memory and Hebrews 11: Outlining a New Investigative Framework." Pages 151–71 in Kirk and Thatcher, eds., *Memory*.

———. *Conflict and Identity in Romans: The Social Setting of Paul's Letter*. Minneapolis: Fortress, 2003.

———. "Paul's Contestation of Israel's (Ethnic) Memory of Abraham in Galatians 3." *BTB* 36, no. 1 (2006): 23–34.

Evans, C. Stephen. *The Historical Christ and the Jesus of Faith: The Incarnational Narrative as History*. Oxford: Clarendon, 1996.

Evans, Craig A. "Context, Family, and Formation." Pages 11–24 in *The Cambridge Companion to Jesus*. Edited by Markus Bockmuehl. Cambridge: Cambridge University Press, 2001.

———. *Fabricating Jesus: How Modern Scholars Distort the Gospels*. Downers Grove: InterVarsity, 2006.

———. "'Have You Not Read…?': Jesus' Subversive Interpretation of Scripture." Pages 182–98 in Charlesworth and Pokorný, eds., *Jesus Research*.

———. *Jesus and His Contemporaries: Comparative Studies*. Leiden: Brill, 2001.

———. "Jewish Scripture and the Literacy of Jesus." Pages 41–54 in *From Biblical Criticism to Biblical Faith: Essays in Honor of Lee Martin McDonald*. Edited by William H. Brackney and Craig A. Evans. Macon: Mercer University Press, 2007.

———. *Luke*. NIBCNT 3. Peabody: Hendrickson, 1990.

Everett, Nicholas. *Literacy in Lombard Italy, c. 568–774*. Cambridge: Cambridge University Press, 2003.

Falk, Harvey. *Jesus the Pharisee: A New Look at the Jewishness of Jesus*. New York: Paulist, 1985.

Fentress, James, and Chris Wickham. *Social Memory*. NPP. Oxford: Blackwell, 1988.

Fitzmyer, Joseph A. *The Gospel According to Luke I–IX*. AB 28. New York: Doubleday, 1970.

———. "The Languages of Palestine in the First Century A.D." *CBQ* 32 (1970): 501–30. Repr. in pages 29–56 in A *Wandering Aramean: Collected Aramaic Essays*. Combined ed. in *The Semitic Background of the New Testament*. BRS. Grand Rapids: Eerdmans, 1997.

Flusser, David. "Jesus, His Ancestry, and the Commandment of Love." Pages 153–76 in *Jesus' Jewishness: Exploring the Place of Jesus in Early Judaism*. Edited by James. H. Charlesworth. SGJC 2. New York: Crossroad, 1991.

Flusser, David, with R. Steven Notley. *The Sage from Galilee: Rediscovering Jesus' Genius*. 4th Eng. ed. Grand Rapids: Eerdmans, 2007.

Fortna, Robert T., and Tom Thatcher, eds. *Jesus in Johannine Tradition*. Louisville: Westminster John Knox, 2001.

Foster, Paul. "Educating Jesus: The Search for a Plausible Context." *JSHJ* 4, no. 1 (2006): 7–33.

Fox, Robin Lane. "Literacy and Power in Early Christianity." Pages 126–48 in Bowman and Woolf, eds., *Literacy and Power in the Ancient World*.

France, R. T. *The Gospel of Mark*. NIGTC. Grand Rapids: Eerdmans, 2002.

France, R. T., and David Wenham, eds. *Gospel Perspectives: Studies of History and Tradition in the Four Gospels*, vol. 1. Sheffield: JSOT Press, 1980.

Fredriksen, Paula. *From Jesus to Christ: The Origins of the New Testament Images of Jesus*. New Haven: Yale University Press, 1988.

Freyne, Sean. *Jesus, A Galilean Jew: A New Reading of the Jesus-story*. London: T&T Clark, 2004.

Fuchs, Ernst. *Studies in the Historical Jesus*. Translated by Andrew Scobie. SBT 42. London: SCM, 1964.

Funk, Robert W. *Honest to Jesus: Jesus for a New Millennium*. New York: HarperCollins, 1996.

Funk, Robert W., and the Jesus Seminar. *The Acts of Jesus: The Search for the Authentic Deeds of Jesus*. New York: HarperCollins, 1998.

Gamble, Harry Y. *Books and Readers in the Early Church: A History of Early Christian Texts*. New Haven: Yale University Press, 1995.

———. "Literacy and Book Culture." *DNTB* 644–48.

Gaventa, Beverly Roberts, and Richard B. Hays. "Seeking the Identity of Jesus." Pages 1–24 in *Seeking the Identity of Jesus*. Edited by Beverly Roberts Gaventa and Richard B. Hays. Grand Rapids: Eerdmans, 2008.

Geldenhuys, Norval. *The Gospel of Luke*. NICNT. Grand Rapids: Eerdmans, 1951.

Gerhardsson, Birger. *Memory and Manuscript: Oral Tradition and Written Transmission in Rabbinic Judaism and Early Christianity with Tradition and Transmission in Early Christianity*. Translated by Eric J. Sharpe. BRS. Grand Rapids: Eerdmans, 1998.

Gijsel, Jan. *Libri de Nativitate Mariae: Pseudo-Matthei Evangelium Textus et Commentarius*. CCSA 9. Turnhout: Brepols, 1997.

Gilbert, M. "Wisdom Literature." Pages 283–324 in Stone, ed., *Jewish Writings of the Second Temple Period*.

Gillis, John R. "Memory and Identity: The History of a Relationship." Pages 3–24 in *Commemorations: The Politics of National Identity*. Edited by John R. Gillis. Princeton: Princeton University Press, 1994.

Glasson, T. Francis. *Moses in the Fourth Gospel*. SBT 40. London: SCM, 1963.

Gnilka, Joachim. *Das Evangelium nach Markus (1,1–8,26)*. EKKNT 2/1. Zurich: Benziger, 1978.

Goodman, M. D. "Texts, Scribes and Power in Roman Judaea." Pages 99–108 in Bowman and Woolf, eds., *Literacy and Power in the Ancient World*.

Goodspeed, Edgar J. *A History of Early Christian Literature*. Chicago: University of Chicago Press, 1942.

———. *Problems of New Testament Translation*. Chicago: University of Chicago Press, 1945.

Goody, Jack. *The Interface between the Written and the Oral*. SLFCS. Cambridge: Cambridge University Press, 1987.

Gould, Ezra P. *A Critical and Exegetical Commentary on the Gospel according to St. Mark*. ICC. Edinburgh: T. & T. Clark, 1897.

Green, Joel B. *The Gospel of Luke*. NICNT. Grand Rapids: Eerdmans, 1997.

Gwynn, John. "Introductory Dissertation: Ephraim the Syrian and Aphrahat the Persian Sage." Pages 119–62 in *NPNF²*. Grand Rapids: Eerdmans, 1956.

Haacker, Klaus. "Die moderne historische Jesus-Forschung als hermeneutisches Problem." *TBei* 31 (2000): 60–74.

———. "'What Must I Do to Inherit Eternal Life?' Implicit Christology in Jesus' Sayings about Life and the Kingdom." Pages 140–53 in Charlesworth and Pokorný, eds., *Jesus Research*.

Haines-Eitzen, Kim. *Guardians of Letters: Literacy, Power, and the Transmitters of Early Christian Literature*. New York: Oxford University Press, 2000.

Halbwachs, Maurice. *Les cadres sociaux de la mémoire*. ES. New York: Arno, 1975.

———. *The Collective Memory*. Translated by Francis J. Ditter, Jr. and Vida Yazdi Ditter. New York: Harper Colophon, 1980.

———. "The Legendary Topography of the Gospels in the Holy Land." Pages 191–235 in *On Collective Memory*.

———. "The Social Frameworks of Memory." Pages 35–189 in *On Collective Memory*.

———. *On Collective Memory*. Translated and edited by Lewis A. Coser. HS. Chicago: University of Chicago Press, 1992.

Halverson, John. "Oral and Written Gospel: A Critique of Werner Kelber." *NTS* 40 (1994): 180–95.

Hamilton, Paula, and Linda Shopes. "Introduction: Building Partnerships between Oral History and Memory Studies." Pages vii–xvii in Hamilton and Shopes, eds., *Oral History*.

———, eds. *Oral History and Public Memories*. Critical Perspectives on the Past. Philadelphia: Temple University Press, 2008.

Hanson, Ann Ellis. "Ancient Illiteracy." Pages 159–98 in Beard et al., *Literacy in the Roman World*.

Haran, Menahem. "On the Diffusion of Literacy and Schools in Ancient Israel." Pages 81–95 in Emerton, ed., *Congress Volume: Jerusalem 1986*.

Hardin, Leslie T. *The Spirituality of Jesus*. Grand Rapids: Kregel, 2009.

Harris, William V. *Ancient Literacy*. Cambridge, Mass.: Harvard University Press, 1989.

Harstine, Stan. *Moses as a Character in the Fourth Gospel: A Study of Ancient Reading Techniques*. JSNTSup 229. Sheffield: Sheffield Academic, 2002.

Hartmann, Lars. "Mk 6,3a im Lichte einiger griechischer Texte." *ZNW* 95 (2004): 276–79.

Haugg, Frigga, ed. *Female Sexualization: A Collective Work of Memory*. Translated by Erica Carter. London: Verso, 1987.

Head, Peter M. *Christology and the Synoptic Problem: An Argument for Markan Priority*. SNTSMS 94. Cambridge: Cambridge University Press, 1997.

Hengel, Martin. *The Charismatic Leader and His Followers*. Translated by James Greig. New York: Crossroad, 1981.

———. *Judaism and Hellenism: Studies in Their Encounter in Palestine during the Early Hellenistic Period*. Translated by John Bowden. 2 vols. Philadelphia: Fortress, 1974.

Herzog II, William R. *Prophet and Teacher: An Introduction to the Historical Jesus*. Louisville: Westminster John Knox, 2005.

Hess, Richard S. "Literacy in Iron Age Israel." Pages 82–102 in *Windows into Old Testament History: Evidence, Argument, and the Crisis of "Biblical Israel"*. Edited by V. Phillips Long, David W. Baker, and Gordon J. Wenham. Grand Rapids: Eerdmans, 2002.

Hezser, Catherine. *Jewish Literacy in Roman Palestine*. TSAJ 81. Tübingen: Mohr Siebeck, 2001.

Hilton, Allen. "The Dumb Speak: Early Christian Illiteracy and Pagan Criticism." Ph.D. diss., Yale University, 1997.

Hodgson, Peter C. "Introduction." Pages xv–l in Strauss, *Life*.

Hooker, M. D. "Christology and Method." *NTS* 17, no. 4 (1971): 480–87.

———. "On Using the Wrong Tool." *Theology* 75 (1972): 574–81.

Höpfl, Hildebrand. "Nonne hic est fabri filius?" *Bib* 4 (1923): 41–55.

Horsley, Richard A. "Introduction." Pages vii–xvi in Horsley, Draper, and Foley, eds., *Performing the Gospel*.

———. *Jesus and Empire: The Kingdom of God and the New World Disorder*. Minneapolis: Fortress, 2003.

———. *Jesus and the Spiral of Violence: Popular Jewish Resistance in Roman Palestine*. San Francisco: Harper & Row, 1987.

———. *Jesus in Context: Power, People, and Performance*. Minneapolis: Fortress, 2008.

————. "Oral Performance and Mark: Some Implications of *The Oral and the Written Gospel*, Twenty-Five Years Later." Pages 45–70 in Thatcher, ed., *Jesus*.

————. "The Origins of the Hebrew Scriptures in Imperial Relations." Pages 107–34 in *Orality, Literacy, and Colonialism in Antiquity*. Edited by Jonathan A. Draper. SemeiaSt 47. Atlanta: Society of Biblical Literature, 2004.

————. "Prominent Patterns in the Social Memory of Jesus and Friends." Pages 57–78 in Kirk and Thatcher, eds., *Memory*.

————. "A Prophet Like Moses and Elijah: Popular Memory and Cultural Patterns in Mark." Pages 166–90 in Horsley, Draper, and Foley, eds., *Performing the Gospel*.

————. *Scribes, Visionaries, and the Politics of Second Temple Judea*. Louisville: Westminster John Knox, 2007.

Horsley, Richard A., Jonathan A. Draper, and John Miles Foley, eds. *Performing the Gospel: Orality, Memory, and Mark*. Minneapolis: Fortress, 2006.

Horst, P. W. van der. "Bibliomancy." *DNTB* 165–67.

Hoskyns, Edwyn Clement. *The Fourth Gospel*. Edited by Frances Noel Davey. 2d rev. ed. London: Faber & Faber, 1947.

Howard, George. "Introduction." Pages vii–ix in *The Teaching of Addai*. SBLTT 16/ECLS 4. Chico: Scholars Press, 1981.

Hurtado, Larry W. *The Earliest Christian Artifacts: Manuscripts and Christian Origins*. Grand Rapids: Eerdmans, 2006.

————. "Early Jesus-Devotion and Jesus' Identity." Unpublished paper.

————. "Greco-Roman Textuality and the Gospel of Mark: A Critical Assessment of Werner Kelber's *The Oral and the Written Gospel*." *BBR* 7 (1997): 91–106.

————. *Lord Jesus Christ: Devotion to Jesus in Earliest Christianity*. Grand Rapids: Eerdmans, 2003.

————. "A Taxonomy of Recent Historical-Jesus Work." Pages 272–95 in *Whose Historical Jesus?* Edited by William E. Arnal and Michel Desjardins. ESCJ 7. Waterloo: Wilfrid Laurier University Press, 1997.

Hurtado, Larry W., and Chris Keith. "Book Writing and Production in the Hellenistic and Roman Era." In *The New Cambridge History of the Bible*. Edited by James Carleton Paget and Joachim Schaper. Cambridge: Cambridge University Press, forthcoming.

Illert, Martin. *Die Abgarlegende: Das Christusbild von Edessa*. Fontes Christiani 45. Turnhout: Brepols, 2007.

Jaffee, Martin S. *Torah in the Mouth: Writing and Oral Tradition in Palestinian Judaism, 200 BCE–400 CE*. New York: Oxford University Press, 2001.

Jensen, Robin M. "The Economy of the Trinity at the Creation of Adam and Eve." *JECS* 7, no. 4 (1999): 527–46.

Johnson, Luke Timothy. *The Gospel of Luke*. SP 3. Collegeville: Liturgical, 1991.

————. "The Humanity of Jesus: What's at Stake in the Quest for the Historical Jesus." Pages 48–74 in Crossan, Johnson, and Kelber, *The Jesus Controversy*.

Judge, E. A. "The Magical Use of Scripture in the Papyri." Pages 339–49 in *Perspectives on Language and Text*. Edited by Edgar W. Conrad and Edward G. Newing. Winona Lake: Eisenbrauns, 1987.

Kähler, Martin. *The So-Called Historical Jesus and the Historic Biblical Christ*. Translated by Carl E. Braaten. SemEd. Philadelphia: Fortress, 1964.

Kannaday, Wayne C. *Apologetic Discourse and the Scribal Tradition: Evidence of the Influence of Apologetic Interests on the Text of the Canonical Gospels*. SBLTCS 5. Atlanta: Society of Biblical Literature, 2000.

Käsemann, Ernst. "The Problem of the Historical Jesus." Pages 15–47 in *Essays on New Testament Themes*. Translated by W. J. Montague. SBT 41. London: SCM, 1964.

Keck, Leander E. *Who is Jesus? History in Perfect Tense*. SPNT. Columbia: University of South Carolina Press, 2000.

Kee, H. C. Introduction to "The Testaments of the Twelve Patriarchs." Pages 1:775–81 in Charlesworth, ed., *Old Testament Pseudepigrapha*.

Keener, Craig S. *The Gospel of John: A Commentary*. 2 vols. Peabody: Hendrickson, 2003.

———. *The Historical Jesus of the Gospels*. Grand Rapids: Eerdmans, 2009.

———. *The IVP Bible Background Commentary*. Downers Grove: IVP, 1993.

Keightley, Georgia Masters. "The Church's Memory of Jesus: A Social Science Analysis of 1 Thessalonians." *BTB* 17 (1987): 149–56.

Keith, Chris. "The Claim of John 7.15 and the Memory of Jesus' Literacy." *NTS* 56, no. 1 (2010): 44–63.

———. "'In My Own Hand': Grapho-Literacy and the Apostle Paul." *Bib* 89 (2008): 39–58.

———. "The Initial Location of the *Pericope Adulterae* in Fourfold Tradition." *NovT* 51 (2009): 209–31.

———. "Memory and Authenticity: Jesus Tradition and What Really Happened." *ZNW* (forthcoming 2011).

———. "A Performance of the Text: The Adulteress's Entrance into John's Gospel." Pages 49–69 in Le Donne and Thatcher, eds., *The Fourth Gospel*.

———. *The* Pericope Adulterae, *the Gospel of John, and the Literacy of Jesus*. NTTSD 38. Leiden: Brill, 2009.

———. "The Role of the Cross in the Composition of the Markan Crucifixion Narrative." *SCJ* 9, no. 1 (2006): 61–75.

———. "The Saliency of a Psalm: The Markan Crucifixion as Social Memory." M.A. thesis, Cincinnati Christian University, 2005.

Keith, Chris, with Larry W. Hurtado. "Seeking the Historical Jesus among Friends and Enemies." In *Jesus among Friends and Enemies: A Historical and Literary Introduction to Jesus in the Gospels*. Edited by Chris Keith and Larry W. Hurtado. Grand Rapids: Baker Academic, forthcoming 2011.

Keith, Chris, and Tom Thatcher. "The Scar of the Cross: The Violence Ratio and the Earliest Christian Memories of Jesus." Pages 197–214 in Thatcher, ed., *Jesus*.

Kelber, Werner H. "The Generative Force of Memory: Early Christian Traditions as Processes of Remembering." *BTB* 36, no. 1 (2006): 15–22.

———. "Introduction." Pages xix–xxxi in *The Oral and the Written Gospel: The Hermeneutics of Speaking and Writing in the Synoptic Tradition, Mark, Paul, and Q*. Bloomington: Indiana University Press, 1997.

———. *The Oral and the Written Gospel: The Hermeneutics of Speaking and Writing in the Synoptic Tradition, Mark, Paul, and Q*. VPT. Bloomington: Indiana University Press, 1983.

———. "The Quest for the Historical Jesus from the Perspectives of Medieval, Modern, and Post-Enlightenment Readings, and in View of Ancient, Oral Aesthetics." Pages 75–115 in Crossan, Johnson, and Kelber, *The Jesus Controversy*.

———. "The Work of Birger Gerhardsson in Perspective." Pages 173–206 in Kelber and Byrskog, eds., *Jesus in Memory*.

Kelber, Werner H., and Samuel Byrskog, eds. *Jesus in Memory: Traditions in Oral and Scribal Perspectives*. Waco: Baylor University Press, 2009.

Kirk, Alan. "The Johannine Jesus in the Gospel of Peter: A Social Memory Approach." Pages 313–21 in Fortna and Thatcher, eds., *Jesus in Johannine Tradition.*
———. "Manuscript Tradition as a *Tertium Quid*: Orality and Memory in Scribal Practices." Pages 215–34 in Thatcher, ed., *Jesus.*
———. "Memory." Pages 155–72 in Kelber and Byrskog, eds., *Jesus in Memory.*
———. "The Memory of Violence and the Death of Jesus in Q." Pages 191–206 in Kirk and Thatcher, eds., *Memory.*
———. "Social and Cultural Memory." Pages 1–24 in Kirk and Thatcher, eds., *Memory.*
Kirk, Alan, and Tom Thatcher. "Jesus Tradition as Social Memory." Pages 25–42 in Kirk and Thatcher, eds., *Memory.*
———, eds. *Memory, Tradition, and Text: Uses of the Past in Early Christianity.* SemeiaSt 52. Atlanta: Scholars Press, 2005.
Kloppenborg Verbin, John S. *Excavating Q: The History and Setting of the Sayings Gospel.* Edinburgh: T. & T. Clark, 2000.
Kraemer, Ross S. "Women's Authorship of Jewish and Christian Literature in the Greco-Roman Period." Pages 221–42 in *"Women Like This": New Perspectives on Jewish Women in the Greco-Roman World.* Edited by Amy-Jill Levine. Atlanta: Scholars Press, 1991.
Kraus, Thomas J. Ad fontes: *Original Manuscripts and Their Significance for Studying Early Christianity—Selected Essays.* TENTS 3. Leiden: Brill, 2007.
———. "(Il)literacy in Non-Literary Papyri from Graeco-Roman Egypt: Further Aspects to the Educational Ideal in Ancient Literary Sources and Modern Times." Pages 107–29 in Ad Fontes. Repr. from *Mnemosyne* 53 (2000): 322–42.
———. "John 7:15B: 'Knowing Letters' and (Il)literacy." Pages 171–83 in Ad Fontes.
Krueger, Derek. *Writing and Holiness: The Practice of Authorship in the Early Christian East.* Philadelphia: University of Pennsylvania Press, 2005.
Kugler, Robert A. *From Patriarch to Priest: The Levi-Priestly Tradition from Aramaic Levi to Testament of Levi.* SBLEJL 9. Atlanta: Scholars Press, 1996.
Kuhn, Karl Allen. *Luke: The Elite Evangelist.* PSN. Collegeville: Liturgical, 2010.
Lane, William. *The Gospel according to Mark.* NICNT 2. Grand Rapids: Eerdmans, 1974.
Le Donne, Anthony. *The Historiographical Jesus: Memory, Typology, and the Son of David.* Waco: Baylor University Press, 2009.
———. "Theological Distortion in the Jesus Tradition: A Study in Social Memory Theory." Pages 163–77 in Stuckenbruck, Barton, and Wold, eds., *Memory in the Bible.*
Le Donne, Anthony, and Tom Thatcher, eds. *The Fourth Gospel in First-Century Media Culture.* ESCO/LNTS 426. London: T&T Clark International, 2011.
Lee, Bernard J. *The Galilean Jewishness of Jesus: Retrieving the Jewish Origins of Christianity.* Conversations on the Road Not Taken 1. New York: Paulist, 1988.
Lemaire, André. *Les Écoles et la Formation de la Bible dans l'Ancien Israël.* OBO 39. Fribourg: Éditions Universitaires, 1981.
———. "Writing and Writing Materials." *ABD* 6:999–1008.
Levine, Lee I. *The Ancient Synagogue: The First Thousand Years.* 2d ed. New Haven: Yale University Press, 2005.
———. *Judaism and Hellenism in Antiquity: Conflict or Confluence?* Peabody: Hendrickson, 1998.
Liddell, Henry George, and Robert Scott. *A Greek–English Lexicon.* Revised by Henry Stuart Jones with Roderick McKenzie. 9th ed. Oxford: Clarendon, 1968.

Lim, Timothy H. *The Dead Sea Scrolls*. VSI 143. Oxford: Oxford University Press, 2005.

Lippman, Thomas W. *Understanding Islam: An Introduction to the Muslim World*. 2d. rev. ed. New York: Meridian, 1995.

Löhr, Hermut. "Jesus und der Nomos aus der Sicht des entstehenden Christentums: Zum Jesus-Bild im ersten Jahrhundert n. Chr. und zu unserem Jesus-Bild." Pages 337–354 in Schröter and Brucker, eds., *Der historische Jesus*.

Luz, Ulrich. "Founding Christianity: Comparing Jesus and Japanese 'New Religions.'" Pages 230–54 in Charlesworth and Pokorný, eds., *Jesus Research*.

———. *Matthew 8–20*. Translated by James E. Crouch. Hermeneia. Minneapolis: Fortress, 2001.

Maccoby, Hyam. *Jesus the Pharisee*. London: SCM, 2003.

Macdonald, M. C. A. "Literacy in an Oral Environment." Pages 49–118 in Bienkowski, Mee, and Slater, eds., *Writing*.

Mack, Burton L. *A Myth of Innocence: Mark and Christian Origins*. Philadelphia: Fortress, 1988.

MacRae, George W. "Introduction." Page 37 in Meyer, ed., *The Nag Hammadi Library in English*.

Malkki, Liisa H. *Purity and Exile: Violence, Memory, and National Cosmology Among Hutu Refugees in Tanzania*. Chicago: University of Chicago Press, 1995.

Marrou, Henri. *A History of Education in Antiquity*. Translated by George Lamb. London: Sheed & Ward, 1956.

Marshall, I. Howard. *The Gospel of Luke: A Commentary on the Greek Text*. NIGTC. Grand Rapids: Eerdmans, 1978.

———. *I Believe in the Historical Jesus*. Grand Rapids: Eerdmans, 1977.

Martin, Ralph. *Mark: Evangelist and Theologian*. Grand Rapids: Zondervan, 1972.

Matson, Mark. "Current Approaches to the Priority of John." *SCJ* 7.1 (2004): 73–100.

Mazar, Amihai. *Archaeology of the Land of the Bible, 10,000–586 B.C.E.* ABRL. New York: Doubleday, 1990.

———. "The Iron Age I." Pag es 258–301 in Ben-Tor, ed., *Archaeology of Ancient Israel*.

McCown, Chester Charlton. "Ο ΤΕΚΤΩΝ." Pages 171–89 in *Studies in Early Christianity*. Edited by Shirley Jackson Case. New York: Century Co., 1928.

McDonald, Lee Martin, and James A. Sanders. "Introduction." Pages 3–20 in *The Canon Debate*. Edited by Lee Martin McDonald and James A. Sanders. Peabody: Hendrickson, 2002.

McKnight, Edgar V. *What is Form Criticism?* GBS. Philadelphia: Fortress, 1969.

McKnight, Scot. *Jesus and His Death: Historiography, the Historical Jesus, and Atonement Theory*. Waco: Baylor University Press, 2005.

Meeks, Wayne A. *The Prophet-King: Moses Traditions and the Johannine Christology*. NovTSup 14. Leiden: Brill, 1967.

Meier, John P. *A Marginal Jew: Rethinking the Historical Jesus*. 4 vols. New York: Doubleday, 1991–2009.

Metzger, Bruce M. *A Textual Commentary on the Greek New Testament*. 2d ed. Stuttgart: Deutsche Bibelgesellschaft, 2000.

Metzger, Bruce M., and Bart D. Ehrman. *The Text of the New Testament: Its Transmission, Corruption, and Restoration*. 4th ed. New York: Oxford University Press, 2005.

Millard, Alan. "Literacy (Israel)." *ABD* 4:337–40.

———. *Reading and Writing in the Time of Jesus*. BS 69. Sheffield: Sheffield Academic, 2001.

Minnen, Peter van. "Luke 4:17–20 and the Handling of Ancient Books." *JTS* 52, no. 2 (2001): 689–90.

Misztal, Barbara A. *Theories of Social Remembering*. ThS. Philadelphia: Open University Press, 2003.

Mohler, S. L. "Slave Education in the Roman Empire." *TAPA* 71 (1940): 262–80.

Moore, George Foot. *Judaism in the First Centuries of the Christian Era: The Age of the Tannaim*. 3 vols. Cambridge, Mass.: Harvard University Press, 1927–30.

Morgan, Theresa. *Literate Education in the Hellenistic and Roman Worlds*. CCS. Cambridge: Cambridge University Press, 1998.

Morris, Nathan. *The Jewish School: An Introduction to the History of Jewish Education*. London: Eyre & Spottiswoode, 1937.

Mournet, Terence C. "The Jesus Tradition as Oral Tradition." Pages 39–61 in Kelber and Byrskog, eds., *Jesus in Memory*.

Moxter, Michael. "Erzählung und Ereignis: Über den Spielraum historischer Repräsentation." Pages 67–88 in *Der historische Jesus: Tendenzen und Perspektiven der gegenwärtigen Forschung*. BZNW 114. Berlin: de Gruyter, 2002.

Mulder, Martin Jan, ed. *Mikra: Text, Translation, Reading and Interpretation of the Hebrew Bible in Ancient Judaism and Early Christianity*. Peabody: Hendrickson, 2004.

Müller, Peter. *"Verstehst du auch, was du liest?": Lesen und Verstehen im Neuen Testament*. Darmstadt: Wissenschaftliche, 1994.

Natanson, Joseph A. *Early Christian Ivories*. London: Alec Turanti, 1953.

Neal, Arthur G. *National Trauma and Collective Memory*. Armonk: M. E. Sharpe, 1998.

Neyrey, Jerome H. "The Trials (Forensic) and Tribulations (Honor Challenges) of Jesus: John 7 in Social Science Perspective." *BTB* 26 (1996): 107–24.

Niditch, Susan. *Oral World and Written Word: Ancient Israelite Literature*. LAI. Louisville: Westminster John Knox, 1996.

Nolland, John. *Luke 1–9:20*. WBC 35a. Nashville: Thomas Nelson, 1989.

Normann, Friedrich. *Christos Didaskalos: Die Vorstellung von Christus als Lehrer in der christlichen Literatur des ersten und zweiten Jahrhunderts*. Münster: Aschendorffsche, 1967.

Oakman, Douglas E. *Jesus and the Economic Questions of His Day*. SBEC 8. Lewiston: Edwin Mellen, 1986.

———. *Jesus and the Peasants*. MBMC 4. Eugene: Cascade, 2008.

Olick, Jeffrey K. *In the House of the Hangman: The Agonies of German Defeat, 1943–1949*. Chicago: University of Chicago Press, 2005.

———. "Products, Processes, and Practices: A Non-Reificatory Approach to Collective Memory." *BTB* 36, no. 1 (2006): 5–14.

Packer, J. I. "Carpenter, Builder, Workman, Craftsman, Trade." *NIDNTT* 1:279.

Paget, James Carleton. "The *Epistle of Barnabas*." Pages 72–80 in *The Writings of the Apostolic Fathers*. Edited by Paul Foster. London: T&T Clark, 2007.

Peabody, David B., with Lamar Cope and Allan J. McNicol, eds. *One Gospel from Two: Mark's Use of Matthew and Luke*. Harrisburg: Trinity, 2002.

Perrin, Norman. *Rediscovering the Teaching of Jesus*. New York: Harper & Row, 1967.

———. *What is Redaction Criticism?* GBS. Philadelphia: Fortress, 1969.

Perrot, Charles. "The Reading of the Bible in the Ancient Synagogue." Pages 137–59 in Mulder, ed., *Mikra*.

Pesch, Rudolf. *Das Markusevangelium I. Teil.* HTKNT 2. Freiburg: Herder, 1980.

Poirier, John C. "Jesus as an Elijianic Figure in Luke 4:16–30." *CBQ* 71 (2009): 349–63.

———. "The Linguistic Situation in Jewish Palestine in Late Antiquity." *JGRChJ* 4 (2007): 55–134.

———. "The Roll, the Codex, the Wax Tablet, and the Synoptic Problem." Unpublished paper.

———. *The Tongues of Angels: The Concept of Angelic Languages in Classical Jewish and Christian Texts.* WUNT 2/287. Tübingen: Mohr Siebeck, 2010.

Pokorný, Petr. "Demoniac and Drunkard: John the Baptist and Jesus according to Q 7:33–34." Pages 170–81 in Charlesworth and Pokorný, eds., *Jesus Research.*

Polkow, Dennis. "Method and Criteria for Historical Jesus Research." Pages 336–56 in *Society of Biblical Literature 1987 Seminar Papers.* Edited by Kent Harold Richards. SBLSP 26. Atlanta: Scholars Press, 1987.

Poltermann, Andreas, ed. *Literaturkanon—Medienereignis—Kultureller Text: Formen interkultureller Kommunikation und Übersetzung.* GBIU 10. Berlin: Eric Schmidt, 1995.

Porter, Stanley E. *The Criteria for Authenticity in Historical-Jesus Research: Previous Discussion and New Proposals.* JSNTSup 191. Sheffield: Sheffield Academic, 2000.

———. "A Dead End or a New Beginning? Examining the Criteria for Authenticity in Light of Albert Schweitzer." Pages 16–35 in Charlesworth and Pokorný, eds., *Jesus Research.*

———. "Reading the Gospels and the Quest for the Historical Jesus." Pages 27–55 in *Reading the Gospels Today.* Edited by Stanley E. Porter. MNTS. Grand Rapids: Eerdmans, 2004.

Powell, Mark Allan. *Introducing the New Testament: A Historical, Literary, and Theological Survey.* Grand Rapids: Baker Academic, 2009.

Puech, Emile. "Les Écoles dans l'Israël Préexilique: Données Épigraphiques." Pages 189–203 in Emerton, ed., *Congress Volume: Jerusalem 1986.*

Purcell, Nicholas. "The *Apparitores*: A Study in Social Mobility." *Papers of the British School at Rome* 51 (1983): 125–73.

Pyper, Hugh S. "Jesus Reads the Scriptures." Pages 1–16 in *Those Outside: Noncanonical Readings of the Canonical Gospels.* Edited by George Aichele and Richard Walsh. London: T&T Clark, 2005.

Renan, Ernest. *The Life of Jesus.* London: Watts & Co., 1935. Repr., San Diego: Book Tree, 2007.

Rhoads, David, Joanna Dewey, and Donald Michie. *Mark as Story: An Introduction to the Narrative of a Gospel.* 2d ed. Minneapolis: Fortress, 1999.

Richards, E. Randolph. *The Secretary in the Letters of Paul.* WUNT 2/42. Tübingen: Mohr Siebeck, 1991.

Ricoeur, Paul. *Memory, History, Forgetting.* Translated by Kathleen Blamey and David Pellauer. Chicago: University of Chicago Press, 2004.

———. *The Symbolism of Evil.* Translated by Emerson Buchanan. Boston: Beacon, 1967.

Riesner, Rainer. *Jesus als Lehrer.* WUNT 2/7. Tübingen: Mohr Siebeck, 1981.

———. "Jesus as Preacher and Teacher." Pages 185–210 in *Jesus and the Oral Gospel Tradition.* Edited by Henry Wansbrough. London: T&T Clark, 2004.

———. "Jüdische Elementarbildung und Evangelienüberlieferung." Pages 209–23 in France and Wenham, eds., *Gospel Perspectives.*

Rius-Camps, Josep. "Origen Lucano de la Perícopa de la Mujer Adúltera (Jn 7,53–8,11)." *Filología Neotestamentaria* 6 (1993): 149–75.

———. "The Pericope of the Adulteress Reconsidered: The Nomadic Misfortunes of a Bold Pericope." *NTS* 53, no. 3 (2007): 379–405.

Roberts, C. H. "Books in the Graeco-Roman World and in the New Testament." Pages 48–66 in Ackroyd and Evans, eds., *The Cambridge History of the Bible*, vol. 1.

Rodríguez, Rafael. "Authenticating Criteria: The Use and Misuse of a Critical Method." *JSHJ* 7 (2009): 152–67.

———. "Reading and Hearing in Ancient Contexts." *JSNT* 32, no. 2 (2009): 151–78.

———. *Structuring Early Christian Memory: Jesus in Tradition, Performance and Text.* ESCO/LNTS 407. London: T&T Clark, 2009.

Rollston, Christopher A. "The Phoenician Script of the Tel Zayit Abecedary and Putative Evidence for Israelite Literacy." Pages 61–96 in *Literate Culture and Tenth-Century Canaan: The Tel Zayit Abecedary in Context.* Edited by Ron Tappy and P. Kyle McCarter. Winona Lake: Eisenbrauns, 2008.

———. "Scribal Education in Ancient Israel: The Old Hebrew Epigraphic Evidence." *BASOR* 344 (2006): 47–74. Repr. pages 91–113 in *Writing and Literacy in the World of Ancient Israel.*

———. *Writing and Literacy in the World of Ancient Israel: Epigraphic Evidence from the Iron Age.* SBLABS 11. Atlanta: Society of Biblical Literature, 2010.

Rubio, Fernando Bermejo. "The Fiction of the 'Three Quests': An Argument for Dismantling a Dubious Historiographical Paradigm." *JSHJ* 7 (2009): 211–53.

Safrai, Schmuel. "Elementary Education, Its Religious and Social Significance in the Talmudic Period." *Cahiers d'Histoire Mondiale* 11 (1968): 148–69.

Saldarini, Anthony J. *Pharisees, Scribes, and Sadducees in Palestinian Society.* BRS. Grand Rapids: Eerdmans, 1988.

Sangster, W. E. *Why Jesus Never Wrote a Book and Other Addresses.* London: Epworth, 1932.

Sawyer, John. *Sacred Languages and Sacred Texts.* RFCC. New York: Routledge, 1999.

Schams, Christine. *Jewish Scribes in the Second-Temple Period.* JSOTSup 291. Sheffield: Sheffield Academic, 1998.

Schmidt, Karl Ludwig. *Der Rahmen der Geschichte Jesu: Literarkritische Untersuchungen zur ältesten Jesusüberlieferung.* Darmstadt: Wissenschaftliche Buchgesellschaft, 1964.

Schnackenburg, Rudolf. *The Gospel of Matthew.* Translated by Robert R. Barr. Grand Rapids: Eerdmans, 2002.

Schnelle, Udo. *Theology of the New Testament.* Translated by M. Eugene Boring. Grand Rapids: Baker Academic, 2009. Translation of *Theologie des Neuen Testaments.* Göttingen: Vandenhoeck & Ruprecht, 2007.

Scholer, D. M. "Writing and Literature: Greco-Roman." *DNTB* 1282–89.

Schröter, Jens. *Erinnerung an Jesu Worte: Studien zur Rezeption der Logienüberlieferung in Markus, Q und Thomas.* WMANT 76. Neukirchen–Vluyn: Neukirchen, 1997.

———. "Geschichte im Licht von Tod and Auferweckung Jesu Christi: Anmerkungen zum Diskurs über Erinnerung und Geschichte aus frühchristlicher Perspektive." Pages 55–77 in *Von Jesus.* Repr. from *BTZ* 23 (2006): 3–25.

———. "The Historical Jesus and the Sayings Tradition: Comments on Current Research." *Neot* 30, no. 1 (1996): 151–68.

———. "Jesus of Galilee: The Role of Location in Understanding Jesus." Pages 36–55 in Charlesworth and Pokorný, eds., *Jesus Research.*

————. "Konstruktion von Geschichte und die Anfänge des Christentums: Reflexionen zur christlichen Geschichtsdeutung aus neutestamentlicher Perspektive." Pages 37–54 in *Von Jesus*. Repr. from pages 202–19 in Schröter with Eddelbüttel, eds., *Konstruktion*.

————. "New Horizons in Historical Jesus Research?: Hermeneutical Considerations Concerning the So-Called 'Third Quest' of the Historical Jesus." Pages 73–85 in *The New Testament Interpreted: Essays in Honour of Bernard C. Lategan*. Edited by Cilliers Breytenbach, Johan C. Thom, and Jeremy Punt. NovTSup 124. Leiden: Brill, 2006.

————. "Von der Historizität der Evangelien: Ein Beitrag zur gegenwärtigen Diskussion um den historischen Jesus." Pages 163–212 in Schröter and Brucker, eds., *Der historische Jesus*. Repr. pages 105–46 in *Von Jesus*.

————. *Von Jesus zum Neuen Testament*. WUNT 204. Tübingen: Mohr Siebeck, 2007.

Schröter, Jens, with Antje Eddelbüttel, eds. *Konstruktion von Wirklichkeit: Beiträge aus geschichtstheoretischer, philosophischer und theologischer Perspektive*. TBT 127. Berlin: de Gruyter, 2004.

Schröter, Jens, and Ralph Brucker, eds. *Der historische Jesus: Tendenzen und Perspektiven der gegenwärtigen Forschung*. BZNW 114. Berlin: de Gruyter, 2003.

Schudson, Michael. "The Present in the Past versus the Past in the Present." *Communication* 11 (1989): 105–13.

————. *Watergate in American Memory: How We Remember, Forget, and Reconstruct the Past*. New York: Basic, 1992.

Schuller, Eileen. The Dead Sea Scrolls: What Have We Learned 50 Years On? London: SCM, 2006.

Schürer, Emil. *The History of the Jewish People in the Age of Jesus Christ (175 B.C.–A.D. 135)*. Translated and edited by Geza Vermes, Fergus Millar, and Matthew Black. 3 vols. Edinburgh: T. & T. Clark, 1979.

Schürmann, H. "Zur Traditionsgeschichte der Nazareth-Pericope Lk 4,16–30." Pages 187–205 in *Mélanges Bibliques en hommage au R. P. Béda Rigaux*. Edited by Albert Descamps and André de Halleux. Gembloux: Duculot, 1970.

Schüssler Fiorenza, Elisabeth. *Jesus and the Politics of Interpretation*. New York: Continuum, 2000.

Schwartz, Barry. *Abraham Lincoln and the Forge of National Memory*. Chicago: University of Chicago Press, 2000.

————. *Abraham Lincoln in the Post-Heroic Era: History and Memory in Late Twentieth-Century America*. Chicago: University of Chicago Press, 2008.

————. "Christian Origins: Historical Truth and Social Memory." Pages 43–56 in Kirk and Thatcher, eds., *Memory*.

Schwartz, Seth. *Imperialism and Jewish Society, 200 B.C.E. to 640 C.E. Jews, Christians, and Muslims from the Ancient to the Modern World*. Princeton: Princeton University Press, 2001.

Schweitzer, Albert. *The Quest of the Historical Jesus: A Critical Study of Its Progress from Reimarus to Wrede*. Translated by F. C. Burkitt. Baltimore: The Johns Hopkins University Press, 1998.

Segbroeck, Frans van. "Jésus rejeté par sa patrie (Mt 13,54–58)." *Bib* 48 (1968): 167–98.

Shils, Edward. *Tradition*. Chicago: University of Chicago Press, 1981.

Smith, Bruce James. *Politics and Remembrance: Republican Themes in Machiavelli, Burke, and Tocqueville*. Princeton: Princeton University Press, 1985.

Smith, D. Moody. *John Among the Gospels: The Relationship in Twentieth-Century Research.* Minneapolis: Fortress, 1992.

———. *The Theology of the Gospel of John.* NTTh. Cambridge: Cambridge University Press, 1995.

Snyder, Graydon F. *Ante Pacem: Archaeological Evidence of Church Life Before Constantine.* Mercer: Mercer University Press, 1985.

Snyder, H. Gregory. Review of Catherin Hezser, *Jewish Literacy in Roman Palestine. Review of Biblical Literature* 8 (2002). No pages. Cited 14 July 2009. Online: http://www.bookreviews.org/bookdetail.asp?TitleId=1564&CodePage=1564.

———. *Teachers and Texts in the Ancient World: Philosophers, Jews and Christians.* RFCC. New York: Routledge, 2000.

Soden, Hermann Freiherr von. Die *Schriften des Neuen Testaments in ihrer ältesten erreichbaren Textgestalt auf Grund ihrer Textgeschichte.* 2 vols. Göttingen: Vandenhoeck & Ruprecht, 1911–13.

Stanton, Graham N. *Jesus and Gospel.* Cambridge: Cambridge University Press, 2004.

Stauffer, Ethelbert. "Jeschu ben Mirjam: Kontroversgeschichtliche Anmerkungen zu Mk 6:3." Pages 119–28 in *Neotestamentica et Semitica: Essays in Honour of Matthew Black.* Edited by E. Earle Ellis and Max Wilcox. Edinburgh: T. & T. Clark, 1969.

Stein, Robert H. "The 'Criteria' for Authenticity." Pages 225–63 in France and Wenham, eds., *Gospel Perspectives.*

———. *Mark.* BECNT. Grand Rapids: Baker Academic, 2008.

Stewart, A. Morris. *The Infancy and Youth of Jesus.* London: Andrew Melrose, 1905.

Stock, Brian. *The Implications of Literacy: Written Language and Models of Interpretation in the Eleventh and Twelfth Centuries.* Princeton: Princeton University Press, 1983.

Stone, Michael E., ed. *Jewish Writings of the Second Temple Period: Apocrypha, Pseudepigrapha, Qumran Sectarian Writings, Philo, Josephus.* Edited by Michael E. Stone. CRINT 2/2. Philadelphia: Fortress, 1984.

Strauss, David Friedrich. *The Life of Jesus Critically Examined.* Edited by Peter C. Hodgson. Translated by George Eliot. LJ. London: SCM, 1973.

Strauss, Mark L. *Four Portraits, One Jesus: An Introduction to Jesus and the Gospels.* Grand Rapids: Zondervan, 2007.

———. "Introducing the Bible." Pages 1–17 in *The IVP Introduction to the Bible.* Edited by Philip S. Johnston. Downers Grove: IVP, 2006.

Stuckenbruck, Loren, Stephen C. Barton, and Benjamin G. Wold, eds. *Memory in the Bible and Antiquity.* WUNT 212. Tübingen: Mohr Siebeck, 2007.

Sullivan, Kevin P., and T. G. Wilfong. "The Reply of Jesus to King Abgar: A Coptic New Testament Apocryphon Reconsidered (P. Mich. Inv. 6213)." *BASP* 42 (2005): 107–23.

Talmon, Shemaryahu. "Hebrew Written Fragments from Masada." *DSD* 3, no. 2 (1996): 168–77.

Taylor, Vincent. *The Formation of the Gospel Tradition.* 2d ed. London: Macmillan & Co., 1960.

———. *The Gospel According to St. Mark.* London: Macmillan & Co., 1963.

Thatcher, Tom. "Beyond Texts and Traditions: Werner Kelber's Media History of Christian Origins." Pages 1–26 in Thatcher, ed., *Jesus.*

———. "Cain and Abel in Early Christian Memory: A Case Study in 'The Use of the Old Testament in the New.'" *CBQ* 72 (2010): 732–51.

————. *Greater than Caesar: Christology and Empire in the Fourth Gospel.* Minneapolis: Fortress, 2009.

————. *Jesus the Riddler: The Power of Ambiguity in the Gospels.* Louisville: Westminster John Knox, 2006.

————, ed. *Jesus, the Voice, and the Text: Beyond the Oral and the Written Gospel.* Waco: Baylor University Press, 2008.

————. "Literacy, Textual Communities, and Josephus' *Jewish War.*" *JSJ* 29 (1998): 123–42.

————. *Why John Wrote a Gospel: Jesus—Memory—History.* Louisville: Westminster John Knox, 2006.

Theissen, Gerd. *The Gospels in Context: Social and Political History in the Synoptic Tradition.* Translated by Linda M. Maloney. Minneapolis: Fortress, 1991.

————. "Jesus as an Itinerant Teacher: Reflections from Social History on Jesus' Roles." Pages 98–122 in Charlesworth and Pokorný, eds., Jesus Research.

Theissen, Gerd, and Annette Merz. *The Historical Jesus: A Comprehensive Guide.* Translated by John Bowden. Minneapolis: Fortress, 1998.

Theissen, Gerd, and Dagmar Winter. *The Quest for the Plausible Jesus: The Question of Criteria.* Translated by M. Eugene Boring. Louisville: Westminster John Knox, 2002.

Tilley, Terrence W. "Remembering the Historic Jesus—A New Research Program?" *TS* 68 (2007): 3–35.

Toit, David S. du. "Der unähnliche Jesus: Eine kritische Evaluierung der Entstehung des Differenzkriteriums und seiner geschicts- und erkenntnistheoretischen Voraussetzungen." Pages 88–129 in Schröter and Brucker, eds., *Der historische Jesus.*

Toorn, Karel van der. *Scribal Culture and the Making of the Hebrew Bible.* Cambridge, Mass.: Harvard University Press, 2007.

Tov, Emanuel. *Scribal Practices and Approaches Reflected in the Texts Found in the Judean Desert.* STDJ 54. Leiden: Brill, 2004.

Tsumura, David Toshio. "'Misspellings' in Cuneiform Alphabetic Texts from Ugarit: Some Cases of Loss or Addition of Signs." Pages 143–53 in Bienkowski, Mee, and Slater, eds., *Writing.*

Tsutsui, Kenji. *Die Auseinandersetzung mit den Markioniten im Adamantios-Dialog: Ein Kommentar zu den Büchern I–II.* PTS 55. Berlin: de Gruyter, 2004.

Tuckett, Christopher. "Form Criticism." Pages 21–38 in Kelber and Byrskog, eds., *Jesus in Memory.*

Turner, E. G. *Greek Papyri: An Introduction.* Oxford: Clarendon, 1968.

Turner, H. E. W. "The Virgin Birth." *ExT* 68 (1956): 12–17.

Twelftree, Graham H. *Jesus the Miracle Worker: A Historical and Theological Study.* Downers Grove: IVP, 1999.

Vermes, Geza. *The Changing Faces of Jesus.* New York: Penguin, 2000.

————. *Jesus the Jew: A Historian's Reading of the Gospels.* Philadelphia: Fortress, 1973.

Walzer, Richard. *Galen on Jews and Christians.* OCPM. London: Oxford University Press, 1949.

Wasserman, Tommy. *The Epistle of Jude: Its Text and Transmission.* ConBNT 43. Stockholm: Almqvist & Wiksell, 2006.

Weaver, Walter P. *The Historical Jesus in the Twentieth Century: 1900–1950.* Harrisburg: Trinity, 1999.

Weber, Hans-Ruedi. *The Cross: Tradition and Interpretation.* Translated by Elke Jessett. Grand Rapids: Eerdmans, 1979.

Weeks, Stuart. *Early Israelite Wisdom*. OTM. Oxford: Oxford University Press, 1999.

Wilken, Robert L. *The Myth of Christian Beginnings*. Notre Dame: University of Notre Dame Press, 1971.

———. *Remembering the Christian Past*. Grand Rapids: Eerdmans, 1995.

Williams, Catrin H. "Abraham as a Figure of Memory in John 8.31–59." Pages 205–22 in Le Donne and Thatcher, eds., *Fourth Gospel*.

Williams, Ritva H. "Social memory and the DIDACHE." *BTB* 36.1 (2006): 35–45.

Winter, Paul. *On the Trial of Jesus*. SJ 1. Berlin: de Gruyter, 1961.

Witherington III, Ben. *The Jesus Quest: The Third Search for the Jew of Nazareth*. 2d ed. Downers Grove: IVP Academic, 1997.

Wright, N. T. *Jesus and the Victory of God*. COQG 2. Minneapolis: Fortress, 1996.

Yerushalmi, Yosef Hayim. Zakhor: *Jewish History and Jewish Memory*. New York: Schocken, 1989.

Young, Brad H. *Jesus the Jewish Theologian*. Peabody: Hendrickson, 1995.

Young, Ian M. "Israelite Literacy: Interpreting the Evidence Part 1." *VT* 48 (1998): 239–53.

Youtie, Herbert C. "Βραδέως γράφων: Between Literacy and Illiteracy." Pages 629–51 in his *Scriptiunculae II*. Amsterdam: Adolf M. Hakkert. Repr. from *GRBS* 12, no. 2 (1971): 239–61.

Zelizer, Barbie. "Reading the Past against the Grain: The Shape of Memory Studies." *Critical Studies in Mass Media* 12 (1995): 214–39.

Zerubavel, Yael. *Recovered Roots: Collective Memory and the Making of Israeli National Tradition*. Chicago: University of Chicago Press, 1995.

Zhang, Tong, and Barry Schwartz. "Confucius and the Cultural Revolution: A Study in Collective Memory." *International Journal of Politics, Culture, and Society* 11, no. 2 (1992): 189–212.

Ziegler, Joseph, ed. *Ezechiel*. LXXG 16/1. Göttingen: Vandenhoeck & Ruprecht, 1952.

Zimmermann, Ruben. "Memory and Form Criticism: The Typicality of Memory as a Bridge between Orality and Literality in the Early Christian Remembering Process." Pages 130–43 in *The Interface of Orality and Writing: Speaking, Seeing, Writing in the Shaping of New Genres*. Edited by Annette Weissenrieder and Robert B. Coote. WUNT 1/260. Tübingen: Mohr Siebeck, 2010.

INDEXES

INDEX OF REFERENCES

INDEX OF AUTHORS